The Impact of Churches
on Political Behavior

Recent Titles in
Contributions in Political Science

Legislators, Law and Public Policy: Political Change in Mississippi and the South
Mary DeLorse Coleman

Provisional Irish Republicans: An Oral and Interpretive History
Robert W. White

The Political World of a Small Town: A Mirror Image of American Politics
Nelson Wikstrom

Ownership, Control, and the Future of Housing Policy
R. Allen Hays, editor

The Presidency in an Age of Limits
Michael A. Genovese

Leftward Ho! V. F. Calverton and American Radicalism
Philip Abbott

Public Administration in China
Miriam K. Mills and Stuart S. Nagel, editors

Public Policy in China
Stuart S. Nagel and Miriam K. Mills, editors

Minority Group Influence: Agenda Setting, Formulation, and Public Policy
Paula D. McClain, editor

Winston Churchill—Architect of Peace: A Study of Statesmanship and the Cold War
Steven James Lambakis

Problems and Prospects for Nuclear Waste Disposal Policy
Eric B. Herzik and Alvin H. Mushkatel, editors

Why the United States Lacks a National Health Insurance Program
Nicholas Laham

Corporatist Decline in Advanced Capitalism
Mark James Gobeyn

The Impact of Churches on Political Behavior

An Empirical Study

Christopher P. Gilbert

Contributions in Political Science, Number 319
Bernard Johnpoll, Series Adviser

Greenwood Press
Westport, Connecticut • London

Library of Congress Cataloging-in-Publication Data

Gilbert, Christopher P.
  The impact of churches on political behavior : an empirical study
/ Christopher P. Gilbert.
    p.   cm.—(Contributions in political science, ISSN 0147-1066
; no. 319)
  Includes bibliographical references and index.
  ISBN 0-313-28757-0 (alk. paper)
    1. United States—Church history—20th century. 2. United States—
Politics and government—1945-1989. 3. Christianity and politics.
4. South Bend (Ind.)—Church history. 5. South Bend (Ind.)—
Politics and government. I. Title. II. Series.
BR526.G55 1993
323'.042'0882—dc20   92-35917

British Library Cataloguing in Publication Data is available.

Library of Congress Catalog Card Number: 92-35917
ISBN: 0-313-28757-0
ISSN: 0147-1066

First published in 1993

Greenwood Press, 88 Post Road West, Westport, CT 06881
An imprint of Greenwood Publishing Group, Inc.

Printed in the United States of America

The paper used in this book complies with the
Permanent Paper Standard issued by the National
Information Standards Organization (Z39.48-1984).

10 9 8 7 6 5 4 3 2 1

Contents

Figures and Tables   vii

Preface   xi

Chapter 1.   INTRODUCTION   1

Chapter 2.   TOWARD A THEORY OF CHURCH CONTEXTUAL
             INFLUENCE ON POLITICAL BEHAVIOR   15

Chapter 3.   COUNTY CONCENTRATIONS OF RELIGIOUS
             ADHERENTS: A TEST OF THREE ELECTION YEARS   27

Chapter 4.   CHURCHES, VOTING, AND PARTY IDENTIFICATION   67

Chapter 5.   CHURCHES AND POLITICAL ATTITUDES   91

Chapter 6.   CHURCH CONTEXTS AND INDIVIDUAL SELF-
             EVALUATIONS   115

Chapter 7.   THE POLITICAL INFLUENCE OF CHURCH
             DISCUSSION PARTNERS   135

Chapter 8.   CONCLUSIONS: THE POLITICAL RELEVANCE OF
             CHURCHES AS CONTEXTS   171

Appendix: VARIABLE CODING SCHEMES   179

Bibliography   185

Index   191

Figures and Tables

FIGURES

4.1   Predicted 1984 partisanship for all
        respondents, Catholics, mainline
        Protestants, and Evangelical
        Protestants   76

4.2   Predicted 1984 presidential vote, all
        respondents, with mean church Reagan
        vote percentage varied against mean
        neighborhood Reagan vote percentage   80

4.3   Probability difference, 1984 presidential
        vote   81

4.4   Probability difference, 1984 presidential
        vote, Catholics   84

4.5   Probability difference, 1984 presidential
        vote, mainline Protestants   86

4.6   Probability difference, 1984 presidential
        vote, Evangelical Protestants   87

5.1   Predicted 1984 support for school prayer,
        responses collapsed to yes/no only,
        frequent and infrequent church
        attenders   110

5.2   Probability difference, 1984 support for
        school prayer, frequent and
        infrequent church attenders   111

6.1   Predicted probability of support for school
        prayer, responses collapsed to yes/no
        only, sorted by family's perceived
        religious difference (collapsed)   131

7.1   Predicted respondent partisanship, same-
        church versus different-church pairs   146

7.2   Predicted discussant partisanship, same-
        church versus different-church pairs   147

7.3   Predicted respondent attitude toward
        abortion, same-church versus different-
        church pairs   151

FIGURES (continued)

7.4   Predicted discussant attitude toward
         abortion, same-church versus different-
         church pairs   152
7.5   Predicted respondent 1984 presidential vote,
         same-church versus different-church
         pairs   156
7.6   Predicted discussant 1984 presidential vote,
         same-church versus different-church
         pairs   157
7.7   Predicted respondent 1984 turnout, same-
         church versus different-church pairs   162
7.8   Predicted discussant 1984 turnout, same-
         church versus different-church pairs   163
7.9   Predicted respondent 1984 presidential vote,
         same-church pairs, for Catholics,
         mainline Protestants, and Evangelical
         Protestants   165
7.10   Predicted discussant 1984 presidential vote,
         same-church pairs, for Catholics,
         mainline Protestants, and Evangelical
         Protestants   166

TABLES

1.1   1984 presidential vote in three South Bend
         Catholic parishes   5

3.1   Estimated 1976 presidential vote   33
3.2   1976 presidential vote by party
         identification (collapsed) and religion   35
3.3   Estimated 1976 party identification   36
3.4   Estimated 1976 general election turnout   38
3.5   Estimated 1976 attention to public affairs   39
3.6   Estimated 1976 attitude toward abortion   40
3.7   1960 presidential vote by party
         identification (collapsed) and religion   44
3.8   Estimated 1960 presidential vote   45
3.9   Estimated 1960 party identification   48
3.10   Estimated 1960 general election turnout   49
3.11   Estimated 1960 attention to public affairs   50
3.12   1980 presidential vote by party
         identification (collapsed) and religion   52
3.13   Estimated 1980 presidential vote   53
3.14   Estimated 1980 party identification   55
3.15   Estimated 1980 general election turnout   56
3.16   Estimated 1980 attention to public affairs   57
3.17   Estimated 1980 attitude toward abortion   58

4.1   1984 South Bend percentage of Republican vote
         by respondents' church attendance,
         attention to campaign, neighborhood
         political context, and church political
         context   69

TABLES (continued)

4.2   1984 South Bend party identification by
         respondents' church attendance,
         neighborhood political context, and
         church political context   71
4.3   Estimated 1984 South Bend party
         identification   72
4.4   Estimated 1984 South Bend party
         identification for Catholics, mainline
         Protestants, and Evangelical
         Protestants   75
4.5   Estimated 1984 South Bend presidential vote   78
4.6   Estimated 1984 South Bend presidential vote for
         Catholics, mainline Protestants, and
         Evangelical Protestants   83

5.1   Estimated 1984 South Bend attitude toward
         importance of national defense   94
5.2   Estimated importance of national defense,
         frequent and infrequent church
         attenders   95
5.3   Estimated 1984 South Bend attitude toward
         government aid to minorities   96
5.4   Estimated attitude toward government aid to
         minorities, frequent and infrequent
         church attenders   98
5.5   Estimated 1984 South Bend expectations for
         the national economy   99
5.6   Estimated 1984 South Bend expectations for
         future personal economic situation   100
5.7   Estimated 1984 South Bend presidential job
         approval   101
5.8   Estimated 1984 South Bend attitude toward
         abortion   103
5.9   Estimated attitude toward abortion, frequent
         and infrequent church attenders   105
5.10   Estimated 1984 South Bend attitude toward
         prayer in public schools   106
5.11   Estimated 1984 South Bend attitude toward
         prayer in public schools, frequent and
         infrequent church attenders   107
5.12   Estimated 1984 South Bend attitude toward
         prayer in public schools, responses
         collapsed to yes/no only   108
5.13   Estimated 1984 South Bend attitude toward
         prayer in public schools, responses
         collapsed to yes/no only, frequent and
         infrequent church attenders   109

6.1   Estimated satisfaction with neighborhood   119
6.2   Estimated satisfaction with neighborhood,
         alternative model specifications   120
6.3   Estimated family interest in politics
         compared with other families in same
         neighborhood   122

TABLES (continued)

6.4   Estimated family interest in politics
            compared with other families in same
            neighborhood, Catholics and non-
            Catholics   123

6.5   Estimated family interest in politics
            compared with other families in same
            neighborhood, frequent and infrequent
            church attenders   124

6.6   Estimated family interest in politics
            compared with other families in same
            neighborhood, sorted by family's
            perceived religious difference
            (collapsed)   126

6.7   Estimated family political activity compared
            with other families in same
            neighborhood   127

6.8   Estimated family political activity compared
            with other families in same
            neighborhood, sorted by family's
            perceived religious difference
            (collapsed)   128

6.9   Estimated family political activity compared
            with other families in same
            neighborhood, frequent and infrequent
            church attenders   129

6.10   Estimated support for prayer in public
            schools, responses collapsed to yes/no
            only, sorted by family's perceived
            religious difference (collapsed)   130

7.1   Estimated party identification, same-church
            pairs   143

7.2   Estimated party identification, different-
            church pairs   144

7.3   Estimated attitude toward abortion, same-
            church pairs   149

7.4   Estimated attitude toward abortion,
            different-church pairs   150

7.5   Estimated 1984 presidential vote, same-church
            pairs   154

7.6   Estimated 1984 presidential vote, different-
            church pairs   155

7.7   Estimated 1984 turnout, same-church pairs   160

7.8   Estimated 1984 turnout, different-church
            pairs   161

7.9   Percent of discussion pairs agreeing on 1984
            presidential vote choice   164

Preface

A book concerned with the importance of contexts should consider the social surroundings and the people who assisted in the development of this study. A handful of individuals deserve special mention.

The National Election Studies data for Chapter 3 was made available through the Inter-University Consortium for Political and Social Research. The South Bend data was made available by John Sprague of Washington University in St. Louis. John's contribution to this project goes well beyond the data, of course. Many political scientists are excellent scholars, and many are great role models; few combine the two as well as John. His substantive contributions to this research have been invaluable; his passion and genuine interest is valued and appreciated particularly.

Others assisting in the St. Louis phase of this project include Jim Davis, Bob Salisbury, William Lowry, Brent Hendry, Christopher Kenny, and Mike McBurnett. In the past two years Shaun Bowler of the University of California-Riverside has been a constant source of intriguing ideas.

At Gustavus Adolphus College, the final phase of this project was supported by a 1992 summer grant from the Faculty Development Committee's Creativity, Research, and Scholarship Fund. My research assistant, Kara Marschke, who has been working with me since early 1992 through the Gustavus Adolphus Partners in Scholarship program, has been both extremely helpful and patient in reading chapter drafts, doing library research, and offering good suggestions. Another student, Mark Vos, has done yeoman work in assisting with compilation of the index. My colleagues inside and outside the political science department, as well as dozens of Gustavus students, have assisted me through their constant curiosity, support, and friendship. Space does not permit listing all their names, but they deserve to be recognized and thanked.

My initial interest in religion and politics was spurred by two undergraduate professors, Steve Gordy and James Hilander, both of Moravian College. I cannot emphasize enough the fact that neither Steve nor Jim is a political scientist by training. Their firm commitment to liberal education, echoed by my own father, two of my brothers, and most of the professors I have encountered as teachers and colleagues, is reflected in the interdisciplinary nature of this book. Politics intersects the world in a myriad of ways, some obvious and some obscure. Absent an understanding of these interconnections, the intricacies of religion's impact on politics are easily overlooked. Making such connections is at the core of liberal arts learning, and it is safe to say that my upbringing and teaching experience in this tradition have made possible the formulation of the ideas contained here.

Finally, I would like to acknowledge the assistance of Greenwood Press staff in seeing this project through to publication.

Chapter 1

Introduction

This book is an empirical study of U.S. churches and the roles
they play in affecting the political attitudes and decisions
of their members. In addressing this question, I seek to
bring together two facets of mass political behavior—religion
and social context—that I believe have been given short shrift
by scholars in the field. To understand the analysis that
constitutes the bulk of this book, it is first necessary to
understand these two facets and to see how their confluence
might help us explain important political questions.

RELIGION AND SOCIAL CONTEXTS: AN OVERVIEW

Religion and Political Behavior

It has become commonplace at academic conferences for
papers and presentations in the field of religion and politics
to be prefaced by laments over the prior lack of serious
attention paid to the subject. In fact, this broad research
area has been inundated in the last decade by new scholarly
activity and innovative approaches to old questions. The
Religion and Politics Organized Section of the American
Political Science Association (APSA) is one of the largest
such groups in the discipline, with over 550 members
(Brintnall 1991: 561). Through its newsletter and other means
the section supports a lively and continuous discussion among
the network of scholars in the field.

Contemporary scholars have explained many important
facets of the connections between religion and political
behavior. These will be discussed at length in the
introductory chapters. For now, the key point is not *what* we
have learned but rather *how* the concept of religion has been
treated by researchers. For the most part, researchers have
been content to operationalize religion as the act of
believing in or professing a certain religious
tradition—usually Catholic, Protestant, Jewish, Orthodox, or
some other broad category—or belonging to a specific
denomination within the broad categories; dividing Protestants

into smaller branches based on their myriad denominations is the best example of this approach.[1] In either case, research shows that the act of belonging to a specific religion or denomination determines particular patterns of belief and behavior, some of which have political consequences.

This mode of thinking, which I call the "labeling" approach, can be appropriate for identifying patterns and increasing our knowledge of religion and its political importance for the average citizen. But the labeling approach also presents a problem, a stumbling block to the accumulation of more knowledge. As Thomas Kuhn pointed out some three decades ago, scientific fields of inquiry inevitably create frameworks, or paradigms, that allow scholars to address important unanswered questions in an efficient manner; however, the creation of paradigms and the conduct of research based on those paradigms also *constrains* the consideration of alternative paradigms (Kuhn 1970: 35-51). Labels such as Catholic, Lutheran, or Greek Orthodox may reveal unique patterns of political attitudes among adherents to those faiths, but the labels also conceal other patterns—patterns that may alter or contradict underlying conceptions of how religion and politics interact.

Why should one be persuaded that the labeling approach constrains a full understanding of religion and political behavior? I argue that the missing element in the labeling approach is the *social* element. Religion refers not only to a specific set of beliefs but also to the practice and expression of those beliefs. Some of this activity takes place in private—Bible reading, personal prayer, quiet reflection. But these activities are almost always accompanied by a public activity, the church service. The dates and times of worship, even the frequency of worship, may vary across religions and denominations (and sometimes within them as well), but the fact remains that religious worship is inherently a *group* activity, directed toward the specific end of creating or strengthening the beliefs of members. Benton Johnson and Richard White discuss this primary goal of forming and maintaining a common consciousness within religious groups:

> Members of religious groups have a common identity, interact with one another regularly, and expect each other to think and act in certain ways. . . . The norms of a religious group constitute its special culture, a culture that is usually distinct in some ways from the culture of other groups in its environment. (Johnson and White 1967: 31)

In short, I wish to draw a distinction between "religion" and "church." In scientific terms, I will operationalize "religion" as self-reported membership in a specific local church or congregation; "church" or "congregation" will therefore refer to these specific places of worship. This book is concerned with what occurs inside the special culture of individual churches or congregations. Hence distinctions across denominations and religions are not the focus here. Rather, I wish to downplay those distinctions and instead explore the common ways in which political attitudes are shaped and influenced within individual churches.

My assertion that religion should be operationalized as membership in a specific church or congregation does not mean that the labeling approach is without merit. In fact, my analysis incorporates both approaches in order to show that even after accounting for differences across denominations, churches as social contexts still exert a unique and measurable effect on their members. The nature of those effects, however, depends to a large extent on what one means by "social contexts." I now turn to this second, equally important facet of my approach.

Social Contexts and Political Behavior

The central problem surrounding the use of social contexts in social science research is that, as with obscenity, we can identify specific examples more readily than we can construct precise definitions. As a starting point, I define social contexts as the environments, groups, or surroundings in which people live and interact with one another; "political context" refers to social contexts insofar as social contexts affect the political attitudes and behavior of individuals within them. This definition probably raises more questions than it answers, and I will have much more to say about the definition of contexts and contextual analysis in the next chapter. For now, however, the more important questions are why one should bother defining social contexts at all, and how religion and social context come together.

As with religion, explanations of mass political behavior based on social contexts have suffered from benign neglect by scholars. But contextual studies of political behavior have also enjoyed a revival in the mainstream of political science research in the last decade. Given the long and storied intellectual history of contextual analysis, one might well conclude that the heightened interest in social factors is long overdue.

As a paradigm for understanding and investigating social and political phenomena, contextual analysis occupies a prominent place in social science research. Emile Durkheim's classic *Suicide* ([1896] 1951) is often cited as the first work to apply a modern empirical approach to quantifying and measuring contextual influences on individuals. Given the sociological nature of the contextual approach, it is not surprising to find many of its signal works coming from disciplines other than political science. What is more surprising is the relative lack of attention paid to the contextual determinants of political behavior by political scientists themselves; for example, a 1989 edited volume on political learning in adulthood, labeled as a "Sourcebook of Theory and Research," never mentions social context or seriously considers it as a significant influence on political behavior (Sigel 1989).

This does not mean that all researchers have ignored social contexts. For example, Herbert Tingsten (1937) uses data from Swedish census districts to show that the propensity for voting socialist increases with working-class density. In

U.S. political research, the most sustained body of work on social context and politics comes from Columbia researcher Bernard Berelson and several of his colleagues. In a series of books analyzing the salience of social group attachments and personal discussion partners, their elegant presentation spells out a basic understanding of how social contexts may affect those embedded in them (Lazarsfeld et al. 1948; Berelson et al. 1954). But despite a few well-known articles in the 1950s and 1960s, most notably by Warren Miller (1956) and Robert Putnam (1966), the work of the Columbia school became less important over time as students of political behavior embraced the individualist, partisanship-based paradigm advanced by *The American Voter* (Campbell et al. 1960).

Political behavior research centered on the theoretical framework and rich data resources of the University of Michigan's Center for Political Studies still defines many of the field's basic research questions over 30 years after Angus Campbell, Philip Converse, Warren Miller, and Donald Stokes first published *The American Voter*. The Michigan approach posits party identification as the key mediating influence on voting. Although group attachments help form individual political identity, stability and durability of partisan attachments are the hallmark of this approach. No specific effects are thought to arise directly from social environments.

Because of the dominance it achieved and continues to hold, albeit with some compelling alternative paradigms now in the literature, the Michigan approach has deterred contextual studies in two ways: on a substantive level, since most researchers have accepted the basic notions of *The American Voter* and have settled into a "normal science" approach (Kuhn 1970) to flesh out specific lingering questions; and on a methodological level, because the data collections normally compiled to test *American Voter*-based hypotheses do not readily yield appropriate measures to test for the salience of contextual factors.

After two decades of keeping a low profile, however, contextual analysis has reemerged in the 1980s and 1990s as a significant and competing conception of how mass political behavior is shaped and determined. The efforts of contemporary scholars utilizing contextual approaches have generated dissertations, articles, books, and, perhaps most significantly, a rich new data source far more appropriate than the Michigan-based National Election Studies (NES) to the task of understanding contextual influences on citizens—the South Bend, Indiana, community study of 1984. That study is the principal basis for my analysis, and its structure I discuss in some detail later. The most compelling work to date has been a series of articles by Robert Huckfeldt and John Sprague, based on their study of neighborhoods in and around South Bend (1987, 1988, 1991, 1992). Huckfeldt and Sprague demonstrate persuasively the salience of local social environments for determining some aspects of individual political behavior.

Combining Religion and Social Context: A Tale of Three Churches

The most important (and most general) finding of contemporary research into contextual effects is that they are neither unpredictable correlates of individual political attitudes nor simply artifacts of improperly specified models and misapplied statistical techniques. A corollary to this finding is the clear recognition that there is nothing simple about contexts—defining them is tricky and assessing their influence is a complex task. An example using churches as contexts is useful to illustrate the problems a researcher faces.

Since the beginning of the New Deal period, Catholics have been considered likely Democratic voters (Wald 1992: 109). By the mid-1980s, however, this allegiance had slipped so acutely that in 1984, only 45 percent of U.S. Catholics voted for Democratic candidate Walter Mondale (Kellstedt and Noll 1990: 360). In South Bend, Indiana, a 1984 community study found stronger support for Mondale: 280 of 541 Catholic voters, or 51.8 percent, voted Democratic (author's calculation). Clearly these summary figures show that by using the labeling approach and some additional thinking, one can make some reasonable conclusions about why and how Catholic voters made their choices in 1984.

But what questions cannot be answered through the summary information provided here? For one, we cannot be sure why more Catholics in the South Bend area voted Democratic than Catholics throughout the United States. This implies that conditions in the local context of South Bend must somehow be different from conditions in the entire nation. The reasons for that are straightforward, given a little knowledge about South Bend, its ethnic and demographic character, and its political history.

A larger question, one that has no simple answer, is how to explain patterns of Catholic behavior in the South Bend area when the data are analyzed parish by parish. Table 1.1 shows 1984 presidential voting patterns for three South Bend Catholic parishes (names of actual churches have been changed).

TABLE 1.1
1984 Presidential Vote in Three South Bend Catholic Parishes

Name of Church	% Mondale	% Reagan
St. Jane (typical parish)	51.5	48.5
St. Walter	75.9	24.1
St. Ronald	21.4	78.6
All South Bend Catholics	51.8	48.2

Source: 1984 South Bend study

Clearly the labeling approach, however well it explains the behavior of the typical Catholic voter, cannot account readily for these voting patterns. The parish served by St. Walter must be very different from the parish served by St. Jane; moreover, both of these parishes obviously must differ somehow from St. Ronald. These differences arise from one or more factors: the ethnicity of the parishes; the social and demographic composition of the parishes; the individual characteristics and attitudes of parish members; and the interaction among members of the parishes, both inside and outside the social context of the church.

This example points to two principal lessons about church members and the congregations to which they belong. First, similar results could have been obtained for Protestants and for specific Protestant denominations. This means that the heterogeneity of voting patterns within churches of the same denomination is *typical*—in other words, aggregate voting statistics for Catholics, Protestants, and most other religious groupings say little or nothing about voting statistics in individual churches and congregations. Second, to understand the salient influences on individual behavior among South Bend church members, Catholics and non-Catholics alike, one must be able to measure and analyze the effects of the church as a political context.

THE PRINCIPAL QUESTIONS

So far I have argued implicitly that individual involvement in religious institutions affects attitudes, beliefs, and behaviors on a whole host of issues. This book specifically seeks to measure and evaluate religious groups and environments—principally churches—as agents of *political* influence. There are two overarching questions to be addressed. First, how does an individual's religious environment affect that individual's political attitudes and behaviors? Second, how might religious environments, specifically churches, shape political attitudes and behaviors in unique ways, different from other social contexts?

Although churches are the primary units of analysis here, they are not the only ones. In fact, I utilize three levels of context to answer these main questions, systematically narrowing the level of context under study by focusing on smaller and smaller contexts in which individuals are embedded. Continually narrowing the context in this manner affords the opportunity to critically evaluate tentative conclusions reached from broader contextual measures. What should emerge from this top-down research strategy is a comprehensive and sophisticated portrayal of the various roles that religion and churches play in relation to individual citizens.

The County as a Social Context

Measures of religious group membership at the county level can assist in identifying and measuring patterns of concentration of denominations throughout the United States

(Gaustad 1976; Newman and Halvorson 1980). Edwin Gaustad, Martin Marty (1986), and other scholars have analyzed the development of political subcultures at local and regional levels, based on the presence of, and interactions among, various denominations. Moving beyond their historical-descriptive approach, I examine individual behavior through county-level measures of the distribution of religious membership. Such an approach offers insight into how membership in such subcultural units creates channels for influencing individual political attitudes. This establishes a strong initial basis for why one should expect religious contexts to influence the political actions of practitioners. A link between religious institutions and individuals at the relatively detached level of the county serves to buttress the hypotheses and results of the investigation at the level of churches.

The Church as a Social Context

Considering their obvious importance as agents of social and political influence, churches are the primary focus of my empirical analysis. The example of St. Walter, St. Ronald, and St. Jane shows that individual churches are an appropriate unit of analysis for the kinds of questions asked here. Therefore I look at churches in South Bend, Indiana, to understand how their members are affected by the church environment. To compare effects from churches with those from other potentially relevant social contexts, I also measure and evaluate the political impact of South Bend neighborhoods. Absent any obvious reason that the South Bend area should differ radically from other communities, I also draw some tentative conclusions about churches as political contexts that may be applied more generally.

The Political Discussion Partner as a Social Context

Finally, the analysis zeroes in at the level of individuals, attempting to measure and evaluate the importance of friends with whom politics is discussed. An individual does not reason through his or her beliefs about politics in a vacuum. Nor is all political information accumulated through reading or watching television. People *talk* about politics, and apparently they talk about politics in almost every setting—at work, at play, at home, even at church. The South Bend community study has identified pairs of individuals who discuss politics with each other. These people are called political discussion partners, and their impact on attitudes and beliefs has been found to be considerable (Kenny 1989).

I focus in particular on the differences between discussion partners who attend the same church and those who attend different churches. Chapter 7 develops a theory to explain influence between discussion partners. The focus on same-church partners is based on the simple notion that two people who share a common church social context—and who therefore are exposed to similar cues and information, albeit not necessarily with equal intensity—might influence each other more than two people experiencing distinct church contexts.

WHAT ATTITUDES AND BEHAVIORS SHOULD BE STUDIED?

The objects under study in this book can be grouped into three major categories: political behaviors such as voting, party identification, and participation; attitudes on political and social issues; and individual self-evaluations of positions relative to those of neighbors and other peers.

These choices are not arbitrary, and the issues surrounding them are worth considering briefly. All the dependent behaviors chosen have been studied before, although not necessarily from a contextual point of view. The existing research on contextual effects shows that it is possible to unearth new information on determinants of individual voting behavior, perhaps the most studied phenomenon in contemporary political science research (Huckfeldt and Sprague 1992). For less explored and less settled subjects such as attitudes on social and political issues, relatively little work has been done on the importance of contexts. Finally, the study of religion and political behavior has been neglected, particularly from a contextual perspective, primarily due to a lack of appropriate data sources. Thus this book aims to do more than place new wine in old bottles; rather, it seeks to integrate the contextual approach with the existing body of knowledge about voting and other attitudes.

As for the third set of dependent behaviors, individual self-evaluations of positions within social environments present an opportunity to assess church influences on an aspect of life that churches explicitly attempt to influence. Within the political literature, these self-evaluations have been found to influence voting and other attitudes (Kernell 1977; Fiorina 1981). Here those questions are turned around: What drives the individual assessments themselves? Because churches confess to attempting such influence on a virtually continuous basis, an analysis of the religious (and more broadly, the social) basis for such individual evaluations is long overdue.

ISSUES OF DESIGN AND RESEARCH METHODOLOGY

Most research on political behavior utilizes data from the National Election Studies or some other nationwide source, and most research also employs the individual as the basic unit of analysis. Thus it is important to note where and why this research chooses to depart from the norm, and what questions are raised by such choices. Since the South Bend area and the 1984 community study by Huckfeldt and Sprague lie at the heart of this work, they deserve careful discussion first.

The South Bend Community Study

Ideally, the data set for this research project would

incorporate the church congregation as the primary sampling unit. Although not precisely what is called for, the South Bend data set meets this requirement better than any other data source.

Moreover, South Bend is a good place to conduct a community study. It has diverse neighborhoods, two relatively strong political parties, no strong electoral majority for either party, both large and small businesses, a major educational institution, and a mix of urban and suburban residential settings. This description does not show South Bend to be distinct from any other U.S. urban area, and that is precisely the point: *Nearly all of us live in places like South Bend*. Thus, in arguing about how South Bend residents act politically, I am implicitly making an argument about all citizens and how their actions and thoughts are determined. Therefore, I use South Bend to reach a broad set of conclusions about churchgoers and what makes them do what they do.

The South Bend study attempts to capture people in the contexts in which they live, work, and worship (Huckfeldt and Sprague 1987). In early 1984, individuals were randomly surveyed in 16 selected neighborhoods and asked about their political views and behavior. Three waves of interviews (A, B, and C) were conducted with approximately 2,100 main respondents; the interviews took place in the late spring, early autumn (preelection), and early winter (postelection) of 1984. Respondents gave detailed information about their residences, their places of work, and the specific churches they attended. Respondents also described their membership and activity levels in a plethora of community and social groups. The end result is a comprehensive portrait of the various social contexts in which people are embedded. There are 16 neighborhoods and 173 churches, which yielded approximately 1,650 usable responses.[2]

An additional component of the South Bend study allows for investigation of the impact of individual political discussion. In the third (C) wave of the interviews, respondents were asked for the names of three people with whom they discussed politics. The fourth (D) wave interviewed as many of these named discussion partners as possible, resulting in approximately 930 pairs of political discussion partners.[3] It turns out that 207 pairs of discussion partners belong to the same church, and thus their behavior can be contrasted to that of the majority of discussion partners who do not attend the same church.

Besides the advantages gained from knowing the specific congregations or parishes that individuals attend, the South Bend data can also be used to assess the merits of alternative explanations for behavior, from both individual and other contextual factors. Using neighborhoods as the primary sampling unit allows for the comparison of effects from neighborhood and church, and of course permits the researcher to control for neighborhood effects and other exogenous variables to ascertain the relative explanatory power of church contextual measures.

Data Sources for County-Level Analysis

To analyze the effects of concentrations of religious memberships in counties, the most diffuse level of context employed, different data sources are required. Three national church censuses were conducted in 1952, 1971, and 1980, by the National Council of Churches of Christ (NCCC) and the Glenmarry Research Center. These censuses counted church adherents for every major U.S. denomination except primarily African American churches; the 1971 and 1980 efforts captured information from even the smallest sects and emerging denominations, offering a wealth of detail.

Information from these church censuses has been appended to National Election Studies data for the 1956-58-60 NES panel study (1952 church census), the 1976 NES panel study (1971 church census), and the 1980 NES panel study (1980 church census). Most of the analysis centers on the 1976 NES panel data set, which asks a broad range of questions and also contains a third data source, collected county- and U.S. census tract-level political and demographic measures. These data sources allow me to introduce control variables and to assess differences in the salience of county contexts over time.

Contextual Analysis: Critical Issues

Few techniques in contemporary political science research are more misunderstood and maligned than contextual analysis. A major reason for this lack of understanding is that, properly speaking, there is and should be no such thing as "contextual analysis," which many scholars take to mean the consideration of social factors to the exclusion of individual factors. That particular misinterpretation was discredited most notably by Robert Hauser (1974), who specifies a set of potential pitfalls to contextual analysis, to which no reasonably careful researcher would fall victim.

The most serious criticism leveled by Hauser and others is the assertion that influences purportedly exerted by social environments are attributable to selection bias: Individuals choose to enter those social contexts whose beliefs and attitudes already correspond to their own (Hauser 1974). This so-called self-selection problem deserves closer attention, and four primary responses come to mind.

First, it is not clear that individuals possess a wealth of information regarding the composition of social groups they desire to join. Terry Moe's work on interest group activity suggests that group joiners tend to stumble into membership (Moe 1980), which belies the sophistication and rational decision making that are implied by an argument for self-selection bias.

Second, self-selection imparts a static quality to social groups that is highly implausible. Individuals change their minds on a wide range of issues and attitudes, an indication of dynamic processes at work within existing social groups and evidence that even quite homogeneous social groups are subject to change.

Third, voluntarily choosing where to live, to work, or to worship defines the dimensions of an individual's social experience in ways that are not completely predictable (Huckfeldt, Plutzer, and Sprague 1990). One does not choose one's future neighbors, even if one did choose to live near the old neighbors in the first place. Unintended political consequences may ensue from apparently unrelated decisions to locate in particular social contexts.

Finally, if self-selection explains why individuals tend to agree with others in their social contexts, how can we explain the voting patterns from the three churches described earlier? Is it plausible to suggest that people joined St. Walter because they heard that most of its members voted Democratic? In fact, it appears that citizens do a poor job of choosing churches based on theology (Wald, Owen, and Hill 1988); it is not likely that they would choose on the basis of politics with any more accuracy.

Proponents of contextual analysis believe that no respectable researcher should exclude *any* potentially meaningful set of factors, whether they are social or individual. In fact, since research has made it clear that social environments do matter for determining individual political behavior, I would argue that there should be no sharp differentiation between individual and contextual approaches. Instead, we must focus attention on how to measure contexts in an effective manner.

Measurement and Modeling Strategies

The nature of the data sources utilized in this study are not straightforward, and the methods used will likely also confound readers at times. Unfortunately, there is no way to get around the fact that some sophisticated statistical techniques are required to test the ideas put forward here. To facilitate understanding, I first address the question of how contexts are to be measured.

If, as I argue, churches should not be identified and characterized solely by their denominational labels, then how is one to characterize the social and political context of a church? The simplest answer is to characterize the church in terms of the attitude or behavior one wishes to study. That is, if one is interested in assessing how much influence a church exerts on the voting choices of its members, one should first measure the aggregate voting patterns of the church.

Consider a church that has 10 of its members surveyed in the South Bend study. Five members of this church voted for Ronald Reagan in 1984, and five members voted for Walter Mondale. Thus we can say that this fictitious church voted 50 percent Republican (or 50 percent Democratic).[4] However, from the point of view of any single individual out of the 10 surveyed, the aggregate voting pattern of the church looks different. Suppose this single individual, Ms. X, voted for Mondale. This would mean that the other nine voters in the church cast five votes for Reagan (56 percent) and only four votes for Mondale (44 percent). Thus Ms. X would be confronted with a church that—excluding her—voted 56 percent Republican, not 50 percent.

Why exclude an individual's behavior from the calculation of the church's behavior in the aggregate?   In effect, the separation of the individual and her behavior from the entire church and its behavior prevents double counting.   It is logically and statistically incorrect to argue that an individual's behavior (a vote, for example) is determined by, among other things, the group's vote when that group's vote also includes the individual's vote.

This is the essence of a *group mean variable*, and contextual measures for churches and neighborhoods in South Bend are constructed using this technique (Boyd and Iverson 1979: 137).   Put more formally, for any individual, a measure of church context for a given attribute is derived from the group mean for that church, subtracting out the individual in question.   The example of Ms. X above shows that for Ms. X in church Y with 10 respondents, the contextual measures for Ms. X are calculated on the other nine respondents from church Y. Measures for neighborhood context are derived in an identical manner.

Once group mean variables have been constructed, rigorous methods are needed to test important hypotheses.   A combination of single-level and multilevel frequency tables and some form of multivariate regression analysis is used in each chapter to conduct such tests (Hanushek and Jackson 1977).   The specific method of multivariate regression depends on the nature of the dependent variable in question: Certain types of dependent variables require techniques different from the standard ordinary least squares (OLS) multiple regression. The most complicated methods employed are logistic models and models of simultaneous systems of equations.   I discuss all these techniques more fully as they are employed in the succeeding chapters.   Where appropriate, graphs are also used to make major points more clearly.

ORGANIZATION OF THE BOOK

The second chapter deals with two major issues, the nature of social contexts and the relationship between churches and their members.   The question to be addressed is in terms of political behavior, what do we already know about contexts in general, and church contexts and individuals in particular, and how does this knowledge inform the analysis to follow?   The relevant literature on religious contexts and political behavior is covered both in this chapter and in the empirical chapters where appropriate.

The empirical analysis begins with Chapter 3.   There are two questions to be answered.   First, can we discern *links at the county level* between religious environments and individual attitudes and behaviors, and if such links exist, what specific individual factors are influenced?   Second, have there been changes over time in the nature of and degree of influence from religious environments?   To answer these questions, the chapter uses the county-level data from national church censuses collected in 1952, 1971, and 1980 to assess a broad range of dependent behaviors, five in all. These findings are the starting point for analysis in succeeding chapters.

Chapter 4 uses churches as the contextual units for analysis (and also considers neighborhoods as contextual units for purposes of comparison and control) to address two aspects of *political behavior*—voting and party identification. Here the South Bend data are utilized as a means to further test the conclusions drawn from the county-level analysis. The central question of Chapter 4 concerns whether the specific church congregation drives individual political behavior. If so, what behaviors appear to be driven by churches, and what effects do specific denominations have?

Chapter 5, which again uses churches as the level of analysis with the South Bend data, focuses on *political attitudes*. The basic questions are, to what extent do church factors drive issue attitudes, and does the presence of other individual or contextual-level factors negate or subsume church influences? The specific dependent variables to be addressed are divided among three general categories: political issues and attitudes on such things as defense spending and government aid to minorities; economic assessments of future prosperity, at both the national and local levels; and issues that might be expected to have salience within churches—abortion and prayer in public schools. For the first two sets of aforementioned issues, a specific church position is not obvious, and one goal is to determine whether any church contextual influence exists on issues not normally considered to be church related.

The sixth chapter retains the church-level focus and looks at *individuals' self-evaluations* of their positions within their South Bend neighborhoods and in comparison to other South Bend neighborhoods and communities. This chapter seeks to determine how citizens perceive and evaluate their social surroundings, and how these perceptions and evaluations might affect the impact of social contexts on behavior. How do people judge themselves in relation to the people around them? And do such judgments provide a clue as to the salience of specific social contexts?

The final empirical chapter, Chapter 7, brings the focus down to the individual level, using the political discussion partners section of the South Bend study to examine the *influence of discussion partners* drawn from the same church. This chapter addresses more than simply influence; I also analyze the mechanisms for transmitting cues within churches. The important question is whether behavior patterns and structures of discussion partners from the same church are similar to those of discussion partners from different churches or partners who share common work or home environments. If so, then I can reach some conclusion as to whether churches operate like other social groups. If not, then I can determine which characteristics of churches contribute to their purportedly unique dimensions and means of influence on members' political views.

The concluding chapter unifies the theoretical framework developed in the opening chapters with the empirical analysis in order to present an overall picture of how churches influence their members, clarifying where the findings of each chapter fit, as well as what aspects of the problem deserve more consideration in the future.

SOME FINAL INTRODUCTORY THOUGHTS

From this study, I hope to derive several conclusions about the place of religion both in individual political decision making and more generally in the U.S. political system. What is really in question here is whether churches matter for political behavior and how differing levels of church context produce different effects on individuals. Much has been written regarding the increasing secularization of advanced industrial societies, yet social science research has also found repeated evidence that religious institutions continue to affect the lives of their members. This research should not only address the question of whether churches matter in contemporary society but also discern the mechanisms through which churches operate. Findings of influence at both the county level and the church level would indicate two means of influence: At the county level, influence is derived from denominational strength, or the propensity for denominations to pursue political influence given their relative numbers in the county; at the church level, influence comes primarily from other individuals within the social context, though this does not preclude signals from the church or denomination at some institutional level above the church.

All the specific findings buttressed by empirical evidence point to a larger goal of contextual research: the reassertion of a social component to political behavior. In seeking an overarching meaning for the research to follow, I point both to the general problem of how groups influence their members politically and to what this may tell us about the groups that appear to exert strong influence on citizens.

NOTES

1. The recent work of Kenneth Wald, Dennis Owen, and Samuel Hill, all of the University of Florida, is the best counterexample to the labeling approach to research I describe here. In fact, it was their 1988 article in the *American Political Science Review* that led to the initial idea for this body of research.

2. Of the 173 churches, 44 had 10 or more members surveyed. After much testing, I decided to use the full set of 173 churches for the analysis, and to date I have found no strong methodological evidence that would cause me to focus only on the churches with larger sample sizes.

3. To be classified as political discussion partners, only one of the two people involved had to name a discussion partner. Approximately 200 true dyadic relationships were found; that is, D-wave respondents named individuals who had named them in the C wave. I have chosen to use all discussion pairs rather than only the subset of true dyads.

4. To keep things simple, I will refer to the levels of Republican voting only.

Chapter 2

Toward a Theory of
Church Contextual Influence
on Political Behavior

This chapter addresses several important issues in order to place the five empirical chapters in their own proper contexts. I begin with a brief look at what churches are, the place they hold in U.S. civil and political life, and how individual religious beliefs come to bear on this research. I then turn to the major findings of recent scholarship on contextual effects and some additional theoretical questions surrounding contextual analysis in general and the nature of churches as contexts in particular.

RELIGION AND THE CHURCH IN U.S. LIFE

Ever since Tocqueville's day, few students of U.S. society have failed to consider the role of religion and its significance for the citizenry. Churches constitute the largest voluntary association extant in the United States, and U.S. levels of attendance and membership surpass those in most other similarly industrialized nations (Bellah et al. 1985: 219). The right to freedom of religion—and increasingly, freedom from religion—continues to be a significant feature of our democratic system of governance. Also important to note is the pluralist character of U.S. religion. The immense number of separate denominations and the story of how they came to be (Mead 1976; H.R. Niebuhr 1929) constitute a prominent component in any explanation of how churches influence the politics of their members.

Investigation of the myriad ways in which religion and politics intersect in the United States has spawned several significant works.[1] My intent is not to discuss all the linkages but rather to pinpoint a framework of analysis that will allow readers to see how individuals perceive their religious lives and how politics enters into those perceptions. The two most important components of this framework are the nature of religious experience and the role of the local congregation.

Religious Experience

Working definitions of religion generally include four
components: a community of believers; a common myth, shared
by the community, that seeks to interpret the values of the
community and promote integration among its members; some
ritual behavior that incorporates individual participation;
and an otherworldly component, the holy, which exists beyond
the reality of everyday life (Hargrove 1979: 12).
Sociologists further note that these four elements are
combined into structures that are not static but dynamic in
form (Hargrove 1979: 12). In the United States, this dynamism
is most evident in the continuous splintering of religious
denominations and the development of new sects and structures.

In their book *Religion and Society in Tension* (1965),
Charles Glock and Rodney Stark identify five dimensions of
religiosity that appear to be common to all groups and
structures characterized as religions. These dimensions and
their basic meanings are the ideological dimension, concerned
with religious beliefs; the ritualistic, based on religious
practice; the experiential, concerned with religious feeling;
the intellectual, dealing with knowledge about one's religion;
and the consequential, addressing the implications of religion
for personal conduct (Glock and Stark 1965: 18-38).
Denominations place unequal emphasis on these five dimensions,
and indeed their importance depends especially on conditions
in the local parish or congregation (Glock and Stark 1965:
138-143).

One can generalize from the five dimensions to say that
the potential impact of religious belief on politics depends
primarily on a church adherent's approach to the consequential
and ritualistic dimensions.   Regardless of what a person
believes or knows about his or her faith, contextual effects
must arise from the application of religious faith to daily
life (and politics), and the degree of involvement in church
life establishes some underlying probability of receiving and
interpreting church teachings or signals about politics.

The Local Congregation

Typologies of religious dimensions are useful in
categorizing what takes place in churches from an individual
perspective, but religion is a social as well as an individual
phenomenon—the community component of the working definition.
Local congregations are often communities unto themselves, a
basis for social relationships and collective identity.
Gerhard Lenski (1961) formulates a theoretical framework from
which to understand the importance of local churches as social
groups.   He argues that religion spawns what he terms
socioreligious subcultures.   These are collections of
individuals who form attachments inside and outside formal
church structures.   Membership in these subcultural units
opens the channels for influencing political attitudes,
supplying the necessary conditions for contextual effects to
occur (Hargrove 1979: 203-204).

For some denominations, these subcultures strongly affect
social networks.   Glock and Stark find that among Southern

Baptists and members of small sects, nearly half of church members report that four or more of their five best friends belong to the same church (1965: 163). More conservative denominations show similar patterns, while Glock and Stark characterize more liberal congregations as "occasional audiences or focused crowds" (1965: 163).

However, despite the primacy of personal relationships within conservative church congregations, Glock and Stark also conclude that congregations in general are extraordinarily heterogeneous in social and class composition (1965: 135-139). Churches by definition seek to appeal to all people, and many denominations actively try to recruit outsiders into their fold. This suggests that congregations should be plagued by centrifugal forces pulling them apart. If so, how do they survive? The short answer is that often they do not, as evidenced by constant splintering or movement by members from one congregation to another. H. Richard Niebuhr offers the classic sociological explication of this process in his landmark book *The Social Sources of Denominationalism* (1929). More recently, contemporary observers have characterized today's church member as a "consumer" of religion, maintaining "brand loyalty" until there is some reason to adopt a different faith (Schaeffer 1990). And a 1978 Gallup poll reported that four in five Americans agreed with the statement that "an individual should arrive at his or her own religious beliefs independent of any churches or synagogues" (Bellah et al. 1985: 228).

It might be anticipated that since congregations appear inherently fragile—common beliefs hold them together, but individuals decide what beliefs they want, and their preferences change over time—there might be relatively little official position taking within congregations: better not to stir the waters and risk losing some members. On the contrary, every important study of congregations finds them to be rife with political messages and other sources that might transmit political cues to members. Kenneth Wald, Dennis Owen, and Samuel Hill provide a typical example:

> In a "mainline" Protestant church, the sanctuary was festooned with posters promoting solidarity with Central American victims of rightist oppression, the minister's sermon lauded the resistance of women to tyranny throughout history, the explanation of harvest symbols stressed the need to combat poverty and hunger, and the choice of hymns included folk songs from the civil rights era. During the announcement period of the service, several congregants encouraged their fellow members to attend demonstrations, meetings, and workshops in support of the causes that had received ministerial endorsement. A cursory inspection of the bumper stickers on vehicles parked around the church suggested that a considerable proportion of church members had indeed been active in such liberal organizations. (Wald, Owen, and Hill 1988: 533)

Wald, Owen, and Hill further note that even with the high degree of defections among individual members, congregations make a concerted effort to foster a sense of community. This includes threats of punitive sanctions and withdrawal of group approval and coercive devices that would impede fissures among members: "This potent array of social influence mechanisms equips congregations with the capacity to promote uniformity in sociopolitical outlook" (1988: 533).

Local congregations clearly have the means at their disposal to influence their members on many topics, including political ones. Specific methods to achieve this are covered below. Whether one concludes that local congregations are fragile communities (Bellah et al. 1985: 232) or more stable social groups (Wald, Owen, and Hill 1988), it cannot be denied that congregations are an appropriate unit of analysis. Questions in the South Bend study offer very little information on the ideological, experiential, and intellectual dimensions of church adherents. However, to the extent that I can characterize the ritualistic and consequential dimensions, the empirical analysis has a great deal to say about the salience of congregations as agents of contextual influence on political behaviors.

CONTEXTUAL INFLUENCES ON POLITICS: FINDINGS AND THEORETICAL CONCERNS

Most researchers choose to concentrate on generating empirical evidence of contextual effects from what are assumed to be relevant contextual units. These units are usually defined spatially or geographically—the county, the census tract, the neighborhood. The advantages to choosing such units are obvious: All can be defined in advance by the researcher (neighborhoods being the most difficult to pinpoint in terms of boundaries), and data on many important indicators already exist for counties and census tracts. Huckfeldt's 1986 book, *Politics in Context*, demonstrates the utility of this type of context definition for understanding attitudes and behaviors in urban neighborhoods.

It is at least arguable that defining the context in geographic terms—one or more environments acting on individuals within the environment(s)—is not the most desirable or appropriate way to approach contextual effects. Why should people identify themselves, for example, in terms of their counties or neighborhoods of residence? And how many people possess enough knowledge about such geographical units to connect political trends with personal attitudes?

Rather than imposing or assuming politically relevant contextual boundaries based on the convenient existence of data, a researcher would be better served by thinking first about how people actually live. The only way to know for sure what contexts might be politically relevant is to *ask* citizens what contexts they interact with on a regular basis. In other words, one should define contexts by starting with the individual: through survey questions, determine all (or the most relevant) of a person's groups, contexts, or environments that might influence individual behavior. This perspective would include other individuals (classified in the South Bend study as discussion partners) with whom a person has regular contact. Such an approach is far more inclusive and less likely to miss salient contexts that affect individual actions.[2]

The structure of the South Bend data reflects both approaches in its pragmatic approach to defining contexts for an individual. Essentially, the South Bend study proceeds from the assumption that some contexts are salient and information should be gathered about the likely salient contexts. The complex answer to the question of what defines a salient context for an individual thus comes from some subset of the contextual ties ascertained for South Bend residents—neighborhood, church, workplace, voluntary groups, talking partners.

Crucial to understanding the potential sources of contextual influence is the point that individuals do not and cannot fully control aspects of their social environments. William McPhee's formalization of political discussion (1963) argues that the environment in which the individual searches for information is biased in favor of the prevailing social structure; hence the modification of beliefs that is likely to result is also biased, in the direction typical of the microenvironment. A recent paper based on the South Bend study expands upon McPhee's argument:

> People locate themselves in neighborhoods, churches, workplaces, clubs and associations. They make these locational choices for good reasons on rational grounds, but in the process they also define the dimensions of their social experience. This social experience has relevance far beyond the basis of the original choice. In particular, it defines the composition of political preferences to which the individual is exposed. (Huckfeldt, Plutzer, and Sprague 1990: 19)

Thus if a particular social context provides salient political cues (how this happens is yet to be discussed), those cues are also likely to be biased in ways that cannot necessarily be anticipated (McPhee 1963). Correlations between characteristics of different contexts in South Bend show that with the exception of Catholics (where parish and neighborhood lines often overlap), there is a strikingly low amount of consistency on basic indicators such as mean education or mean partisanship (Gilbert and Hendry 1989; Huckfeldt, Plutzer, and Sprague 1990). Examining patterns among political discussion partners also shows that individuals do not always choose talking partners with whom they agree (Kenny 1989), further demonstrating that unintended political consequences may ensue from apparently unrelated decisions concerning where to live, work, or worship or whom to befriend. Even the simple acts of observing bumper stickers on neighbors' cars, campaign signs, or petitioners canvassing a neighborhood demonstrate behaviors that an individual can neither control nor easily ignore.

CHURCHES AS SALIENT POLITICAL CONTEXTS

Turning from this discussion of contextual findings to churches in particular, it is time to consider assumptions about how these contextual processes work within a congregation. In considering church contextual influences on political attitudes and behavior, two theoretical components of the problem must be addressed: the means and mechanisms through which church contexts influence such behaviors, and the ways in which the church as a political and social context interacts and interrelates with the other contexts in which individuals are embedded.

Mechanisms of Contextual Effects

The religious context in which an individual interacts and worships with his or her fellow congregants offers similar opportunities for transmission of political signals as do other social groups. As I have noted earlier, religion in this country is both an individual and a group activity, and attendance at church implies for the worshiper adherence to a carefully defined set of behaviors, rituals, and practices. It is therefore expected that political cues are transmitted in religious settings much as they would be in other contexts: through social interaction; shared experience; communications from elites; direct observation; and the transmission of norms, values, and doctrines between generations (Wald 1992). What exactly are the mechanisms for transmission of contextual effects? Both McPhee (1963) and Sprague (1982) suggest reinforcement as the basis for transmitting influence from person to person. McPhee argues that political discussion reveals to an individual that her beliefs either agree or do not agree with those of her discussion partner. If she finds agreement, the attitudes under discussion are positively reinforced. If disagreement is found, she engages in a reconsideration of her own views, then seeks out additional information in order to resolve the dissonance. Sprague further argues that the consequences of social interaction depend on three factors: attention to the interaction, which is necessary for information to be processed; motivation to learn; and interaction patterns, which determine with whom an individual interacts as well as the frequency of the interaction and reinforcement. Empirical evidence to support this conception of influence transmission and attitude change is now widespread and considered quite persuasive (Huckfeldt 1986; Huckfeldt and Sprague 1987, 1988; Kenny 1989).

From the perspective of religious contexts, involvement in the church must be a crucial mediating factor in the strength of contextual influences (Guth et al. 1988). Gerhard Lenski (1961), Seymour Martin Lipset (1963), and others provide empirical support for this contention, and Lenski further demonstrates that defining church involvement in different ways produces different impacts on individual behavior. The salience of church attendance for partisanship and voting behavior is shown by David Knoke (1974), who found that in the 1968 presidential election, church attendance was significantly related to party identification and presidential vote. The findings of Knoke and others appear to contradict Philip Converse's assertion (1966) that church attendance is connected to vote choice only when some issue makes religion salient—in 1960, for example, with Catholics and John F. Kennedy.

Sorting among Multiple Contexts

The second theoretical concern poses a thornier problem when considering the nature of contextual effects. Citizens have ties to several political and social contexts, and there seems to be no easy way to discern which contexts will be salient for specific aspects of daily life. Moreover, the bases for membership or connection to various social contexts probably differ for each individual. It is not plausible to argue, for example, that an individual joins a church, lives in a certain neighborhood, and holds a specific job all for the same underlying reason (Wald, Owen, and Hill 1988).

Recent work in religion and political behavior recognizes the problem of multiple contexts and the difficulty of hypothesizing in advance about their respective strengths. Standard responses fall into two general categories. Some, most notably Steven Peterson (1990a, 1990b), place a strong emphasis on church attachments as being more salient than attachments to other groups. Peterson argues for what he terms a spillover effect: "participation in decision-making within the church could be expected to spill over and enhance the odds of an individual becoming more involved in political activities" (1990a: 4). Peterson finds some statistical evidence to support his hypothesis that increasing participation in church decision making leads to heightened levels of political participation, interest, and efficacy and to greater status quo orientation. This approach is in the spirit of Lenski's (1961) famous assertion that churches reach out to touch all facets of individual lives, not just those facets directly addressed inside churches.

The more common approach is to argue for the selective importance of church contexts—that is, churches matter for some political behaviors but not others. Wald, Owen, and Hill (1988) show that the positions of congregation members influence the behavior of their fellow members, specifically in regard to links between theological conservatism and political conservatism. Wald, Owen, and Hill do not argue that such links between context and individual apply across a broad range of behaviors, but rather that churches can influence their members on certain things, depending on the political and social orientation of the church. Thus in a congregation that does not actively involve itself in politics, little contextual influences should be found. This general approach posits some form of behavioral contagion within congregations (or social groups in general) that serves to make an issue salient and heighten the transmission and reception of cues surrounding the issue (Wald, Owen, and Hill 1988; MacKuen and Brown 1987).

This latter conception of the church as a salient political context under certain conditions and for certain attitudes is a more fruitful starting point for the empirical analysis to follow. Contextual analysis generally holds that effects arise from individual interaction with one *or more* contexts, and that there can be interactive effects among contexts as well. Therefore, since it is believed (and empirically supported to an extent) that the church can be a salient context, and since it is also known (and empirically supported) that other contexts matter as well, I have chosen to operationalize church contexts in various ways—different levels of analysis, different contextual measures at each level of analysis—and evaluate the presence of contextual effects across a range of dependent behaviors. At the same time, other contexts must be considered as potentially salient, and they too must be operationalized and tested in concert with church contextual measures. The question of potential interactions among contexts can also be addressed within this framework.

NOTABLE RESEARCH ON CHURCHES AS POLITICAL CONTEXTS

Discussion of church contextual influences on political behavior must begin with the work of Gerhard Lenski. Beginning with his path-breaking book, *The Religious Factor* (1961), Lenski legitimizes the idea that religion influences politics and specifies the inherently social nature of this influence:

> [T]hrough its impact on individuals, religion makes an impact on all the other institutional systems of the community in which these individuals participate. *Hence the influence of religion operates at the social level as well as at the personal level* [emphasis added]. (1961: 289)

Lenski analyzes religious factors in Detroit in 1957 and 1958 and finds that increasing church attendance, his measure of associational involvement, is positively correlated with increasing Republican support for working-class and middle-class Protestants. Further, Catholics support Democrats more than Republicans, but frequent Catholic attenders are more likely to support Republicans than infrequent attenders. Lenski does not find a correlation between increasing attendance and Democratic preference for white Catholics.

Seymour Martin Lipset builds upon Lenski's empirical findings, as well as his theoretical notions concerning religious subcultures, and finds that lower-status church members are more likely to vote for conservative parties as the average socioeconomic status of their fellow church members increases (1963: 242). J. M. Bochel and D. T. Denver (1970) find evidence in Scotland to support Lipset's assertion. Echoing Lenski, they argue for treating church adherents as group members seeking to conform to the norms of the group, be they spiritual, political, or anything in between (1970: 216).

That churchgoers may be treated as group members is not a radical proposition. Nevertheless, posing the question of church effects on political variables in this manner diminishes the need to resort to arguments based on religious doctrine or ritual and instead allows the church to be considered as a unit of political socialization operating in concert with other groups and institutions to guide an individual's political activities.

Although the dominant approach in the study of religious characteristics and political behavior has been to analyze different denominations and the varying ways in which each denomination affects the political behavior of its members, even this research has occasionally included consideration of contextual effects. For instance, David Segal and Marshall Meyer (1974) argue that Catholics, who constitute a cohesive religious group and traditionally support the Democratic party, are thus "most immune to political currents in the local community" (1974: 226). Protestants, on the other hand, are theorized to be more responsive to their environments (1974: 228). Segal and Meyer attribute this to the fact that Protestantism as a doctrine is not a cohesive body of beliefs and norms. Within the group "Protestants," however, other researchers have demonstrated strong effects of group membership for ascetic Protestant denominations, which do fit the mold of cohesive religious environments (Johnson 1964). More recent research has found that the conclusions of Segal and Meyer hold more for Evangelical Protestants than for all Protestants (Gilbert and Hendry 1989; Gilbert 1991).

No discussion of U.S. religion and political behavior research is complete without mention of the 1960 presidential election. In acknowledging the salience of religion as an issue in 1960, however, most researchers downplay religion's importance in other national elections. The principal sources for this view are the authors of *The American Voter* (Campbell et al. 1960). In their 1966 book, *Elections and the Political Order*, Campbell, Converse, Miller, and Stokes devote two chapters to the meaning and implications of the 1960 contest. They find that Kennedy's Catholicism cost him approximately 1.5 million popular votes, or 2.2 percent of the total popular vote in 1960 (1966: 92). Protestant Democrats defecting from their party's candidate were the main reason, especially in the South, and church attendance played a crucial intervening role—more regular attendance correlated with a decreased probability of voting for Kennedy (1966: 88-89). The final conclusion, though, is that normal partisan loyalties were reinstated in 1960 after two successive Republican victories, and that religion mitigated the strength of the Democratic partisan resurgence (1966: 122-124).

It must be noted that not all researchers relegate religion to secondary importance when interpreting presidential voting patterns. Paul Lopatto (1985) has investigated voting behavior by denominations in presidential elections from 1964 to 1984. Although Lopatto finds vast differences in the effects of religion from election to election, his study does yield some interesting and consistent results. Lopatto finds that increasing social class appears to diminish the effects of religion on vote choice: A voter with higher levels of income and education is more likely to vote Republican regardless of his or her religion (1985: 73-78). Translating this into contextual terms, one would expect to find that in contexts that can be defined as high in social status, individuals are more likely to vote and act Republican, regardless of their own religious preferences. A recent analysis by Lyman Kellstedt and Mark Noll (1990) further elaborates on differences among major groups of denominations, and the next chapter discusses these findings in more detail.

The story told by previous research on the interplay between religious contexts and political behavior is that less attention is paid to the relationship than the existing work would indicate is warranted. This benign neglect may simply reflect the deemphasis on religion among increasingly secular scholars. Or it may mean that alternative paradigms, which admittedly do a more than creditable job of explaining many types of political behavior, have crowded religion out of the mainstream. Regardless of the reason, religious contexts, like social contexts in general, deserve to be more strongly emphasized as important influences on political behavior. To ignore them is to omit what has historically been a signal factor in explaining the political activities and beliefs of Americans.

CONCLUDING THOUGHTS

The existing research clearly suggests that religious environments matter for some individuals, and that contextual analysis is an appropriate means of investigating exactly how religious environments matter. The analysis to follow systematically attempts to isolate and explain how religious factors and the context of the church affect political attitudes and behavior. It adopts the idea that churches influence members selectively and that some contagion process must drive the influence.

In order to understand the impact of church contexts, both in absolute terms and in relation to other salient contexts, it is necessary to operationalize and measure at least one other context for the South Bend survey respondents and for the National Election Studies survey respondents in Chapter 3. I have chosen the neighborhood (in Chapter 3, some other aspect of the county) as this other context, primarily on methodological grounds. Indeed, even with the South Bend data the options are limited. Hence the analysis in Chapters 4 through 6 includes contextual measures for both church and neighborhood, thus allowing for investigation of the interaction between contexts. The neighborhood is not a perfect measure of an alternative context; it is not clear that an individual interacts often or at all with his or her neighbors, and compared to the church the residential context is arguably more detached from the individual. However, other contextual research does make a persuasive case for neighborhood effects, meaning that at the very least, my results offer a counterpoint to existing findings.

In Chapter 7, the idea of considering alternative contexts takes a different tack. Instead of considering the interplay between church and neighborhood, I divide political discussion partners into those pairs who attend the same church and those who attend different churches. Thus Chapter 7 investigates contextual effects in two ways: the salience of discussion partners in general, and the possible heightened salience of discussion partners sharing another common context, the church.

Justifications and hypotheses for dependent variables are offered at the beginning of each empirical chapter. As outlined in Chapter 1, each empirical chapter stands alone as an analysis of some aspect of church context and political behavior. Taken separately, each chapter's findings strengthen the case for the salience of churches as contexts; taken together with the theoretical components discussed here, the empirical research offers a solid and broadly based response to questions about the role of religion in both individual and social terms. As scholars of U.S. political behavior begin to reconsider cultural interpretations of behavior patterns (Leege, Lieske, and Wald 1989), these findings are well worth considering.

NOTES

1. Kenneth Wald (1992) and Mark Noll (1990) offer the best recent overviews for readers new to this field.

2. On the other hand, in attempting to be inclusive of all salient contexts, a researcher may end up with a hopeless conundrum of conflicting findings produced by unwieldy statistical models. There is no simple formula to determine where to place limits on specification of contexts.

Chapter 3

County Concentrations of Religious Adherents: A Test of Three Election Years

The distribution of religious denominations across the United States has drawn the attention of many students of U.S. politics, from the writings of Tocqueville in the nineteenth century to a windfall of recent articles and books in the late 1980s. Regardless of the analytic techniques employed, the central points to be made are (1) that a remarkable degree of diversity exists in U.S. religious life, and (2) that the patterns of distribution and concentration of denominations throughout the United States have important social and political ramifications for the body politic. This chapter seeks to assess the salience of denominational concentrations for individual political behavior. There are two questions to be answered: Based on county-level measures of religious context, are there links between religious environments and individual attitudes and behaviors? If such links exist, what specific individual factors are influenced, and why do religious contexts seem to matter for some behaviors but not others?

Answers to these questions will come from analysis of three election years—1960, 1976, and 1980—using three sets of National Election Studies survey data, supplemented by data from three national church censuses and from collected county- and U.S. census tract-level political and demographic measures. The data sets are constructed as follows:

> *1960*: 1956-58-60 NES panel study; 1952 NCCC/Glenmarry church census; 1960 county election returns
>
> *1976*: 1976 NES panel study; 1971 NCCC/Glenmarry church census; 1976 county election returns; 1970 U.S. census demographic data for counties and census tracts
>
> *1980*: 1980 NES panel study; 1980 NCCC/Glenmarry church census; 1980 county election returns

The advantage of using three data sets rather than one is that I can assess differences in religious contextual influences over time. The results from the 1976 NES investigation can be compared and contrasted with the 1956-58-60 NES panel series and with the 1980 NES panel. A further advantage of this approach is that each of the presidential elections covered by the NES data differs in terms of the importance of religion and its bearing on individual vote decisions; whether those differences affect the salience of religious context is an empirical question to be addressed.

EXISTING RESEARCH USING COUNTY-LEVEL DATA

Although research utilizing the NCCC/Glenmarry church census data is relatively limited in political science, two works stand out as examples of what can be done with this rich information source. In the first, William Newman and Peter Halvorson (1980) utilize factor analytic techniques to derive new classifications of U.S. denominations, based on geography and historical and ethnic ties among the groups classified together. They describe their four major groupings (out of six total) as follows:

Northeast and Metropolitan Protestant-Catholic-Jew: located in major cities and constituting one body of urbanized believers as opposed to the traditional sorting of these three groups; major denominations are Episcopal, Methodist, United Church, Presbyterian

Midwest and Northwest, Northern European Protestant: primarily Germanic and Scandinavian, Continental Reform churches such as Lutheran and Evangelical

Southern Anglo-Calvinist: Baptist, Methodist, and Presbyterian, British in background, the source of strong Southern religious adherence

Central and Western, Native Protestant: mostly born in this country, U.S. branches of Protestant faiths such as Adventist, Nazarene, some Baptist, and Presbyterian

Newman and Halvorson separately categorize subregional groups such as Germanic pietists (Mennonites, for example), the Dutch Reformed churches, and the Church of Jesus Christ of Latter-Day Saints (Mormons). They use their findings to argue for a demographic theory of religious adherence, tracing changes in denominational strength to changes in population patterns. Their work stands out as a unique way of examining the distribution of U.S. denominations and its implications for politics.

A more direct look at the salience of religious contexts using county-level data has been undertaken by Robert Salisbury, John Sprague, and Gregory Weiher (1984). They attach the Glenmarry 1971 church census data to several national surveys conducted between 1964 and 1976, thus constructing a large data file for analysis. The authors create a five-level typology of county religious concentrations, ranging from a monopolistic county (one denomination claims over 75 percent of all religious adherents) to a pluralist one (no denomination claims more than 35 percent of total adherents), and test whether these levels have an impact on individual party identification. They find that living in a pluralist county is not a significant predictor of partisanship when other individual-level factors are controlled for; county pluralism does, however, correlate with a party vote. Further, Catholics are more likely to participate in politics when surrounded by Protestants, who do not themselves show the same inclination when surrounded by Catholics. This elegant analysis demonstrates the potential of county data for uncovering religious context influences on political behavior.

Although contextual studies utilizing county data are rare in the literature, most of the early work in contextual studies is conducted at levels of analysis larger than the neighborhood or parish. For example, Warren Miller (1956) finds that Democrats living in highly Democratic counties are more likely to vote Democratic than Democrats living among high concentrations of Republicans. Robert Putnam (1966) and Kevin Cox (1974) report similar results on the importance of group memberships within contexts. Although much of this research cannot directly address questions about the means and mechanisms of contextual influence, they do establish that even at the county level links exist between contexts and individual behavior.

POINTS OF DEPARTURE

This chapter differs from the existing research on religious concentrations by attempting to explicitly link county-level measures of the distribution of religious membership to individual political behavior. Such an approach should offer insight into the composition of political subcultures based on religious membership and how membership in such subcultural units opens the channels for influence on political attitudes.

Given what is known about aggregation problems and the so-called ecological fallacy (see Robinson 1950), conclusions drawn at this level must be subject to more rigorous examination within smaller contextual units. Two potential sources of difficulty stand out: the detachment of the contextual level of analysis from the individual, and the extent to which evidence of influence at the county level corresponds with influence at the church or individual level. Measuring context at the county level certainly does not preclude the detection of contextual influences on individuals (Miller and Putnam clearly find such influences), yet arguments for a direct or causal link between county environments and individuals require more evidence. Moving to the church and neighborhood level may produce findings that differ from county-level findings, and such differences will have to be explained.

DEPENDENT MEASURES AND MODELING TECHNIQUES

    To gain a broad sense of how religious context interacts
with individual actions, several dependent measures are
utilized. These measures have been chosen for three principal
reasons: They are interesting behaviors in and of themselves;
specific factors influencing the behaviors might differ over
time; and comparable or identical measures for each can be
obtained in the three different NES panels under study. Based
on these factors, I examine presidential voting, partisanship,
abortion attitudes,[1] voting turnout, and interest in public
affairs. For each of the dependent behaviors in question, I
construct regression models that include both individual
demographic characteristics and contextual variables to fully
explore exactly which factors influence these behaviors.
    The measures of religious context, based on county-level
data, calculate the total number of adherents of a given
religion divided by the county population. Using the county
population as the base figure instead of the total number of
religious adherents in the county gives a more accurate
portrait of county composition. In this manner, measures are
obtainable for virtually every denomination available in the
Glenmarry census data; in practice, however, only a few
religions or denominations achieve any large concentration
within counties. Hence most of the models estimated rely on
a set of summary measures, collapsing denominations into three
primary categories: Catholics, Evangelical Protestants, and
mainline Protestants.[2] A third group of Protestants,
nontraditional Protestants, is also available, as are measures
for Orthodox religions and for Jews. Little information is
obtainable for sects that are neither Christian nor Jewish, as
this information is not gathered in full by Glenmarry.
Finally, predominantly African American churches are
underrepresented in the Glenmarry census data. Hence I will
not pursue hypotheses concerning the impact of black churches
on the political behavior of county residents, though the
historical evidence demonstrates that such impact can be quite
significant.

A Further Methodological Note

    The question of causation becomes paramount in a
statistical model explaining political behavior using
aggregate measures such as the ones employed here. For
example, the number of Catholics may indeed influence voting
choices, but it seems obvious that such influence may work in
many directions at once. Consider a hypothetical county that
is 50 percent Catholic, 20 percent mainline Protestant, 7
percent scattered among many denominations, and 23 percent
nonchurch adherents. Does the presence of many Catholics
cause other Catholics to vote for the same candidate? Do
Protestants then vote in line with the Catholic majority (two
out of every three churchgoers in this county), or do they
hold more strongly to their political predispositions, which
likely run counter to Catholics'? And how do the smaller
denominational groups react to the situation presented to
them? If we hypothesize that minority groups hold to their

predispositions in the face of (possibly hostile) majorities, this means that the presence of so many Catholics strengthens prevailing Catholic *and* prevailing Protestant behavior patterns. Clearly one variable, "percent Catholic in county," will not be able to capture the complexity of this situation in one complete model.

In practice, the hypothetical situation just described repeats itself for virtually every county. The solution is to utilize several *interaction terms* to measure the effect of a particular religious group concentration on members of specific denominations or groups. Thus, using the example above, a prudent strategy would test three variables rather than one:

> *Catholic times percent Catholic*: tests for the effect of the county Catholic concentration on Catholics alone

> *Mainline Protestant times percent Catholic*: accounts for the effect of the county Catholic concentration on mainline Protestant adherents; this variable tests the hypothesis that large Catholic numbers cause mainliners to "stick to their guns" and resist pressures to vote with the (Catholic) majority

> *Percent Catholic*: accounts for the effect of the Catholic concentration on members of all other religions and on nonadherents, for they too may be affected by the religious character of their surroundings

This range of variables is far more likely to capture the entire spectrum of contextual effects and will produce results that should be far easier to interpret as well.

In addition to the interaction terms, variables representing particular denominations (percent Lutheran or percent Episcopalian, as opposed to simply using summary measures such as percent mainline Protestant) are included where appropriate, or where existing research suggests a relationship. It must also be noted that when individual measures of religious membership (all such variables are coded as dichotomous—1 indicates membership and 0 indicates nonmembership) are used in interaction terms, interpretation of the former is no longer straightforward. If Catholic is interacted with percent Catholic and percent Jewish, then the coefficient on the individual variable Catholic represents the impact of being Catholic that is *not* captured in either of the interaction terms. In practice the symptoms of this situation will be counterintuitive signs on the individual variables.

A final note regarding the models in this and all succeeding chapters is in order. For all dependent variables that are structured by party, I have coded variables so that a positive sign indicates a pro-Republican effect and a negative sign indicates a pro-Democratic effect.[3] This is done primarily to maintain consistency and ease of readability; since the models are not always simple to digest, this coding scheme intends to add clarity to the presentation.

MODELS OF ATTITUDES AND BEHAVIORS IN 1976

Recall that for the 1976 NES survey respondents, contextual measures for county political and religious characteristics as well as census tract demographic measures are available. Thus I look at this NES survey first and in the most detail.

The demographic variables used in the 1976 models include education, personal income, gender, age, race, ideology, social class identification, political activity, and union membership. Some combination of these is used in each model. In addition, census tract measures of mean education, percent high school graduates, and mean income are utilized. The primary county political variable is percent Republican vote in county, in keeping with the coding scheme for individual presidential voting.[4]

Variables measuring the religious context, including interaction terms, are included in each model, as are individual measures of religious identification. Church attendance is also included, and several interaction terms are constructed to measure how changes in attendance influence different denominations. Finally, a dichotomous variable for county religious pluralism is included, based on the work of Salisbury, Sprague, and Weiher (1984). This variable is also introduced through interaction terms to test how specific denominations may react to a pluralist religious environment.

Presidential Voting

The 1976 election provides some important events for the student of religion and politics to consider—the presence of a Southern Evangelical candidate, combined with the activation of Evangelicals as a political force, for example. But other factors also weigh heavily in the 1976 election, primary among them Watergate and its aftermath, including Gerald Ford's pardon of Nixon and the negative public reaction to the pardon. Rarely in modern times has the public known so little about the two candidates before the campaign itself. Jimmy Carter was a complete unknown on the national scene, and Ford's 20-year career in Congress prior to his elevation had registered only on the most informed. Thus it can be hypothesized that with less information available from the outset, social contexts may become more salient as both information sources and influences on vote choice.

Table 3.1 provides an empirical test for this hypothesis. Table 3.1 shows that county levels of Republican voting influence Democratic partisans to vote Republican.[5] This finding is consistent with the hypothesis that Democrats are more inclined to follow the prevailing trend and vote with a particular context; on the other hand, the effect of county GOP voting on Republicans and independents is negligible and not statistically significant.

Beyond the county political context, all the demographic measures included in the voting model are significant predictors of vote choice, and the signs on the coefficients point in expected directions. Self-reported working-class individuals and nonwhites tend to vote Democratic, and

TABLE 3.1
Estimated 1976 Presidential Vote
                    (Logit Estimates)

Independent Variable	Coefficient
Intercept	-3.71 (1.88)**
Party identification	0.86 (0.12)***
Income	0.23 (0.13)*
Personal economic future	0.20 (0.07)***
Nonwhite respondent	-1.43 (0.71)**
Working class	-0.68 (0.27)***
Ideology self-placement	0.55 (0.11)***
Census tract mean education	-0.20 (0.12)
Percent GOP vote in county	0.17 (1.50)
Democrat X percent GOP vote in county	1.86 (0.82)**
Catholic	2.24 (1.32)*
Mainline Protestant	0.86 (0.75)
Evangelical Protestant	-0.04 (0.73)
Southern Evangelical Protestant	-0.92 (0.90)
Church attendance	0.14 (0.11)
Catholic X church attendance	-0.07 (0.18)
Catholic X pluralist county	-0.64 (0.54)
Mainliner X pluralist county	0.49 (0.47)
Evangelical X pluralist county	0.56 (0.58)
Jewish X pluralist county	0.14 (1.01)
Percent Catholic in county	-0.19 (1.40)
Catholic X pct. Catholic in county	-1.96 (2.57)
Percent mainliners in county	-0.72 (1.49)
Mainliner X pct. mainline Protestant in county	-2.36 (2.45)
Evangelical X percent Evangelical in county	4.02 (4.01)
Mainliner X percent Evangelical in county	-0.01 (2.80)
Catholic X percent Evangelical in county	-3.48 (4.15)
Total number of cases	603
Percent of cases correctly predicted	82.4
Model chi-square	357.05 with 26 df

Source: 1976 National Election Study.
Note: Standard errors in parentheses.
    *=Significant at 0.10 level.
    **=Significant at 0.05 level.
    ***=Significant at 0.01 level.

variables assessing partisanship, income, ideology, and beliefs about future personal economic situations drive voters in a Republican direction.

As for religious influences on voting, the model in Table 3.1 shows no significant effects, save for Catholic religious identification. Recall that the interpretation of this variable is not straightforward; Catholic identification is interacted with four other variables, so that the individual measure gives the effect from being Catholic *after* controlling for the effects of church attendance, county religious pluralism, percent Catholic in county, and percent Evangelical in county. All other things being equal, the positive, or pro-Republican, sign on the dichotomous Catholic variable means that Catholics have a residual propensity to vote Republican.

If 1976 represents an election in which religious factors play a significant role, why are no effects from county religious concentrations discovered in the voting model? It is certainly possible that the short-term character of an election or campaign precludes strong influence from a county-level measure; if that is the case, then little or no significant findings should appear in either the 1960 or 1980 voting model, although one could still expect county religious context to have an impact on the other dependent measures.

A second explanation for the null results is that because 1976 appears to represent the beginning of the political activism of Evangelical Christian voters, the effects of this activism do not yet appear in a study of 1976, or their impact is obscured by post-Watergate factors and other significant predictors. If this hypothesis is correct, then the 1980 elections may well show important county religious contextual effects.

Pursuing the 1976 election for a moment, Table 3.2 displays aggregated voting patterns for the three major religious groups utilized in the analysis. Table 3.2 shows that although each of the three religious groups votes in a unique way, the deviations across party groupings are quite small. In fact, although 14.1 percent of Republican partisans voted for Carter, the range among Republicans across religious groups deviates only four percentage points either way (Catholics, 18.0; Evangelicals, 10.0). Similarly, for Democrats who voted for Carter, the range across religious groups is less than four percentage points. Only mainline Protestant independents show any significant deviation, voting 39.3 percent Democratic as opposed to 46.5 percent for all independents. Hence the differences in the aggregate religious group voting totals arise almost entirely from the partisan distribution within those groups. There are more Republicans among mainline Protestants (36.2 percent) than among Catholics (16 percent) or Evangelicals (21 percent), so a small difference in the percentages across groups masks the larger differences due to dissimilar group composition.

The story Table 3.2 tells is that religion as an individual trait makes only a small difference in 1976. Breaking down by religious context, with and without interaction terms, provides no further explanatory power. A final verdict on religious context and voting, then, must wait for the 1960 and 1980 results.

TABLE 3.2
1976 Presidential Vote by Party Identification (Collapsed) and Religion

Category/Party	Percent Carter	Percent Ford	N
All Voters	51.4	48.6	1,342
Democrats	82.2	17.8	527
Independents	46.5	53.5	439
Republicans	14.1	85.9	376
Catholics	58.9	41.1	338
Democrats	79.8	20.2	173
Independents	48.1	51.9	104
Republicans	18.0	82.0	61
Mainline Protestants	40.2	59.8	478
Democrats	78.8	21.2	137
Independents	39.3	60.7	150
Republicans	13.1	86.9	191
Evangelical Protestants	55.4	44.7	374
Democrats	85.4	14.6	164
Independents	48.3	51.7	120
Republicans	10.0	90.0	90

Source: 1976 National Election Study.
Note: Figures may not add to 100 percent due to rounding off.

Party Identification, Turnout, and Attention to Public Affairs

These three dependent behaviors represent a range of political attitudes. Partisanship is presumed to be a long-term attachment, indicative of an individual's political history and outlook, and is affected or altered by short-term forces, particularly during presidential election years. Attention to public affairs measures an overall interest in the political process. Turnout represents a willingness to participate in that process.[6] Of the three, partisanship should be the most responsive to county religious context, for partisanship develops over time and partly in response to external and contextual forces (Leege, Lieske, and Wald 1989; Campbell et al. 1960; Berelson et al. 1954). Previous research has concluded that turnout and political interest are largely individually determined, hence not responsive to context. But some religious groups do affect turnout, especially in a negative sense; consider that many Pentecostal denominations actively discourage participation in politics (Kellstedt and Noll 1990; Johnson and White 1967). Further, one can hypothesize that interest and participation may well be activated by political activity emanating from particular

TABLE 3.3
Estimated 1976 Party Identification
            (OLS Regression Estimates)

Independent Variable	Coefficient
Intercept	2.85 (0.76)***
Father's party identification	0.31 (0.04)***
Income	0.07 (0.04)*
Nonwhite respondent	-0.05 (0.15)
Working class	-0.14 (0.08)*
Ideology self-placement	0.34 (0.03)***
Census tract mean education	-0.24 (0.08)***
Tract mean pct. high school grads	2.10 (0.55)***
Percent GOP vote in county	2.58 (0.45)***
Democrat X pct. GOP vote in county	-5.65 (0.18)***
Catholic	0.44 (0.27)
Mainline Protestant	0.13 (0.22)
Southern Evangelical Protestant	-0.31 (0.25)
Church attendance	0.06 (0.03)*
Mainline Protestant X church attendance	0.04 (0.06)
Pluralist county	-0.07 (0.09)
Percent Catholic in county	-0.45 (0.45)
Catholic X pct. Catholic in county	-1.67 (0.72)**
Mainliner X percent mainline Protestant in county	-0.60 (0.57)
Evangelical X pct. Evangelical in county	1.01 (1.03)
Mainliner X percent Evangelical in county	-2.06 (0.93)**
Catholic X percent Evangelical in county	-2.87 (1.24)**
Total number of cases	716
Adjusted R-square	.76

Source: 1976 National Election Study.
Note: Standard errors in parentheses.
   *=Significant at 0.10 level.
   **=Significant at 0.05 level.
   ***=Significant at 0.01 level.

religious groups; a heightened interest would then stem from
some perceived threat or response to the activities of others,
either inside or outside one's own religious group.

With these hypotheses in mind, Table 3.3 analyzes the
determinants of party identification. Partisanship is
affected by all demographic measures except race; note
particularly that an individual's father's party
identification is a strong predictor. Further, two census
tract contextual measures are significant: mean tract
education and percent high school graduates. Curiously, a
higher percentage of high school graduates has a strong
positive (Republican) effect on individual partisanship, and

mean education (measured in years of school completed) has a negative (Democratic) influence on partisanship.

The use of interaction terms pays off with the partisanship model, as three separate interaction variables are statistically significant. This means the following:

- The presence of Catholics in increasing numbers within a county means that individual Catholics are more likely to be Democrats; and

- Increasing numbers of Evangelicals within a county drive *both* Catholics and mainline Protestants to be Democratic.

What do these findings say about the effect of county religious distributions? Catholics find two reasons to adhere to their traditional political allegiances: the presence of other Catholics, which creates a natural reinforcement mechanism; and a rising number of Evangelicals—a newly emerging political force in 1976. Mainline Protestants also appear more driven to Democratic attachments when there are more Evangelicals in a given county.

The county political variables also offer interesting results. Increased Republican voting is positively related to partisan identification (drives individuals in a Republican direction), but for Democratic partisans, increased Republican voting reinforces their Democratic attachment. The voting model showed precisely the opposite result for Democrats. Thus, Democratic partisans may be influenced to vote Republican with their Republican and independent neighbors, but Democrats *do not* change partisan attachments; in fact, their Democratic ties are strengthened in the presence of heavy Republican voting.

Table 3.4 examines 1976 voter turnout, and the model indicates that turnout is influenced by all demographic factors except one; race has no impact on turnout in 1976. Democrats are more likely to turn out as the vote in their counties becomes increasingly Republican. Mainline and Evangelical Protestants are more likely to vote as their church attendance increases—further indications that these churches are becoming politically active in the mid-1970s. And Evangelicals in particular are motivated to cast ballots by two other factors: the percentage of Catholics and the percentage of other Evangelicals in the county. Both these factors are sizable in magnitude and positively related to turnout. Evangelicals thus appear to be motivated to vote not by the mere fact of being Evangelicals but in response to specific aspects of their county environments and to repeated attendance at their churches.

Findings such as these should put to rest once and for all the simple—and simplistic—notion that religious attachment alone constitutes a sufficient reason for particular behavior patterns among denominations.

Attention to public affairs is a measure of the degree to which an individual is interested in politics, perhaps an indicator of individual receptiveness to cues from surrounding social and political contexts. However, in Table 3.5 the only contextual variable influencing attention to public affairs is

TABLE 3.4
Estimated 1976 General Election Turnout
(Logit Estimates)

Independent Variable	Coefficient
Intercept	-9.03 (1.22)***
Party identification	0.04 (0.10)
Age	0.02 (0.01)***
Male	0.72 (0.25)***
Union member	0.54 (0.27)**
Education	0.32 (0.12)***
Income	0.21 (0.13)*
Follows public affairs	0.61 (0.12)***
Nonwhite respondent	0.19 (0.41)
Middle class	0.56 (0.24)**
Discussion partners also voted	1.04 (0.16)***
Census tract mean income	0.10 (0.04)**
Percent GOP vote in county	0.79 (1.31)
Democrat X pct. GOP vote in county	1.99 (0.82)**
Catholic	-0.96 (0.89)
Mainline Protestant	0.38 (0.87)
Evangelical Protestant	-1.34 (0.95)
Catholic X church attendance	0.18 (0.14)
Mainliner X church attendance	0.49 (0.19)***
Evangelical X church attendance	0.24 (0.15)*
Pluralist county	-0.20 (0.27)
Catholic X percent Catholic in county	2.94 (1.99)
Mainliner X percent Catholic in county	-1.14 (2.05)
Evangelical X percent Catholic in county	6.57 (3.14)**
Evangelical X percent Evangelical in county	4.85 (2.75)*
Mainliner X percent Evangelical in county	-4.82 (3.15)
Catholic X percent Evangelical in county	2.60 (4.10)
Total number of cases	798
Percent of cases correctly predicted	85.0
Model chi-square	222.38 with 26 df

Source: 1976 National Election Study.
Note: Standard errors in parentheses.
    *=Significant at 0.10 level.
    **=Significant at 0.05 level.
    ***=Significant at 0.01 level.*

tract mean education, which has a negative influence. That
is, as a census tract is more educated on average, individuals
are less interested in public affairs. Individual educational

TABLE 3.5
Estimated 1976 Attention to Public Affairs
                    (OLS Regression Estimates)

Independent Variable	Coefficient
Intercept	1.57 (0.29)**
Interest in election	0.19 (0.02)***
Political activity	0.32 (0.05)***
Age	0.00 (0.00)
Education	0.07 (0.02)***
Nonwhite respondent	-0.04 (0.08)
Watches television news about election	0.11 (0.02)***
Reads newspapers about election	0.24 (0.02)***
Census tract mean education	-0.05 (0.02)**
Percent GOP vote in county	0.26 (0.27)
Catholic	-0.13 (0.11)
Church attendance	0.02 (0.02)
Mainliner X church attendance	-0.00 (0.02)
Pluralist county	-0.03 (0.05)
Catholic X pct. Catholic in county	0.11 (0.31)
Total number of cases	1071
Adjusted R-square	.44

Source: 1976 National Election Study.
Note: Standard errors in parentheses.
    *=Significant at 0.10 level.
    **=Significant at 0.05 level.
    ***=Significant at 0.01 level.

attainment is positively related to attention; thus the impact of education depends on the measurement unit. None of the county religious context variables is significant, and in fact only the dichotomous Catholic variable is even close to being statistically significant.

Hence attention to public affairs does not seem to rely on county religious concentrations, or on specific denominational membership, in any meaningful way. Social context apparently does compel voting for some groups in some situations, but it does not affect overall levels of interest in politics.

Attitudes toward Abortion

In the wake of the 1973 Supreme Court decision Roe v. Wade, abortion became a salient political issue for many individuals and groups in the United States. Although abortion was not a heated topic during the 1976 elections, it had at least pricked the public consciousness and risen to the national agenda, spurred on by the beliefs and actions of both ministers and laypeople in religious institutions. Thus the regression model predicting abortion attitudes for 1976 could

TABLE 3.6
Estimated 1976 Attitude Toward Abortion
           (OLS Regression Estimates)

Independent Variable	Coefficient
Intercept	1.01 (0.68)
Education	-0.17 (0.03)***
Income	-0.11 (0.03)***
Ideology self-placement	0.02 (0.03)
Male	0.15 (0.07)**
Supports Equal Rights Amendment	-0.37 (0.09)***
Census tract mean education	0.12 (0.07)*
Tract mean pct. high school grads	-0.91 (0.50)*
Percent GOP vote in county	0.45 (0.41)
Democrat X pct. GOP vote in county	0.10 (0.16)
Catholic	-0.58 (0.24)*
Jewish	-0.72 (0.21)***
Evangelical Protestant	-0.57 (0.36)
Southern Evangelical Protestant	-0.48 (0.24)**
Catholic X church attendance	0.30 (0.04)***
Mainliner X church attendance	0.10 (0.04)**
Evangelical X church attendance	0.18 (0.05)***
Mainliner X pluralist county	-0.20 (0.11)*
Evangelical X pluralist county	-0.28 (0.17)
Catholic X percent Catholic in county	-0.26 (0.44)
Mainliner X percent Catholic in county	-0.89 (0.43)**
Evangelical X percent Catholic in county	0.74 (0.80)
Catholic X percent mainline Protestant in county	0.51 (0.54)
Mainliner X percent Evangelical in county	-1.13 (0.80)
Evangelical X percent Evangelical in county	2.35 (1.09)**
Percent Episcopal in county	-7.95 (3.38)**
Total number of cases	679
Adjusted R-square	.28

Source: 1976 National Election Study.
Note: Standard errors in parentheses.
*   *=Significant at 0.10 level.*
*   **=Significant at 0.05 level.*
*   ***=Significant at 0.01 level.*

well produce evidence of religious contextual influences on individual attitudes.

Positive signs on the coefficients in Table 3.6 denote increasingly pro-life, anti-abortion attitudes; negative signs denote increasingly pro-choice, pro-abortion attitudes. Most of the demographic variables are significantly related to abortion attitudes, and the results conform to expectations. As for the church variables, with so many variables competing for attention in Table 3.6, the following discussion of the results focuses in turn on each of the five denominations specified in the model.

Catholics

Catholic adherence appears in four separate variables—by itself and interacted with church attendance, percent Catholic in county, and percent mainline Protestant in county. Increasing church attendance is a significant predictor of pro-life attitudes, a sure sign that an individual Catholic is receptive to the strong, official institutional position of the church hierarchy. The presence of other Catholics, or of mainline Protestants, in the county has no bearing on individual Catholic attitudes about abortion.

With the effect of those three intervening factors separated out through the OLS model, the dichotomous Catholic variable is significant and negatively related to pro-life attitudes. In other words, when church attendance and Catholic and mainline Protestant county concentrations are controlled for, Catholics are more likely to be pro-choice. Evidently Catholic adherents require church attendance to reinforce pro-life attitudes; otherwise they are certainly receptive to pro-choice attitudes from personal beliefs or other aspects of their social surroundings.

Jews

Jewish respondents are included in only one variable, the dichotomous variable for Jewish adherence. This is statistically significant and drives the Jewish respondent in a definite pro-choice direction, in line with expectations about this group.

Episcopalians

This group also appears separately once in the model: Percent Episcopal in a county is significant and shows a strong pro-choice influence. This same finding is replicated in every estimated permutation of this model (other estimations not reported). However, the dichotomous variable for Episcopal adherence is never a significant predictor of abortion attitudes. Although no county in the study ever has more than 15 percent Episcopalians, it certainly appears that high concentrations (in relative terms) have a definite effect, even if ready explanations for the effect are not at hand.

Mainline Protestants

The effect of mainline Protestant adherence is divided among four separate variables: church attendance, pluralist county environment, percent Catholic in county, and percent Evangelical Protestant in county. As with Catholics, increasing church attendance is correlated with pro-life attitudes among mainliners. However, the coefficient for

Catholics is three times greater than that for mainliners, probably because there is no single, consistent mainline church view on abortion. Second, in pluralist counties, mainline Protestants are more likely to be pro-choice. Perhaps in this case, the pluralist religious situation promotes less rigid abortion attitudes as well. Pluralist counties have no differentiating effects for any other denominational grouping except mainliners. Third, as the percentage of Catholics rises, mainliners are increasingly pro-choice; this may well be evidence of a reaction by mainliners against a Catholic majority that may be actively hostile to legalized abortion. Finally, the percentage of Evangelicals does not significantly affect mainliner attitudes. Thus there are environmental factors—either no dominant religion or a dominant Catholic presence—that drive mainliners to adopt more pro-choice positions, while mainliners, like Catholics, become more pro-life with greater exposure to their church environments.

Evangelical Protestants

Six separate variables attempt to capture the reasons why adherents to Evangelical faiths believe what they believe on abortion, and three of these show significant results. Church attendance has a positive (pro-life) effect (smaller in magnitude than for Catholics, larger than for mainliners), and the percentage of other Evangelicals in the county also has a strong pro-life effect. Two dichotomous variables—Evangelical adherence alone, and Southern Evangelical membership—are negative (pro-choice) in sign, though only the latter is statistically significant. Finally, a pluralist county environment and the percentage of Catholics in a county have no significant statistical effect on Evangelical abortion attitudes.

Apparently Evangelicals have pro-life, anti-abortion attitudes strengthened by the presence of other Evangelicals, both in churches and in the county environment. The negative coefficient for Southern Evangelicals suggests that living in the South has no additional pro-life impact, and indeed this coefficient appears to mitigate the strong positive effects of Evangelical concentration within counties.

Summary of Findings on Abortion

In 1976, with the exception of the interaction between Evangelical and percent Evangelical, the contextual influences all work in a pro-choice direction; that is, they mitigate the pro-life influence of church attendance (all religions) and official church positions (especially Catholics and Evangelicals). It is clearly difficult to explain all the determinants of individual attitudes toward abortion, but the findings do point to an active assessment of the social environment when individuals consider this issue.

MODELS OF ATTITUDES AND BEHAVIORS IN 1960

The presidential election of 1960 represents a signal event for students and scholars of religion and political behavior. John F. Kennedy's Catholicism was a visible and contentious issue to many in the electorate, and its effects on the final outcome have been well documented for Catholics and non-Catholics alike. The most well known analysis is that of Philip Converse (1966), who argues that the Kennedy candidacy had a polarizing and mobilizing effect, causing Catholics to turn out in greater numbers to vote Democratic, and causing many Protestants to cast ballots against Kennedy. This result is not generally questioned in the literature on 1960, and indeed fits well with the Converse normal vote analysis. My 1960 vote model attempts to replicate the existing findings and uses county concentrations and interaction variables to understand more clearly how contextual forces may have influenced the vote decisions of religious adherents.

Presidential Voting

I begin with a table of aggregated voting patterns, again breaking down NES respondents by religion and party affiliation to find relevant trends. Table 3.7 clearly shows the strength of partisan ties in 1960, as Republican and Democratic partisans voted in high percentages for their party's candidate, regardless of religious affiliation. Unlike in 1976, the variance of partisans across religious groups is sizable. For example, 21 percent of Catholic Republicans voted for Kennedy, while less than 3 percent of Republicans in the two Protestant groups voted for Kennedy. A general pattern of different aggregated results by religious groups, due to the distribution of partisans within those groups, is present here as it was in 1976. But the extreme percentages in some cells suggests that significant contextual effects are at work in 1960. The logistic regression model will test explicitly for these effects.

The 1960 voting model (Table 3.8) correctly predicts 86.2 percent of the vote, which is not surprising since partisanship is such a strong indicator. Income and race join partisanship as significant demographic variables. As in 1976, the interaction between Democratic partisans and the percent of Republican vote in the county is a significant and positive influence on Nixon voting; Democrats thus appear susceptible to heavy Republican voting trends in their counties.

Unlike the model estimating 1976 vote choice, this model produces some significant results on the contextual variables. Since the model includes so many interaction terms to assess contextual effects, the findings for religious groups again deserve close examination one by one.

Catholics

Catholics are not affected by the percentage of other Catholics in their counties, but they are affected by the

TABLE 3.7
1960 Presidential Vote by Party Identification (Collapsed) and Religion

Category/Party	Percent Kennedy	Percent Nixon	N
All Voters	50.4	49.6	1,122
Democrats	84.4	15.6	514
Independents	46.5	53.5	245
Republicans	4.7	95.3	363
Catholics	80.1	19.9	271
Democrats	96.0	4.0	174
Independents	74.6	25.5	55
Republicans	21.4	78.6	42
Mainline Protestants	34.4	65.7	492
Democrats	79.7	20.3	153
Independents	37.3	62.7	110
Republicans	2.6	97.4	229
Evangelical Protestants	44.0	56.0	284
Democrats	72.4	27.6	152
Independents	26.4	73.6	53
Republicans	1.3	98.7	79

Source: 1960 National Election Study.
Note: Figures may not add to 100 percent due to rounding off.

percentage of mainliners. In fact, there is a very strong pro-Kennedy effect among Catholics who live in counties with large numbers of mainline Protestants. If this finding is coupled with another significant coefficient, on the Catholic dichotomous variable, a clear explanation for Catholic behavior emerges. Not surprisingly, simply being Catholic in 1960 predisposes an individual to vote for Kennedy, but no additional reinforcement to that predisposition comes from the presence of other Catholics; rather, Catholics bind together in the face of mainline Protestants to support Kennedy. This insulating effect is identical to the phenomenon described by Finifter (1974) in her classic study of Republican auto workers, who were found to join groups primarily with one another rather than with their mostly Democratic coworkers, whose group ties did not strongly correlate with party preferences. Further, findings of Catholic cohesion and resistance to the prevailing views of the social environment replicate the work of Segal and Meyer (1974), who reached the same conclusion.

Mainline Protestants

Although the presence of mainliners appears to affect the behavior of other religious groups, their own behavior is less

TABLE 3.8
Estimated 1960 Presidential Vote
(Logit Estimates)

Independent Variable	Coefficient
Intercept	-5.18 (1.03)***
Party identification	1.25 (0.12)***
Income	0.06 (0.03)**
Personal economic future	0.05 (0.08)
Nonwhite respondent	-0.90 (0.54)*
Working class	0.25 (0.25)
Percent GOP vote in county	-0.38 (1.23)
Democrat X pct. GOP vote in county	3.02 (0.83)***
Catholic	-0.64 (0.21)***
Mainline Protestant	1.11 (1.02)
Evangelical Protestant	-0.50 (0.95)
Church attendance	0.11 (0.15)
Mainliner X church attendance	0.18 (0.20)
Evangelical X church attendance	0.62 (0.23)***
Pluralist county	0.61 (0.34)*
Mainliner X pluralist county	-1.39 (0.52)***
Jewish X pluralist county	-1.46 (0.90)*
Catholic X percent Catholic in county	-0.85 (2.04)
Mainliner X percent Catholic in county	0.90 (1.38)
Evangelical X percent Catholic in county	-1.22 (1.81)
Catholic X percent mainline Protestant in county	-6.28 (3.72)*
Mainliner X percent mainline Protestant in county	-2.13 (1.61)
Evangelical X percent Baptist in county	1.06 (1.97)
Total number of cases	897
Percent of cases correctly predicted	86.2
Model chi-square	690.38 with 22 df

Source: 1960 National Election Study.
Note: Standard errors in parentheses.
   =Significant at 0.10 level.
   **=Significant at 0.05 level.*
   ***=Significant at 0.01 level.*

affected by contextual influences. Church attendance, percent Catholic in a county (a variable analogous to percent mainliners for Catholics), percent mainliners in a county, and the dichotomous variable for mainline adherence are not significant in the full 1960 model.

Mainline Protestants show environmental effects only from living in counties that are pluralist in their distribution of

religious adherents.   In such counties, mainline Protestants
are more likely to vote for Kennedy.   Now, since mainliners
are strongly Republican and vote that way to begin with (as
the initial frequency table demonstrates), it can be surmised
that any anti-Catholic feelings among mainliners might be
mitigated or perhaps missing altogether when their county
environment has no strong concentration of any particular
religion.   The coefficient on the mainliner-pluralist county
interaction suggests that all other things being equal
(meaning that the average mainliner is likely to vote
Republican in the first place), pluralist counties weaken the
mainliner-Republican bond in some way, such that other vote
options become viable.

Evangelicals

Perhaps some Evangelical denominations saw an even
greater threat from a Catholic president than did other
Protestants in 1960, for a strong connection between
increasing church attendance and Republican voting is seen for
Evangelicals.   No other variable significantly predicts the
behavior of Evangelicals.   Evangelicals thus are the only
group to show an effect from church exposure, leading to
speculation that perhaps some direct proscriptions were
emanating from the pulpit against the Kennedy candidacy.   The
frequency distribution of votes shows that Evangelical
independents vote Republican in greater numbers than mainliner
independents, even though mainliners as a group vote
Republican more than do Evangelicals.

Other Religions

After testing alternative specifications, only an
interaction between pluralist county and Jewish adherence
proved to be a significant predictor of voting.   As with
mainliners, Jews in pluralist counties voted strongly
Democratic.   Given the tendency of Jewish adherents to vote
Democratic in the first place, this result may not reflect a
true contextual effect.

Summary of Findings on 1960 Voting

Social context, specifically religious context, clearly
matters in the 1960 race.   Given the salience of religion as
a campaign issue, it is not surprising that contextual effects
are uncovered.   The precise nature of those effects suggests
that at the county level, religious context has little power
as a reinforcement mechanism.   Catholics do not respond to
having more Catholics around them, nor does either group of
Protestants. However, religious context has substantial power
as a means of enforcing cohesion (Catholics as a minority) or
weakening existing ties (mainliners in the pluralist
situation).   At the church level, included only indirectly
through the effects of attendance, there may be direct
contextual influence (Evangelicals), and this finding can be
pursued further and tested more directly in Chapters 4 and 7.

Partisanship, Turnout, and Attention to Public Affairs

As in 1976, partisanship in 1960 is hypothesized to be more responsive to contextual factors than the other two dependent measures. In 1960, however, with the salience of religion as a campaign issue, religious context should be more likely to affect turnout and interest in public affairs. One can hypothesize greater numbers of both Catholics and Protestants mobilizing, the former to support Kennedy and the latter to support his opponent.

The partisanship model for 1960, displayed in Table 3.9, produces results identical to those for 1976 on the county political context variables. Democratic partisans strengthen their allegiance to the Democratic party as their counties vote Republican in greater numbers; independents and Republican partisans go with the county flow. Recall again the findings in both the 1960 and 1976 voting models: Democrats are influenced by the political character of the county to *vote* Republican, but are not influenced to *become* Republicans.

As for county religious context effects, Jews show stronger Democratic ties in pluralist counties, a finding repeated from the vote model. Only church attendance appears to affect the partisanship of Catholics, but the negative (Democratic) effect contradicts Lenski's assertion that church attendance correlates with conservative political preferences among Catholics. Again, the Kennedy candidacy and the feelings of pride stirred among Catholics may have altered the distinction between church and community life that forms the basis for Lenski's findings.

The most interesting county religious context findings concern mainline Protestants. Four significant variables have an impact on their partisan identification. Mainliners are driven in a Republican direction by three factors: church attendance, percent Catholic in county, and percent other mainliners in county (percent Evangelical, which was significant for mainliners in 1976, is not significant in 1960). Clearly mainline Protestants are predisposed to identify with the Republican party; these results show that some specific contexts enhance this predisposition. Finally, the dichotomous mainliner variable is negatively related to partisanship, a sensible finding only after the other three positively related interaction variables are considered.

The 1976 turnout model revealed that Evangelicals were more likely to vote given certain conditions in their county religious contexts; it may not have been a coincidence that an Evangelical ran for president in 1976. The 1960 findings provide support for an analogous argument: that a Catholic's candidacy, when religion is an issue, can mobilize more voters to go to the polls. In fact, the turnout findings in Table 3.10 demonstrate a mobilization effect based on Kennedy's presence in the race. Catholics are more likely to vote in 1960 regardless of other factors. Additionally, increasing concentrations of Catholics in counties make the likelihood of voting rise for all voters, including Catholics but especially mainline Protestants.

Finally, Catholics are less likely to vote as the percentage of mainliners in a county increases. This finding

TABLE 3.9
Estimated 1960 Party Identification
                    (OLS Regression Estimates)

Independent Variable	Coefficient
Intercept	1.47 (0.27)***
Father's party identification	0.35 (0.04)***
Income	0.00 (0.01)
Nonwhite respondent	-0.44 (0.16)***
Working class	-0.09 (0.08)
Percent GOP vote in county	5.07 (0.34)***
Democrat X pct. GOP vote in county	-7.24 (0.16)***
Catholic	0.10 (0.17)
Mainline Protestant	-1.32 (0.30)***
Evangelical Protestant	-0.46 (0.28)*
Catholic X church attendance	-0.16 (0.07)**
Mainliner X church attendance	0.21 (0.05)***
Evangelical X church attendance	0.10 (0.06)
Pluralist county	0.09 (0.09)
Catholic X pluralist county	0.20 (0.17)
Jewish X pluralist county	-0.74 (0.29)***
Catholic X percent Catholic in county	0.48 (0.58)
Mainliner X percent Catholic in county	2.71 (0.49)***
Evangelical X percent Catholic in county	1.03 (0.56)*
Mainliner X percent mainline Protestant in county	1.16 (0.53)**
Mainliner X percent Evangelical in county	1.09 (0.85)
Total number of cases	999
Adjusted R-square	.81

Source: 1960 National Election Study.
Note: Standard errors in parentheses.
    *=Significant at 0.10 level.
    **=Significant at 0.05 level.
    ***=Significant at 0.01 level.

should be considered in tandem with the effect of percent mainliner on Catholics' vote choices (strong Democratic influence; see Table 3.8). According to this analysis, the presence of Mainliners in the county environment depresses Catholic turnout; but those Catholics who do cast votes are the most committed Democratic or Kennedy supporters. Hence one can speculate that in 1960 some Catholics who otherwise would not have voted did so because Kennedy was running; other Catholics had the added impetus to vote by virtue of residing within large Catholic communities. But those Catholics not fortunate enough to have strength in numbers went to the polls only if they were strongly committed to Kennedy; those who

TABLE 3.10
Estimated 1960 General Election Turnout
(Logit Estimates)

Independent Variable	Coefficient
Intercept	-3.93 (0.90)***
Party identification	0.09 (0.09)
Income	0.10 (0.04)***
Age	0.03 (0.01)***
Union member	0.17 (0.23)
Education	0.50 (0.13)***
Follows public affairs	0.26 (0.08)***
Nonwhite respondent	-0.93 (0.28)***
Middle class	0.10 (0.26)
Talked with someone about election	0.53 (0.27)**
Percent GOP vote in county	1.01 (0.94)
Democrat X percent GOP vote in county	0.36 (0.74)
Catholic	0.85 (0.49)*
Mainline Protestant	-1.19 (0.69)*
Church attendance	0.04 (0.13)
Mainliner X church attendance	0.32 (0.22)
Catholic X church attendance	0.14 (0.16)
Pluralist county	0.22 (0.27)
Percent Catholic in county	1.84 (1.09)*
Mainliner X percent Catholic in county	4.34 (1.68)***
Percent mainliners in county	2.31 (1.50)
Catholic X percent mainliners in county	-3.64 (2.18)*
Percent Evangelicals in county	0.41 (1.30)
Total number of cases	1031
Percent of cases correctly predicted	84.4
Model chi-square	223.00 with 23 df

Source: 1960 National Election Study.
Note: Standard errors in parentheses.
    *=Significant at 0.10 level.
    **=Significant at 0.05 level.
    ***=Significant at 0.01 level.

lacked strong predispositions reduced the conflict between themselves and their Protestant neighbors by not participating.

Table 3.11 examines 1960 determinants of attention to public affairs. In 1976, no contextual influence on attention to public affairs was found. In 1960, two interaction terms provide significant contextual influences. Catholic times percent Catholic in the county is positively related to attention to public affairs—clearly evidence of religion's salience and perhaps the level of interest and conversation

TABLE 3.11
Estimated 1960 Attention to Public Affairs
(OLS Regression Estimates)

Independent Variable	Coefficient
Intercept	-0.58 (0.31)*
Interest in election	0.39 (0.04)***
Talked about election with others	0.25 (0.09)***
Age	0.01 (0.00)**
Education	0.06 (0.04)*
Watches television news about election	0.03 (0.04)
Reads newspapers about election	0.23 (0.03)***
Nonwhite respondent	0.18 (0.14)
Percent GOP vote in county	-0.23 (0.33)
Catholic	0.04 (0.18)
Mainline Protestant	0.84 (0.33)***
Jewish	0.28 (0.25)
Church attendance	0.00 (0.04)
Catholic X church attendance	-0.12 (0.08)
Pluralist county	0.09 (0.11)
Mainliner X pluralist county	-0.30 (0.19)
Catholic X percent Catholic in county	1.56 (0.64)**
Mainliner X percent Catholic in county	-0.86 (0.58)
Catholic X percent Mainline Protestant in county	0.77 (0.79)
Mainliner X percent mainliner in county	-0.82 (0.64)
Percent Evangelicals in county	0.63 (0.54)
Mainliner X percent Evangelical in county	-2.11 (1.05)**
Total number of cases	1077
Adjusted R-square	.31

Source: 1960 National Election Study.
Note: Standard errors in parentheses.
*   *=Significant at 0.10 level.*
*   **=Significant at 0.05 level.*
*   ***=Significant at 0.01 level.*

within Catholic subcultures as well. Mainline Protestants are more interested in politics simply by their affiliation (as shown by the dichotomous variable coefficient for mainliners), but this interest is mitigated by the percentage of Evangelicals in the county. Perhaps this is evidence of the same effect manifested in Evangelical Republican voting: Mainliners in such counties respond to anti-Kennedy feelings by withdrawing from political affairs.

MODELS OF ATTITUDES AND BEHAVIORS IN 1980

The presidential election of 1980 marked the first time since 1932 (Herbert Hoover) that a sitting elected president was defeated in his reelection bid. Jimmy Carter's loss has been attributed to several obvious factors, including economic troubles, the national humiliation from Iran's hostage taking and defiance, the presence of a third major candidate who pulled 7 percent of the vote largely from Carter, and the personal appeal of Ronald Reagan. Along with these usual suspects, we must look for county religious context as a factor activated by some of the above issues. Analysis of the 1976 election revealed no such contextual effects, but 1960 displayed several interesting findings. Accordingly, the same dependent measures are again tested for the presence of church contextual effects.

Presidential Voting

For purposes of this analysis, votes for independent candidate John Anderson are excluded from the analysis, so that interpretation of models and findings more closely parallels that of the other two elections studied. Table 3.12 details the frequency breakdown of 1980 voting by partisanship and religious preference. Jimmy Carter's share of the two-party vote slips for all major religious groups from 1976 to 1980; his share of Evangelical votes slips the least, and he does maintain a plurality over Reagan within this group. But mainline Protestants shift strongly to Reagan, giving him more than a two-to-one advantage over Carter. Examining the partisan breakdown, Carter loses eight percentage points from 1976 to 1980, and the loss in percentage terms is between 7 and 13 percentage points for each partisan category. Despite the changes from 1976 to 1980, Table 3.12 presents a pattern common to all three elections studied: clear differences across religious groups, and consistent patterns within the partisan breakdowns of the religious groups. In other words, Catholic Republicans appear just as likely as Evangelical Republicans to vote Republican; the difference in aggregated totals comes from differences in partisan distributions across groups.

Table 3.13 formally models the determinants of vote choice in 1980. Economic factors in the 1980 election are reflected in the lack of significance of the working-class variable. Normally this self-reported description is a reliable correlate of Democratic voting, but it is not in 1980. Partisanship, race, and ideology are the relevant individual-level factors. Additionally, the now-familiar response of Democrats to county voting appears again; Democrats are more likely to vote against their partisan preferences as the share of Republican votes in their counties increases. In 1980, the only GOP victory of the three elections studied, Republicans and independents are also influenced by the county political context.

Evangelical Protestants appear most susceptible to county religious context in the 1980 election. Recall from 1976 that no significant findings regarding Evangelicals were found,

TABLE 3.12
1980 Presidential Vote by Party Identification (Collapsed) and Religion

Category/Party	Percent Carter	Percent Reagan	N
All Voters	43.5	56.5	621
Democrats	74.0	26.0	273
Independents	33.3	66.7	162
Republicans	7.5	92.5	186
Catholics	47.5	52.5	139
Democrats	66.7	33.3	72
Independents	39.5	60.5	38
Republicans	10.3	89.7	29
Mainline Protestants	32.2	67.8	202
Democrats	75.0	25.0	68
Independents	22.9	77.1	48
Republicans	3.5	96.5	86
Evangelical Protestants	52.4	47.6	191
Democrats	79.8	20.2	99
Independents	39.5	60.5	38
Republicans	11.1	88.9	54

Source: 1976 National Election Study.

even though one of their own was a candidate. But in 1980, after examining the relevant interaction and dummy variables, the following can be said about Evangelical behavior:

— In pluralist counties, and in the presence of many Catholics in the county, Evangelicals are more probable Republican voters.

— Southern Evangelicals are also more likely Republican voters.

— Having controlled for all of the above, the average Evangelical is more likely to vote Democratic.

Certainly the so-called "Religious Right" becomes a political force in 1980, and the issues salient to this group lead them to the GOP. According to the analysis here, that movement toward the Republican party is stronger than ties to Carter (who is Southern, conservative on social issues, and an Evangelical himself), especially in counties dominated by no other denomination or group. Kellstedt and Noll (1990) argue that Evangelicals undergo a realignment in the late 1970s and early 1980s, shifting primary allegiance to the Republican party. The model in Table 3.13 appears to be a snapshot of

TABLE 3.13
Estimated 1980 Presidential Vote
                    (Logit Estimates)

Independent Variable	Coefficient
Intercept	-8.70 (2.04)***
Party identification	1.22 (0.21)***
Income	0.08 (0.05)
Personal economic future	0.10 (0.13)
Nonwhite respondent	-2.21 (0.92)**
Working class	-0.57 (0.39)
Ideology self-placement	0.67 (0.18)***
Percent GOP vote in county	4.57 (2.58)*
Democrat X percent GOP vote in county	2.77 (1.33)**
Catholic	-1.41 (1.87)
Mainline Protestant	-0.33 (1.48)
Evangelical Protestant	-5.01 (1.82)***
Southern Evangelical Protestant	2.74 (1.19)**
Church attendance	-0.10 (0.18)
Catholic X church attendance	0.50 (0.29)*
Catholic X pluralist county	-3.53 (1.50)**
Mainliner X pluralist county	0.22 (0.79)
Evangelical X pluralist county	1.60 (0.95)*
Jewish X pluralist county	-5.37 (0.76)***
Catholic X percent Catholic in county	0.98 (1.64)
Mainliner X percent Catholic in county	2.94 (2.02)
Evangelical X percent Catholic in county	7.38 (3.03)**
Catholic X percent mainliners in county	-0.10 (2.91)
Mainliner X percent mainliners in county	-1.08 (2.10)
Evangelical X percent mainliners in county	3.72 (3.29)
Total number of cases	316
Percent of cases correctly predicted	85.8
Model chi-square	223.93 with 24 df

Source: 1980 National Election Study.
Note: Standard errors in parentheses.
      *=Significant at 0.10 level.
      **=Significant at 0.05 level.
      ***=Significant at 0.01 level.

this realignment in progress in 1980, with specific religious contexts playing a role in the depth of this shift.
    Catholics abandon Carter in large numbers in 1980, and Catholic Democratic partisans are less inclined to vote the

party line than any other partisan group (only a two-to-one margin). However, pluralist counties still produce strong Democratic influences on Catholics. More significantly, increasing church attendance is related to GOP voting among Catholics. This result replicates the finding reported by Lenski in 1961. But in 1980, the likely explanation for the relationship between attendance and voting is issue advocacy, in particular the salience of abortion and the clear embrace of the Catholic Church's position by the Republican party and its candidate. This explanation is more specific (and perhaps time bound) than the one offered by Lenski, but it fits the case of 1980 well.

Partisanship, Turnout, and Attention to Public Affairs

Fewer demographic variables explain partisanship in 1980, according to Table 3.14. Only ideology and an individual's father's party identification are significant. The model further replicates the 1960 and 1976 findings that Democratic partisans maintain their allegiance to their party, but not to their party's presidential candidate, in the face of strong Republican voting in the county.

As for contextual measures, Catholics respond to county context differently in 1980 than they did four years ago. They are more likely to be Republican partisans if they live among rising levels of Evangelicals or mainline Protestants. Having controlled for those measures, the dichotomous Catholic variable takes on a strong negative coefficient. These findings reflect the weakening of Democratic ties among Catholics, so that any shift in the distribution of religious adherents is correlated with shifts to Republican partisanship. As Catholics no longer vote Democratic automatically, they become more susceptible to contextual forces pulling them to the GOP.

The only other significant contextual variable in Table 3.14 is the interaction between Evangelical adherence and percent mainline Protestant in the county. The effect of this is to drive Evangelicals toward Democratic party identification. It is not clear why this should be the case in contextual terms, but since Evangelical partisanship is still skewed toward the Democratic end, some variable should reflect that distribution.

The 1980 election shows little county religious contextual influence on turnout, according to Table 3.15. This is the dominant finding of other researchers, though the other two turnout models examined in this chapter do show some contextual effects. As in 1976, Democrats are more likely to cast ballots as the percentage of Republican voters in a county rises. In addition, increasing church attendance among mainliners raises the probability of their voting. Beyond these two findings, the turnout model produces solid if unspectacular findings, significant results from several individual-level measures and an 81 percent correct prediction of respondent turnout.

Table 3.16 reveals that no contextual measure is significantly related to attention to public affairs for 1980. A host of individual factors make a difference, but no church

TABLE 3.14
Estimated 1980 Party Identification
                (OLS Regression Estimates)

Independent Variable	Coefficient
Intercept	0.48 (0.52)
Father's party identification	0.38 (0.07)***
Income	-0.01 (0.01)
Nonwhite respondent	-0.18 (0.26)
Working class	-0.05 (0.13)
Ideology self-placement	0.23 (0.05)***
Percent GOP vote in county	4.39 (0.66)***
Democrat X percent GOP vote in county	-5.94 (0.25)***
Catholic	-8.65 (4.59)*
Mainline Protestant	-1.26 (1.62)
Evangelical Protestant	0.85 (0.97)
Southern Evangelical Protestant	0.26 (0.30)
Church attendance	0.10 (0.07)
Mainliner X church attendance	0.09 (0.10)
Evangelical X church attendance	0.04 (0.10)
Catholic X pluralist county	-0.03 (0.41)
Mainliner X pluralist county	0.11 (0.23)
Evangelical X pluralist county	0.18 (0.25)
Jewish X pluralist county	-0.69 (0.76)
Catholic X percent Catholic in county	9.40 (4.73)**
Mainliner X percent Catholic in county	1.44 (1.71)
Evangelical X percent Catholic in county	-0.55 (1.16)
Catholic X percent mainline Protestants in county	7.74 (4.69)*
Mainliner X percent mainline Protestants in county	0.61 (1.64)
Evangelical X percent mainline Protestants in county	-2.31 (1.18)**
Catholic X percent Evangelicals in county	8.34 (4.74)*
Mainliner X percent Evangelicals in county	1.66 (1.71)
Evangelical X percent Evangelicals in county	-0.76 (0.97)
Total number of cases	346
Adjusted R-square	.77

Source: 1980 National Election Study.
Note: Standard errors in parentheses.
*   *=Significant at 0.10 level.*
*   **=Significant at 0.05 level.*
*   ***=Significant at 0.01 level.*

TABLE 3.15
Estimated 1980 General Election Turnout
(Logit Estimates)

Independent Variable	Coefficient
Intercept	-3.29 (1.09)***
Party identification	0.28 (0.11)**
Age	0.02 (0.01)**
Male	-0.16 (0.25)
Union member	0.23 (0.27)
Education	0.49 (0.13)***
Income	0.00 (0.04)
Follows public affairs	0.47 (0.13)***
Middle class	0.37 (0.25)
Talked with others about election	1.20 (0.27)***
Percent GOP vote in county	-1.58 (1.41)
Democrat X percent GOP vote in county	2.09 (0.82)***
Catholic	0.51 (0.43)
Mainline Protestant	-0.32 (0.66)
Evangelical Protestant	1.22 (0.81)
Church attendance	0.01 (0.09)
Mainliner X church attendance	0.50 (0.21)**
Pluralist county	-0.16 (0.28)
Percent Catholic in county	-0.06 (0.65)
Evangelical X percent Evangelicals in county	-0.78 (0.97)
Evangelical X percent mainline Protestants in county	-1.70 (1.49)
Total number of cases	608
Percent of cases correctly predicted	81.1
Model chi-square	132.09 with 20 df

Source: 1980 National Election Study.
Note: Standard errors in parentheses.
  *=Significant at 0.10 level.
  **=Significant at 0.05 level.
  ***=Significant at 0.01 level.

connection can be seen. The model explains 43 percent of the variance, almost the same as 1976, but little else can be discerned from the results. This model and its relation to the other public affairs models will be discussed further in the concluding section.

Attitudes Toward Abortion

The 1976 model produced a long list of significant findings for many denominations and groups. The 1980 model, reported in Table 3.17, is somewhat easier to interpret,

TABLE 3.16
Estimated 1980 Attention to Public Affairs
(OLS Regression Estimates)

Independent Variable	Coefficient
Intercept	1.85 (0.31)***
Interest in election	0.23 (0.02)***
Age	-0.004 (0.002)**
Education	0.09 (0.02)***
Watches television news about election	0.17 (0.03)***
Reads newspapers about election	0.19 (0.03)***
Nonwhite respondent	-0.16 (0.09)*
Percent GOP vote in county	-0.39 (0.31)
Democrat X percent GOP vote in county	0.09 (0.10)
Catholic	-0.07 (0.11)
Mainline Protestant	-0.03 (0.11)
Jewish	0.04 (0.19)
Church attendance	-0.01 (0.02)
Pluralist county	0.00 (0.07)
Percent Catholic in county	-0.10 (0.25)
Percent mainline Protestants in county	0.11 (0.30)
Evangelical X percent mainline Protestants in county	0.15 (0.31)
Percent Evangelicals in county	-0.07 (0.24)
Total number of cases	669
Adjusted R-square	.43

Source: 1980 National Election Study.
Note: Standard errors in parentheses.
*   *=Significant at 0.10 level.*
*   **=Significant at 0.05 level.*
*   ***=Significant at 0.01 level.*

though in this case only the three main religious groups can be discussed in detail. Note that the two abortion models explain the same amount of variance and show statistical significance on the same basic set of individual-level independent measures. (As in 1976, positive coefficients denote pro-life or anti-abortion attitudes.)

Church attendance again is correlated with pro-life positions for Catholics, Evangelicals, and mainliners: More frequent attenders are more opposed to abortion. After controlling for attendance, Evangelicals are more likely to be pro-choice, again suggesting that Evangelicals strengthen their opposition to abortion with increased exposure to the church environment. No other significant variables explain Evangelicals' attitudes on abortion.

Catholics adopt more pro-choice attitudes when in pluralist counties—evidence perhaps that a softening of the

TABLE 3.17
Estimated 1980 Attitude Toward Abortion
              (OLS Regression Estimates)

Independent Variable	Coefficient
Intercept	-1.26 (0.43)***
Education	-0.04 (0.04)
Income	-0.05 (0.01)***
Ideology self-placement	0.15 (0.04)***
Male	0.26 (0.11)**
Supports Equal Rights Amendment	-0.10 (0.05)**
Percent GOP vote in county	0.21 (0.52)
Democrat X percent GOP vote in county	0.16 (0.19)
Catholic	-0.13 (0.72)
Jewish	-0.06 (0.34)
Evangelical Protestant	-0.90 (0.44)**
Catholic X church attendance	0.24 (0.06)***
Mainliner X church attendance	0.22 (0.05)***
Evangelical X church attendance	0.23 (0.07)***
Pluralist county	-0.06 (0.12)
Catholic X pluralist county	-0.59 (0.36)*
Catholic X percent Catholic in county	-0.38 (0.84)
Mainliner X percent Catholic in county	-1.32 (0.34)***
Evangelical X percent Catholic in county	-0.24 (0.61)
Catholic X percent Evangelicals in county	-0.71 (1.10)
Mainliner X percent Evangelicals in county	-0.99 (0.43)**
Evangelical X percent Evangelicals in county	0.66 (0.58)
Total number of cases	338
Adjusted R-square	.28

Source: 1980 National Election Study.
Note: Standard errors in parentheses.
      *=Significant at 0.10 level.
      **=Significant at 0.05 level.
      ***=Significant at 0.01 level.

reinforcing mechanisms of the Catholic religious subculture also softens adherence to official church teachings. Public opinion polls reveal that Catholics are by no means united on the abortion issue (Plutzer 1986). Thus it is plausible to argue that their surrounding context might exert a pro-choice influence on Catholics.

Mainline Protestants are influenced to adopt more pro-choice attitudes in the presence of large numbers of

Catholics—the same result as in 1976. It is difficult to tell whether this is a reaction to individual Catholics or to the strength of the official Catholic church in a given county, but the effect on mainliners is clear. The presence of Evangelicals, another group whose leadership advocates a strong pro-life stance, also pushes mainliners to the more accommodating pro-choice position.

As with 1976, the abortion model shows that the county context measures appear to provoke reactions among some members of religious groups, and these reactions soften or work against the prevailing pro-life trend engendered by church attendance. More speculation on this is forthcoming below.

CONCLUSIONS AND IMPLICATIONS

Two overriding tasks emerge at the end of this long journey through three very different elections. First I pull together the findings, organized by dependent behavior, to assess what the data analysis reveals about county context and political behavior. The findings are further considered for their utility as guides to what might be expected in the next four chapters. Then I turn to the question of what effects might be endemic to religious contexts at the county level, and what effects might simply appear in the presence of specific salient events or issues in one particular election year. This also has implications for the chapters to follow.

Major Findings and Comparisons Across Elections

Voting

The key findings from the statistical analysis of voting behavior in 1960, 1976, and 1980 can be summarized as follows:

— Democrats are more likely to vote Republican as GOP voting in their counties increases.

— Partisanship plays a major role in determining vote choice, and other individual characteristics also are salient for voting.

— Concentrations of religions in counties have significant effects in 1960 and 1980, but not in 1976. Specifically, pluralist counties strengthen Democratic ties for Jewish voters and weaken mainline Protestant attachments to Republican candidates.

— Little evidence of county religious concentrations as a reinforcement mechanism is produced.

— Dichotomous religious measures and church attendance are powerful predictors of voting preferences, although these variables do not always achieve statistical significance.

Chapters 4 and 7 further examine church contexts and voting. Because vote choice is necessarily a short-term decision at the national level (different sets of candidates each time, with few exceptions), and because the presidential race receives a disproportionately large share of attention in the news, churches are well positioned to act as communicators of cues in an election year. Although the reaction of religious adherents to particular county configurations (1980) or specific election years (1960) may turn out to occur for idiosyncratic reasons, the individual church or discussion partner in a church appears to be a more stable context through which an individual can determine which candidate he or she prefers. Thus I expect the church to be a significant context for vote choice and discussion partners from the same church to strongly influence each other's decision.

Partisanship

A recent study of religion, partisanship, and voting in the post-World War II era (Kellstedt and Noll 1990) found Catholic-Democratic ties weakening, mainline Protestants remaining a Republican mainstay, and Evangelicals shifting allegiance from the Democrats to the GOP. Although Kellstedt and Noll are reluctant to specify microlevel causes for these macrolevel changes, the partisanship models here offer some clues. Specifically, they reveal the following:

— In 1960 the dual mobilization noted by Converse (1966) is found—Catholics and Protestants are drawn to their traditional party allegiances (Democratic and Republican, respectively) by attendance and exposure to county religious concentrations.

— In 1976 and 1980, county religious concentrations have the opposite effect (pro-Republican) on Catholics, perhaps evidence that Catholic partisan attachments are weakening.

— Evangelicals and mainliners generally do not respond much to contextual factors.

— Democrats strengthen their existing ties to the Democratic party in the face of increasing GOP voting in counties.

The end result of the partisanship analysis is that these models explain most of the variance in partisanship (R-squares .81, .76, and .77); contain many significant individual-level predictive factors; provide one consistent contextual effect, though not for a religious trait (Democratic partisan strength in GOP-voting counties); and show some promising leads but no consistent findings for county religious context measures.

Since partisanship arises from some combination of short- and long-term factors, one explanation for these findings is that in 1960, the short-term salience of the Kennedy candidacy pops out of the strong individual explanatory factors, while in the other years any contextual influence appears to be minimal. Thus, at the church and discussion partner levels, it is more likely that a contextual effect will be uncovered. With recent research arguing persuasively that partisanship is far more responsive to short-term forces than was previously thought (MacKuen, Erikson, and Stimson 1989), a closer look at South Bend in 1984 may show how churches and discussion partners can affect partisan attitudes within a specific time frame. With partisanship holding such a prominent position in the study of U.S. political behavior, further investigation into the role of church contexts is clearly warranted.

Turnout

Though previous research casts doubt on a strong relationship between context and turnout, the models here provide a small set of significant findings:

— For mainline Protestants, attending church compels higher turnout in 1976 and 1980; interestingly, no such encouragement is forthcoming in 1960.

— Besides this result, leaving the findings in the 1960 race aside, only Evangelicals show any inclination to respond to contextual factors when contemplating casting a ballot in 1976.

— Democrats are more likely to cast ballots as the percentage of Republican voters in a county rises.

Two things can be said about context and turnout. First, when religion is at all salient, or when certain groups feel threatened or obscured by other larger groups, turnout is heightened as a response to external pressures. Second, apart from that situation (1960, 1976) or from the direct activation of previously dormant political groups (Evangelicals in 1976 is the example from this analysis), individuals determine whether to vote without consideration for their social surroundings. Only mild effects would therefore be expected when turnout is further examined at the discussion partner level (Chapter 7).

Attention to Public Affairs

On this dependent measure, the findings are easy to summarize:

— Only in 1960 was any contextual factor found to be a significant influence on this attitude; in that year, Catholics are more interested in politics when located among other Catholics, and mainliners pay less attention in the presence of Evangelicals.

— In general, individuals either care or do not care about politics for reasons unrelated to

religious adherence or to county concentrations of
religious adherents.

These results suggest that churches normally play no role
or at best an indirect role as a conduit or clearinghouse for
political   discussion   that   presumably   sparks   political
interest. But Wald, Owen, and Hill (1988) describe the church
as a political community and argue for a contagion process at
work within churches for the transmission of political cues.
My results support the view that the contagion process should
operate primarily on those already motivated to care about the
issues in question. Motivation is one of the factors that
affect the salience of political discussion (Sprague 1982),
and motivation explains the positive results in the 1960
models, where the salience of the Catholic candidate issue
provokes a response from county religious contexts that
affects certain individuals in those contexts.
    Although attention to public affairs does not reappear as
a dependent measure in succeeding chapters, I pursue the
importance of motivation and the ability of the church itself
to foster political discussion and transmit cues among its
members. For now, my conclusion is that the findings on this
dependent measure support the contention that only in
extraordinary circumstances can churches activate those who do
not otherwise care about public affairs, though on a regular
basis churches may well affect those individuals already
interested or motivated to learn.

Abortion Attitudes

There are many results here worthy of further discussion:

— Church attendance promotes pro-life views for
members of all faiths.

— With one exception (1976—Evangelicals in the
presence of other Evangelicals), all other
significant county contextual factors are
correlated with pro-choice attitudes.

— Mainliners (1976) and Catholics (1980) are
influenced toward pro-choice positions by residence
in pluralist counties, implying that weak religious
concentrations are related to a more tolerant
position on this charged issue.

— Mainliners further appear to support abortion
rights more when faced with Catholic strength,
further evidence that abortion attitudes are
affected by the social environment.

— Only Evangelicals show a strong reinforcement
mechanism from their social contexts, becoming more
pro-life in the presence of other Evangelicals.

According to the findings in this chapter, examining
abortion attitudes at the church and individual levels
(Chapters 5 and 7, respectively) should show that Catholic and

Evangelical churches promote pro-life attitudes, meaning that attendance will be the most salient independent measure. But the response of individuals to the distribution of cues in the larger county environment may not appear at the church, neighborhood, or individual level. It is plausible to suggest that individuals make up their own minds on this often emotional issue, and a neutral stance is perhaps the most difficult position to maintain. Hence the attitudes of fellow church members or of discussion partners may carry less weight on abortion than on voting or partisan attitudes. Indeed, one might expect to find that when all denominations are included in one model, the attitudes of fellow churchgoers will be related to individual abortion attitudes, but if Catholics or Evangelicals are examined in isolation, the relationship will turn on the religion itself, not the views of other religious adherents. Hence little or no contextual effect will be present when modeling specific denominations.

Concluding Thoughts: Generalizing from These Three Elections

If all the findings described above have their roots in unique, short-term features of the political landscape—the Kennedy candidacy, post-Watergate cynicism, the Iran hostage crisis, and political malaise—then what we have are three interesting cases where events combine with characteristics of social and religious contexts to affect some behaviors and not others. The cases are interesting in and of themselves, but not necessarily indicative of a more generally applicable theory linking churches and political behavior. Since the second chapter argues for the viability of just such a theory and since the next four chapters depend on findings in a single year, 1984, the question of how much can be generalized from the findings in this chapter needs to be addressed.

The evidence for the effect of county contexts in general is demonstrated strongly by the consistent relationship among vote choice, party identification, and the county political context. With other significant findings repeated from election to election—for example, the pro-choice response of mainliners to Catholic concentrations in counties—the preponderance of the evidence favors the conclusion that these county religious contextual effects are not random, nor are they produced only coincidentally by the specific nature or context of the election under study. If the same contextual measure affects behavior in two separate elections, but the reasons for the effects in each election are different, then one can still argue that the context is a meaningful influence on political behavior.

For further support of that conclusion, consider again the reasoning surrounding the inclusion of interaction variables in the regression models. There are two competing hypotheses: an embattlement process (minority status compels heightened attention to church group norms) and a bandwagon process (minorities go along with the prevailing or majority group norms). The models here produce results that support both hypotheses, depending on the denomination and dependent behavior under study. The abortion attitudes of mainline

Protestants, for example, appear to conform to the latter hypothesis. Catholic voting and turnout in 1960 in the face of increasing mainliner concentrations demonstrate the reaction of an embattled group; the behavior of Democratic partisans in increasingly Republican counties shows the embattlement hypothesis even more clearly.

These points are worth noting, for in Chapters 4 through 6 I attempt to define more than one context for an individual (usually church and neighborhood). In sorting out the reactions of citizens to multiple sets of political cues, it is useful to remember that Catholics appear far more likely to band together when faced with minority status, while Protestants seem more likely to take on the character of their surroundings. Clearly these hypotheses can be extended to the church and neighborhood levels from these and other findings at the county level (Salisbury, Sprague, and Weiher 1984; Segal and Meyer 1974).

The county-level findings represent the weakest links in the case for religious contextual influences on political behavior, since the channels of causation are necessarily based on educated speculation. Yet the presence of a large number and rich variety of significant findings, even if a convincing or elegant explanation for them is not always at hand, is an encouraging sign for the chapters to follow. The 1984 South Bend data will provide a more detailed look at the processes uncovered from this look at the entire nation.

NOTES

1. Abortion attitudes are analyzed for 1976 and 1980 only; there are no questions regarding abortion attitudes in the 1956-58-60 NES study.

2. Classification into the two Protestant categories relies on a scheme developed by Kellstedt and Noll (1990), who discuss in some detail the relative merits of alternative classifications of Protestant denominations. Where Kellstedt and Noll term their second category "other Protestants," I choose "mainline Protestants," also an accurate representation of the composition of this category. The full list of denominations in each of the three Protestant categories can be found in the Appendix.

3. This means that all presidential election votes are coded 0 for Democratic candidates (1980 Anderson voters are excluded) and 1 for Republicans; party identification uses the standard 0 (strong Democrat) to 6 (strong Republican) scale; and abortion attitudes run from 0 (pro-choice, usually a Democratic position) to 6 (pro-life, usually associated with Republicans). The participation variables are not structured by party, obviously; they simply run from less (or no) interest or participation to more interest or participation.

4. Again, readers will find complete coding schemes for all variables in the Appendix. It may be useful to scan these coding schemes before perusing the model results.

5. This model as well as other models estimating either voting or turnout are logistic regression models. When a dependent variable has only two possible values (Carter or Ford, voted or not voted), ordinary least squares (OLS) regression does not produce efficient or reliable estimates. Hence a logit model, which calculates probabilities based on the relationship between the independent variables and the dichotomous dependent variable using the equation $P = 1/(1+e^{-Xb})$, is the more

appropriate choice.   Among its many advantages, this function can only take on values from 0 through 1 (Hanushek and Jackson 1977: 187-203).

    6.   Each of these dependent measures is analyzed using a full model that considers individual as well as contextual traits.   As with the voting model for 1976, the behavior of the individual demographic variables is noted only briefly.   I include those measures to construct a parsimonious, properly specified model, and I discuss those findings in detail only if they are counterintuitive or directly relevant to the religious context measures.

Chapter 4

Churches, Voting, and Party Identification

Do churches themselves play a role in driving individual political behavior? If so, what behaviors appear to be most susceptible to church influence, and what effects do specific denominations have? In addressing these questions, one crucial factor to keep in mind is individual political involvement generally—that is, the individual's relationship to all facets of the social environment must be characterized as fully as possible. To what other groups, for example, does an individual belong, and how would this broad picture of involvements in other social networks impact church influences specifically?

This chapter uses churches as the contextual units of analysis and also considers neighborhoods as contexts for purposes of comparison and control to address two facets of political behavior, voting and partisanship. The central hypothesis is straightforward: An individual's religious affiliation and involvement, as well as the political context of his or her religious environment, influences that individual's vote choice and partisanship. The theoretical concerns raised by this hypothesis have been covered in earlier chapters. The analysis presented here demonstrates and assesses the effects of other individual- and contextual-level variables on voting and partisanship, in concert with investigation of the roles that churches play in influencing these attributes.

DESIGN SPECIFICS

Utilizing data from the 1984 South Bend community study allows me to define and measure several social contexts for each individual, creating group mean variables (recall Chapter 1) for use in statistical models. Using the A, B, and C waves of the 1984 South Bend study, four initial measures of context are calculated for each respondent:[1]

— Church political context; calculated as the church (group) mean of the seven-point party identification scores for each respondent (0 = strong Democrat, 6 = strong Republican).

— Church socioeconomic status context; the church (group) mean of a five-level measure of individual educational attainment (1 = less than high school, 5 = postcollege).

— Neighborhood political context; calculated in the same manner as the church political context.

— Neighborhood socioeconomic status context; calculated in the same manner as the church socioeconomic status context.

Respondents who report no religious preference and no church affiliation are excluded from the analysis, since no comparison between their church and neighborhood contexts is possible; approximately 1,700 church members remain for study.

A FIRST CUT: DETERMINANTS OF VOTING PREFERENCES

Table 4.1 shows the 1984 presidential vote in South Bend, broken down by contextual and individual factors. Entries in the cells denote the percentage of the vote for Ronald Reagan for the specified conditions. The table reveals patterns of voting by controlling for neighborhood political context, church political context, church attendance, and attention paid to the campaign. Churches and neighborhoods have been classified as Democratic, mixed, or Republican. Democratic and Republican neighborhoods and churches are those whose mean partisanship suggests a strong preference for one party; mixed neighborhoods and churches have mean partisanship that fall in the middle range of the seven-point party identification scale.
If some contextual effect from the church environment were present, one would expect increasing percentages moving from left to right (increasing Republican voting) across the cells; this is the case in nearly all categories. The largest effect from church political context in all categories occurs for respondents who attend church often and do not pay attention to the campaign: in Democratic neighborhoods, a 52 percentage point difference between Democratic and Republican church political environments; in mixed neighborhoods, 26 percentage points; in Republican neighborhoods, 50 percentage points. This is initial evidence for the presence of church political contextual effects. These respondents do not pay a great deal of attention to the campaign, which is dominated by Republicans; nevertheless, they vote for Ronald Reagan in increasing numbers across church political contexts, regardless of their neighborhood political context.
Another noteworthy feature of Table 4.1 is the behavior of individuals living in mixed neighborhood political contexts. It might be expected that these individuals would be more susceptible to influence from contexts other than their neighborhood, since no clear signal is being transmitted through the neighborhood. Table 4.1 would suggest that

TABLE 4.1
1984 South Bend Percentage of Republican Vote by Respondents'
Church Attendance, Attention to Campaign, Neighborhood
Political Context, and Church Political Context

Neighborhood/Category	Dem. Church Context	Mixed Church Context	Repub. Church Context
Democratic Neighborhoods			
Attends frequently, pays attention to campaign	31.2 (77)	41.7 (12)	73.3 (15)
Attends frequently, does not pay attention to campaign	31.1 (103)	37.5 (8)	83.3 (6)
Does not attend frequently, pays attention to campaign	27.6 (29)	50.0 (10)	22.2 (9)
Does not attend frequently, does not pay attention to campaign	56.6 (53)	66.7 (12)	71.4 (14)
Mixed Neighborhoods			
Attends frequently, pays attention to campaign	50.0 (36)	68.4 (57)	62.5 (40)
Attends frequently, does not pay attention to campaign	51.4 (35)	72.3 (83)	77.4 (31)
Does not attend frequently, pays attention to campaign	32.0 (25)	51.4 (37)	62.1 (29)
Does not attend frequently, does not pay attention to campaign	48.4 (31)	59.2 (49)	59.3 (27)
Republican Neighborhoods			
Attends frequently, pays attention to campaign	68.4 (19)	71.4 (49)	80.6 (36)
Attends frequently, does not pay attention to campaign	36.4 (11)	62.8 (43)	86.4 (22)
Does not attend frequently, pays attention to campaign	15.4 (13)	66.7 (24)	83.3 (24)
Does not attend frequently, does not pay attention to campaign	53.3 (15)	75.0 (20)	90.9 (22)

Source: 1984 South Bend study.
Note: N = 1,126. Parenthetical entries are total cases in each cell.

churches may not be transmitting a clear signal either. For frequent attenders, those paying attention to the campaign do not vote increasingly for Reagan across church political contexts; in fact, a smaller share in Republican churches voted for Reagan than in mixed churches. Moving down the mixed neighborhood columns, frequent attenders not paying attention to the campaign do behave as expected. Nonattenders also exhibit shifts toward Reagan, but this could be due to their paying attention to campaign talk, and not to signals from the church. Those at the bottom, nonattenders who do not pay attention, predictably show the smallest movement toward Republican voting across church political contexts.

One more point about this table bears notice, primarily because it motivates part of the analysis to follow. Individuals in Republican neighborhood contexts and either mixed or Republican churches vote most heavily for Reagan. This is not unexpected, given the outcome of the 1984 election, but the level of Reagan support, particularly among those attending church and paying attention, is high across the board. In Republican neighborhoods, individuals would appear to be overwhelmed by the signals around them favoring the GOP, and thus perhaps are less susceptible to cross-pressures from other contexts or from other individual attributes.

Accordingly, there is reason to surmise that the driving forces behind the Reagan vote choice, and behind the difference between an individual's attitudes and those of others around him or her, will differ according to an individual's *neighborhood* political climate. That is, for people living in Democratic neighborhoods, the factors influencing their party identification are *not* likely to be identical to the factors that affect people living in Republican neighborhoods. Republicans already vote Republican in such high numbers that some factors significant for Democrats and independents will not significantly increase identification with Republicans. The fact that other researchers have found magnified religious effects on voting within high-status denominations (Lopatto 1985) further strengthens the argument that Republican neighborhood residents should be treated separately from their fellow South Bend residents.

PARTY IDENTIFICATION AND CONTEXTUAL EFFECTS

Party identification, long the staple of research into mass political behavior, has traditionally been thought to be a more stable indicator of political preferences than voting. More recent evidence of its apparent short-term volatility (MacKuen, Erikson, and Stimson 1989, 1992) suggests, however, that party identification is susceptible not only to transient factors but also to contextual factors. Thus it is worth considering how party identification breaks down by church and neighborhood political context.

Table 4.2 follows the same basic structure as Table 4.1, this time showing party identification across neighborhood and church political contexts. Church attendance is included as an additional control variable. The table clearly shows that

TABLE 4.2
1984 South Bend Party Identification by Respondents' Church Attendance, Neighborhood Political Context, and Church Political Context

Neighborhood/Category	Dem. Church Context	Mixed Church Context	Repub. Church Context
Democratic Neighborhoods (15.9% Republican)			
Frequent church attenders	11.9 (268)	28.1 (32)	41.7 (24)
Infrequent church attenders	12.1 (99)	20.6 (34)	30.0 (20)
Mixed Neighborhoods (26.0% Republican)			
Frequent church attenders	18.1 (138)	27.1 (218)	49.0 (100)
Infrequent church attenders	16.0 (119)	19.5 (164)	37.4 (91)
Republican Neighborhoods (42.4% Republican)			
Frequent church attenders	31.7 (41)	34.5 (138)	54.3 (81)
Infrequent church attenders	26.8 (41)	42.9 (77)	62.1 (58)

Source: 1984 South Bend study.
Note: N = 1,743. Parenthetical entries are total cases in each cell.

people living in Republican neighborhoods are more likely to identify with the GOP than residents in Democratic or mixed neighborhoods. This pattern is analogous to the previous table showing voting trends.

More importantly, this table shows that in Democratic and mixed neighborhoods, frequent church attendance is associated with higher levels of Republican partisanship. Further, in these neighborhoods, people who frequently attend Republican churches are far more likely to be Republicans themselves. For example, Democratic neighborhoods are 16 percent Republican on average, but frequent attenders of mixed and Republican churches are about two to three times as likely as their neighbors to be Republicans. The more Republican the neighborhood is, the smaller this difference is when looking at Republican churches; nevertheless, it is clear that church political contexts exert an influence on individuals that may outweigh the effects from their residential environments.

TABLE 4.3
Estimated 1984 South Bend Party Identification
              (OLS Regression Estimates)

Independent Variable	Coefficient
Intercept	-0.78 (1.80)
Individual education	0.07 (0.07)
Individual income	0.14 (0.06)***
Male	0.22 (0.14)*
Lifelong resident of South Bend	-0.22 (0.18)
White	1.45 (0.31)***
Pays attention to campaign	-0.05 (0.13)
Active in a neighborhood group	-0.27 (0.22)
Mainline Protestant	0.87 (0.33)***
Evangelical Protestant	0.76 (0.33)**
Catholic	-0.10 (0.30)
Neighborhood mean party identification	-0.08 (0.27)
Neighborhood mean education	0.40 (0.29)
Church mean party identification	0.20 (0.07)***
Church mean education	-0.04 (0.12)
Index of church activity	0.04 (0.02)***
Catholic density of neighborhood	-0.54 (1.88)
Protestant density of neighborhood	0.30 (2.10)
Pluralist neighborhood	0.24 (0.22)
Total number of cases	925
Adjusted R-square	.18

Source: 1984 South Bend study.
Note: Standard errors in parentheses.
   *=Significant at 0.10 level.
   **=Significant at 0.05 level.
   ***=Significant at 0.01 level.

A More Formal Test for Party Identification

Table 4.3 presents results from an OLS regression model of party identification. At the individual level, it is hypothesized that party identification is influenced by demographic factors such as education, income, gender, and race; attention to the campaign; length of residence in South Bend; church attendance and activity in a church-connected group (combined in one variable termed "index of church activity"); and individual involvement and level of activity in various community groups and organizations. Dichotomous variables testing the effects of Catholic, mainline Protestant, and Evangelical Protestant church membership are also included.[2]

Most of these variables are not novel indicators of partisanship; indeed, education and religion (specifically, denomination) are two of the most common factors that are thought to influence partisanship. The other variables are included because they address the central question: How can one explain partisanship in terms of the environments in which an individual lives, works, and worships? Clearly, paying attention to the campaign indicates the inclination to receive and interpret the political signals encountered in daily routines (Huckfeldt and Sprague 1987). Church attendance similarly indicates the extent to which an individual may receive political signals from church. If one attends church only at Easter and Christmas, one will probably not be influenced by the church environment on any front; on the other hand, repeated interaction with fellow churchgoers or with the pastor or priest, in formal or informal settings, greatly increases the likelihood of political discussion and of the transmission of political signals from church to individual.

At the contextual level I include the four previously defined variables that define contexts for the individual: mean partisanship and socioeconomic status (education) for both church and neighborhood. Additionally, variables measuring the density of Catholics and Protestants in a given neighborhood are used, based on the Segal and Meyer hypothesis that Catholics are more likely to vote and behave as a cohesive religious group. Finally, a variable characterizing the degree of homogeneity among religious groups in a neighborhood is included; a neighborhood is defined as pluralist if no more than 35 percent of its residents belong to any one religion.[3]

The results from Table 4.3 support the argument for significant church political contextual influences on partisanship. Several demographic variables are significant predictors of partisan attachment—income, gender, race, and belonging to either a mainline or Evangelical Protestant denomination. More importantly, church mean partisanship is a significant predictor, but mean neighborhood partisanship is not. In addition, the level of involvement in the church is significant.

The regression model in Table 4.3 also supports the preliminary conclusions from Table 4.2. Church political context has a definite impact on individual partisanship, though not an overwhelming impact compared with that of other individual-level influences.

Readers who are accustomed to conceiving of religious influences on partisanship in terms of denominational memberships might wonder here whether the presumed effect of church political contexts is caused by specific denominations that are predisposed to prefer one party or the other. Indeed, the existing literature on church contextual influences suggests that this is so. Both Lenski (1961) and Berelson, Lazarsfeld, and McPhee (1954) find that Catholics may not be driven in a Republican direction by increasingly Republican church contexts. To address the question, I have divided South Bend respondents into three denominational groups (Catholics, mainline Protestants, and Evangelicals), reestimated regression equations, and constructed a graph to show the relative effects of church political context on each group.

Table 4.4 presents only the coefficients for the four contextual variables and overall church involvement, in order to compare the three religious groupings with one another. The results are most easily discussed by religion.

Catholics

For Catholics, none of the contextual measures is significant, apparently demonstrating that the partisanship of Catholics does not respond to the partisanship of their fellow parishioners. However, activity within the church, measured as attendance and other group activity, causes Catholics to strengthen their partisan ties *in the direction of the group as a whole*. This is a contextual effect, even if the effect does not arise directly from the measures provided. It is derived from the same sources and motivations described by Finifter's classic study of Republican auto workers (Finifter 1974). Considering the minority status of many Catholics in their social surroundings, their ties to church produce a definite strengthening of political preferences consistent with the group norm.

Evangelicals

Like Catholics, Evangelicals are not significantly affected by their church political contexts, or any other context for that matter. However, increasing involvement in the church subculture reinforces the propensity for Evangelicals to think and act as the subculture does. In this case, the more an Evangelical citizen attends church and interacts with other members, the more likely that Evangelical is to be Republican.

Mainline Protestants

Mainliners show the strongest cross-pressures from competing contexts. Neighborhood socioeconomic status, church mean partisanship, and church mean socioeconomic status are all significant and positive (Republican) influences. However, mean neighborhood partisanship is a significant Democratic influence. What explains this apparent contradiction?

The principal explanation is a statistical one. Since mainline Protestants are predisposed to be Republican partisans, there is a strong, though not fatal, level of correlation among the independent variables (multicollinearity), particularly the contextual measures. Proper methodological techniques require that relevant variables be included for a properly specified model, meaning that multicollinearity must be tolerated.

Beyond the technical explanation, substantively it can be argued that the model for mainline Protestants overestimates the Republican influence of the contextual measures, hence the negative sign on neighborhood mean partisanship attempts to mitigate the positive (Republican) influence from the other contextual measures. In practice, this means that for highly

TABLE 4.4
Estimated 1984 South Bend Party Identification for Catholics,
Mainline Protestants, and Evangelical Protestants
(OLS Regression Estimates)

Independent Variable	Catholics Coefficient	Mainliners Coefficient	Evangelicals Coefficient
Neighborhood mean party identification	0.35 (0.40)	−2.15 (0.81)***	0.27 (0.72)
Neighborhood mean education	0.27 (0.58)	3.32 (1.14)***	0.78 (0.89)
Church mean party identification	−0.23 (0.25)	0.33 (0.14)**	0.01 (0.13)
Church mean education	−0.27 (0.24)	0.38 (0.23)*	−0.05 (0.22)
Index of church activity	−0.22 (0.11)**	0.07 (0.03)**	0.07 (0.03)**
Total number of cases	434	242	198
Adjusted R-square	.11	.11	.24

Source: 1984 South Bend study.
Note: Standard errors in parentheses. Only contextual coefficients are
reported.
*=Significant at 0.10 level.
**=Significant at 0.05 level.
***=Significant at 0.01 level.

Republican environments, the model compensates by driving the predicted partisanship of individuals downward. The bottom line is that, statistical anomalies notwithstanding, mainline Protestants are responsive to the partisan character of their churches, more so than either Catholics or Evangelicals.

The important results from the models in Table 4.4 are displayed graphically in Figure 4.1. This figure shows the effects of mean church partisanship (the horizontal axis) on individual partisanship (vertical axis) for each of the religions considered in Table 4.4. Here the picture described by the regression models is clarified. First, Catholics show the modest downward (Democratic) trend predicted by Lenski and the Columbia researchers: They become more Democratic, and hence more like other Catholics, even as their church environment becomes increasingly Republican. Second, an increasingly Republican church political context drives mainline Protestants to be increasingly Republican. Mainliners are highly susceptible to church influences even after neighborhood influences are controlled for statistically. Finally, Evangelicals show a nearly flat line with no slope; this suggests that Evangelicals identify with their neighbors more than with their fellow churchgoers, although the question of what is driving their behavior warrants further investigation.

FIGURE 4.1
**Predicted 1984 Partisanship for All Respondents, Catholics,
    Mainline Protestants, and Evangelical Protestants**

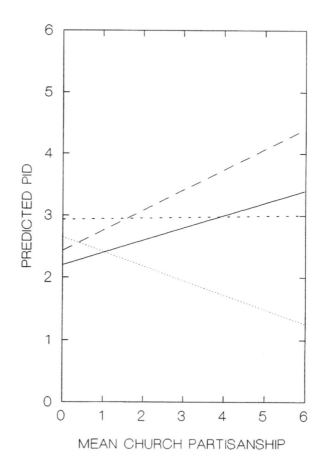

LEGEND

All respondents	───────────
Catholics	················
Mainline Protestants	─ ─ ─ ─ ─ ─
Evangelical Protestants	- - - - - - - -

A final point should be noted in regard to church contextual influences on party identification. For all religions analyzed, increasing church involvement is a significant influence on partisanship. Clearly, levels of church activity influence contextual effects, as predicted by McPhee's (1963) and Sprague's (1982) theory based on motivation and frequency of interaction. Moreover, greater activity in a church political context that offers a clear signal as to its partisan leanings (highly Democratic or highly Republican) magnifies the impact of that context and strengthens the propensity for individuals to agree with the general leanings of the church.

VOTING BEHAVIOR AND CHURCH CONTEXTS

Table 4.1 considered possible contextual determinants of voting. I now return to this subject possessing some stronger hypotheses based on Table 4.1 and buttressed by the results from the investigation of partisanship. Specifically, four preliminary assertions can be made:

— There is reason to suspect that church political context is an important factor in voting, although the magnitude and direction of its impact might differ by religion.

— The results based on county-level contextual data from Chapter 3 suggest that members of some religions respond to disagreement within contexts by strengthening their ties to the prevailing or historical stance of their church.

— Involvement in the church should be an important indicator of whether or not contextual influences will exist.

— Individuals living in Democratic or mixed neighborhoods may react differently to stimuli in their church or neighborhood contexts than individuals living in Republican neighborhoods.

In keeping with my strategy for defining relevant contexts in terms of the dependent behavior under study, logit models[4] estimating voting behavior utilize two additional contextual measures in addition to the ones already employed in this chapter. They are the group mean variables measuring the Republican (Reagan) percentage of the vote in both churches and neighborhoods. Since partisanship and vote choice are not identical, these contextual measures of voting are the key variables of interest. Of course, other relevant explanatory variables such as education and race remain in the models.

Table 4.5 provides evidence of a definite contextual component to voting. Contextual variables measuring the effect of church and neighborhood levels of Reagan voting are significant and positive. This means that individuals are more likely to vote Republican as their churches and

TABLE 4.5
Estimated 1984 South Bend Presidential Vote
(Logit Estimates)

Independent Variable	Coefficient
Intercept	-6.80 (2.48)***
Percent Reagan vote in church	9.78 (0.90)***
Percent Reagan vote in neighborhood	6.28 (2.65)**
Individual education	0.16 (0.08)*
Individual income	0.15 (0.07)**
Male	0.48 (0.18)***
Lifelong resident	-0.13 (0.23)
White	1.80 (0.54)***
Pays attention to campaign	-0.35 (0.17)**
Active in a neighborhood group	-0.01 (0.28)
Mainline Protestant	0.92 (0.49)*
Evangelical Protestant	0.64 (0.51)
Catholic	0.35 (0.61)
Neighborhood mean party identification	-1.50 (0.66)**
Neighborhood mean education	0.73 (0.41)*
Church mean party identification	-1.21 (0.18)***
Church mean education	-0.24 (0.18)
Index of church activity	0.04 (0.02)*
Catholic church attendance	-0.10 (0.10)
Catholic density of neighborhood	1.10 (2.52)
Protestant density of neighborhood	1.58 (2.77)
Total number of cases	868
Percent of cases correctly predicted	75.3
Model chi-square	268.37 with 20 df

Source: *1984 South Bend study.*
Note: *Standard errors in parentheses.*
     *=Significant at 0.10 level.
     **=Significant at 0.05 level.
     ***=Significant at 0.01 level.

neighborhoods vote increasingly Republican—a contextual influence on behavior. Moreover, the effect from church levels of voting appears to outweigh the effect from neighborhood levels. This will be shown more clearly in graphic form.

Table 4.5 reveals that other individual factors (education, income, gender, race) significantly predict voting choices, and all these variables behave in expected ways. In addition, increasing church activity is associated with increasing Republican voting preferences, generally in line with the preliminary hypothesis. Further, church mean partisanship becomes a powerful negative (Democratic) influence on voting. Finally, the dichotomous variables for each religious group are not significant, with the exception of the mainline Protestant dichotomous variable, which barely achieves statistical significance. This indicates that when church contexts are specified and measured, the direct effects from membership alone virtually disappear. In 1984 at least, the labeling approach to religion and political behavior appears inadequate.

Because the contextual measures for Republican voting in churches and neighborhoods are measured on the same scale, this model offers a rare opportunity to directly compare and assess the relative influence of churches and neighborhoods on voting.[5] Figure 4.2 traces the probability of voting for Reagan against the mean Republican vote in the church and neighborhood contexts. Some specifics on interpreting this figure will be helpful:

— The *solid line* represents the probability of a Reagan vote as the *church vote* for Reagan varies.

— The *broken line* represents the probability of a Reagan vote as the *neighborhood Reagan vote* is allowed to vary.[6]

— The *horizontal (X) axis* represents variations in the measured contexts—the levels of Reagan voting in both church and neighborhood, ranging from 0 to 100 percent.

— The *vertical (Y) axis* represents for each individual the probability of voting Republican, ranging from 0 to 1.

It should be noted that since only votes for the two major candidates are included, an individual with a 0.5 probability of voting for Reagan would also have a 0.5 probability of voting for Mondale. Hence this figure can be read in both a Republican (probability increasing toward 1) and a Democratic (probability decreasing toward 0) direction.

The best place to begin reading Figure 4.2 is at the point where the two lines cross. This point falls at roughly a 0.6 probability of voting for Reagan on the vertical scale, and a level of church/neighborhood Reagan voting of 60 percent on the horizontal scale. This point represents the likelihood of a Republican vote in the absence of any explanatory factors; in other words, the average person in the South Bend sample has an underlying probability of voting for Ronald Reagan of 0.6.

The rest of the figure shows what happens to this underlying probability when churches and neighborhoods vote in varying amounts for Reagan. With all other variables held constant, any change in individual probability of Reagan voting must be attributable to changes in church and/or neighborhood levels of Republican voting.

At the upper (right) end of the curves, as the church mean vote for Reagan increases toward 100 percent, individuals in such churches become more likely to vote for Reagan. As mean neighborhood voting for Reagan increases, individuals

FIGURE 4.2
**Predicted 1984 Presidential Vote, All Respondents, with Mean
    Church   Reagan   Vote   Percentage   Varied   Against   Mean
    Neighborhood Reagan Vote Percentage**

LEGEND

Mean church Reagan vote
    percentage   ———————

Mean neighborhood Reagan
    vote percentage   – – – – – – – –

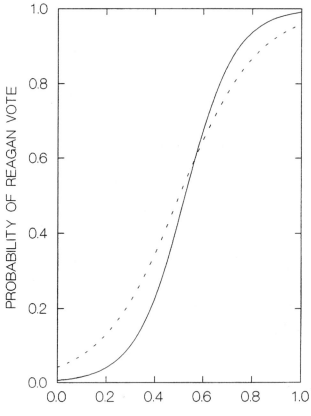

MEAN CHURCH, NEIGHBORHOOD REAGAN VOTE

FIGURE 4.3
Probability Difference, 1984 Presidential Vote

(Probability of Republican vote, church mean Reagan
vote varying, minus probability of Republican vote,
neighborhood mean Reagan vote varying)

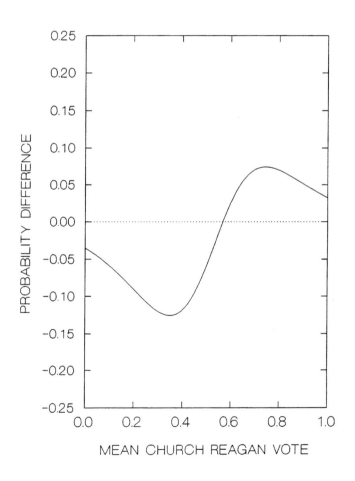

also increase their probability of voting for Reagan. However, the increasing vote in the church has a greater impact than does the increasing vote in the neighborhood. The gap between the curves demonstrates that the effect of church and neighborhood contexts is unequal. Both contexts amplify the underlying propensity to vote Republican, but the church context provides a stronger amplification than the neighborhood context.

At the lower (left) end of the figure, a similar gap between the curves is found, although its meaning is a little different. As the church mean Reagan vote decreases—in other words, the church votes more Democratic—an individual's probability of voting Republican also decreases, and it decreases faster when churches vote less Republican than when neighborhoods vote less Republican. This is also an amplification effect, but in this case the amplification is in a Democratic, or Mondale, direction.

To better illustrate the magnitude of the differences shown in Figure 4.2, Figure 4.3 simply subtracts the probability trace generated by the mean church Reagan vote from the probability trace generated by the mean neighborhood Reagan vote (solid line minus broken line, from Figure 4.2). The vertical axis in Figure 4.3 now gives the value of this difference.

Figure 4.3 reveals that the impact of mean church voting versus mean neighborhood voting can produce as much as a 10 percentage point impact on an individual's probability of voting Republican or Democrat. The largest Reagan boost has a magnitude of 0.07 and occurs at 65 percent levels of Reagan voting in the two contexts. The greatest effect in a Democratic direction is 0.12, a 12 percentage point difference in probability between church and neighborhood contexts; this largest boost in the direction of Mondale occurs at roughly 35-40 percent levels of church and neighborhood Reagan voting. Figure 4.3 dramatically illustrates that even relatively minor differences in the strength of contextual effects can produce substantial boosts in voting probabilities.

Voting by Religions

Table 4.6 analyzes 1984 South Bend voting for the three religious groups previously considered: Catholics, mainline Protestants, and Evangelicals. The table reports results only for the relevant contextual variables and church activity, and the results reveal some interesting patterns across the three groups.

Catholics

According to the model in Table 4.6, the average vote of their church is nearly twice as powerful an influence on Catholics as the average vote of the neighborhood. Figure 4.4 plots this difference, and the pattern is identical in shape to the entire sample (recall Figure 4.3). Note the sizable amplification of probable Republican voting for Catholics in churches with Reagan majorities. The probability boost in such churches is a whopping 0.25, compared with an

TABLE 4.6
Estimated 1984 South Bend Presidential Vote for Catholics,
Mainline Protestants, and Evangelical Protestants
(Logit estimates)

Independent Variable	Catholics Coefficient	Mainliners Coefficient	Evangelicals Coefficient
Percent Reagan vote in church	12.40 (2.33)***	11.85 (1.86)***	10.82 (1.94)***
Percent Reagan vote in neighborhood	6.31 (3.79)*	9.88 (6.36)	8.92 (8.87)
Church mean party identification	-2.47 (0.59)***	-1.33 (0.34)***	-1.35 (0.36)***
Church mean education	-0.38 (0.36)	0.25 (0.36)	-0.29 (0.45)
Index of church activity	0.10 (0.14)	-0.32 (0.20)*	-0.54 (0.29)*
Catholic density of neighborhood	-1.41 (4.05)	13.37 (6.22)**	-7.04 (7.94)
Protestant density of neighborhood	-0.91 (4.35)	12.60 (6.82)*	-5.89 (9.80)
Total number of cases	398	234	189
Percent of cases correctly predicted	67.3	82.5	89.4
Model chi-square	77.24 with 18 df	87.92 with 18 df	102.77 with 18 df

Source: 1984 South Bend study.
Note: Standard errors in parentheses. Only contextual coefficients are
reported.
*=Significant at 0.10 level.
**=Significant at 0.05 level.
***=Significant at 0.01 level.

amplification of no more than 0.08 in Catholic Democratic churches. When a Catholic church leans Republican in its voting patterns, individual members are highly inclined to go with the group.

The remainder of the results for Catholics yield less clear information. There is no significant effect from church involvement. And among the included contextual measures, only church mean partisanship is significant, with a negative (Democratic) sign. This finding also arose in the model of Catholic partisanship (Table 4.4). Apparently the long-term attribute of partisanship exerts a pull back toward the traditional Catholic-Democratic voting pattern, while the actual votes of contemporaries drives individual Catholics toward the majority—in other words, they become Reagan voters.

FIGURE 4.4
Probability Difference, 1984 Presidential Vote, Catholics

(Probability of Republican vote, church mean Reagan
vote varying, minus probability of Republican vote,
neighborhood mean Reagan vote varying)

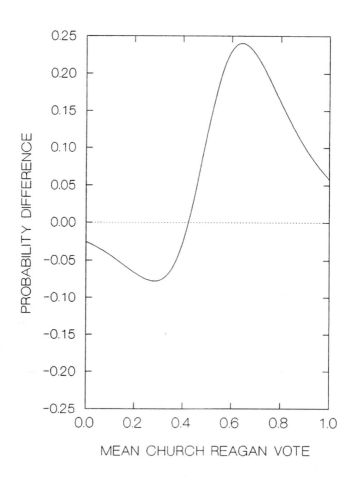

Mainline and Evangelical Protestants

For both groups, church mean Reagan vote is significant, and neighborhood mean Reagan vote is not. In fact, no neighborhood contextual measure is significant, except for the measures of religious density among mainliners. Is the church then the only contextual factor driving Protestant voting? This could well be the case, especially since the church involvement variables become significant predictors among Protestants. Church activity has a negative, Democratic effect on voting for both groups of Protestants. It would appear from Table 4.6 that mainliners and Evangelicals respond to their church political environments more so than to their neighborhood political environments when it comes to voting behavior.

The significance of the findings on density measures for mainline Protestants also merits discussion. As the percentage of either Catholics or Protestants in a neighborhood rises, mainliners are more disposed to vote Republican. The Catholic density measure may have an explanation similar to those offered by Putnam (1966) and Finifter (1974). Both Putnam and Finifter found that individuals in minority situations tend to band together in their group involvements, and in this case their behavior as well, in the face of hostile neighborhood surroundings. As for the significance of rising Protestant density, the more conventional explanation of higher concentrations leading to amplified influence makes sense.

Figures 4.5 and 4.6 again plot the probability differences between church and neighborhood mean Reagan vote for mainliners and Evangelicals, respectively. These figures resemble each other closely but do not resemble the corresponding figures for the entire sample and for Catholics alone. Specifically, there is no amplification effect in a Republican direction. This means that although increasing levels of Republican voting in churches and neighborhoods appear to amplify an individual's likelihood of voting Republican, it cannot be said that one context matters more than the other.[7]

Figures 4.5 and 4.6 also show that at roughly equal levels of church and neighborhood Reagan voting (50 percent), there is an amplification of magnitude 0.2 to 0.25 in a Democratic direction. The underlying propensity of mainliners and Evangelicals to vote Republican thus can be mitigated by their church political environments. Once again, dividing the sample by religions does not alter the direction or intensity of the contextual effects from churches.

SUMMARY OF FINDINGS AND CONCLUSIONS

Significant findings from Chapter 4 are numerous and worth repeating here:

— The analysis indicates that there are effects from the church environment on political behavior, and these effects exist independent of effects from other aspects of an individual's environment.

FIGURE 4.5
Probability Difference, 1984 Presidential Vote, Mainline Protestants

(Probability of Republican vote, church mean Reagan vote varying, minus probability of Republican vote, neighborhood mean Reagan vote varying)

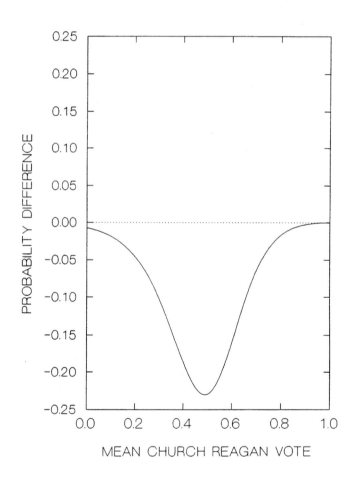

FIGURE 4.6
Probability Difference, 1984 Presidential Vote, Evangelical Protestants

(Probability of Republican vote, church mean Reagan
vote varying, minus probability of Republican vote,
neighborhood mean Reagan vote varying)

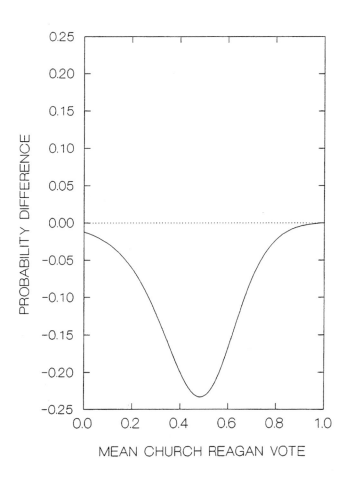

— Dividing the sample in different ways—by neighborhood political environment and by religion, for example—alters the nature of the contextual effects in nonobvious ways.

— Church contextual variables are found to play a relatively weak role in influencing partisanship.

— The voting behavior of the church as a whole, however, plays a strong role in determining individual voting choices. This influence does not vary across religions; it is very consistent in direction and quite consistent in intensity.

— Church attendance and church involvement are significant predictors of party loyalty and voting, usually working to strengthen the existing or underlying attachments between individuals and their church.

— The effects and direction of effects from attendance and involvement are consistent across religions, thus suggesting that the mechanisms for contextual influence do not vary across religions.

Attendance and involvement influence political behavior by reinforcing signals from the church environment, whether explicit or subtle, that shape political attitudes and actions. Such signals likely are not direct attempts to influence partisan attitudes or exhortations to vote a certain way. Rather, the effect comes from repeated interaction with the environment of the church and its members and leaders.

In regard to voting, it must be reiterated that the level of Republican voting within churches produces strong influences on the individual vote decisions of church members; this is true regardless of the religion in question. And for all three religious groups considered (especially Protestants), neighborhoods clearly have less contextual influence than do churches.

A final theoretical question raised by these results concerns the significance of the differing findings on the dependent variables. Partisanship, usually considered to be a relatively stable, long-term attitude with a short-term component, responds to neighborhood context more than to church context; on the other hand, vote choice, a short-term decision with a long-term component (partisanship, past voting history), responds to church context more than to neighborhood context. What theory of contextual influences might account for this dichotomy?

I would speculate that if partisanship is predominantly a long-term attitude, then religion will be a significant and steady influence, since its effects are also likely to be long term in nature. Thus the religious (moral and/or spiritual) dimension of partisanship works its influence over time and is not necessarily evident in a cross-sectional analysis. Further, the low correlations (on the order of 0.3 for Protestants, 0.55 for Catholics) between church and neighborhood contextual measures demonstrate that cross-pressures do indeed exist, and the empirical findings here and in other research show their importance (Bowler and Gilbert 1992).

As for voting, the brief length of the campaign season (relative to an attitude such as partisanship) places an emphasis on observation and interaction with other potential voters. If partisanship does not waver much over time, then the individual voter may have a solid grasp of how his or her neighbors will behave (or at least a fixed perception of how they will behave), but a far less clear picture of how fellow churchgoers will behave. This suggests that an individual's long-term church "memory" is stronger on attitudes (hence less obvious to the researcher using cross-sectional data) and weaker on behavior; the need, then, to reevaluate the church's voting patterns at each election makes the church a *more* influential actor on voting decisions—and makes the consequences of that influence, and the consequent behavior of the voter, more obvious to the researcher.

Although changing patterns of church attendance and adherence among younger generations surely point to reduced church influence on mass political behavior, the findings here imply that for those individuals who do take an active role in their faiths, the church will continue to act as a source of political cues. At the very least, the church's salience for determining political outcomes cannot be ignored.

NOTES

1. Refer to the Appendix for specific coding schemes for all variables used in this chapter.

2. The division of Protestants into these two categories follows a scheme used in other religion and politics research (Kellstedt 1989a; Wilcox 1986). Complete lists of denominations in each group can be found in the Appendix. A third group, nontraditional Protestants, including Jehovah's Witnesses and Mormons, yielded few cases and was not used.

3. Once again, all variables are coded so that a positive coefficient is associated with an influence toward Republican voting and partisanship, and a negative coefficient means a push toward Democratic voting and partisanship.

4. As described previously for Chapter 3, the dichotomous nature of the dependent variable (Reagan or Mondale) necessitates the use of a logit model.

5. In general, regression coefficients generated through either OLS or logistic models cannot be directly compared unless the variables in question are measured with precisely the same scale.

6. The effects of all other variables in the model from Table 4.5 are held constant to produce these probability traces.

7. This conclusion is tentative, since in the full models for mainliners and Evangelicals, the coefficient for mean neighborhood Reagan vote is not statistically significant. In a bivariate logit model (results not reported), the mean neighborhood Reagan vote was a statistically significant predictor of individual voting, and its magnitude was similar to those reported in Table 4.6. Caution in interpreting these results is probably still warranted.

Chapter 5

Churches and
Political Attitudes

This chapter, which again uses churches as the level of analysis, focuses on the individual and contextual determinants of political attitudes. The basic questions to be addressed are, to what extent do church factors drive issue positions, and does the presence of other individual- or contextual-level factors negate or subsume church influences? Because churches are manifestly concerned with such things as worldviews and future expectations, not to mention morality and social issues, it is expected that the church is sending signals on important issues of the day; however, such signals must be processed in tandem with those emanating from other institutions and social contexts. Thus the causal link between church and individual is once again difficult to discern empirically.

The dependent variables in this chapter cover a range of policy domains and social concerns. Expectations of how churches influence these attitudes therefore differ across those domains and issues. For example, attitudes toward abortion and prayer in public schools are more likely to display evidence of significant church influences, since churches have played a leading role in public discussion on these issues. For an issue such as defense spending, however, a specific church position is generally not obvious. Hence one aim of this chapter is to determine whether any contextual influence exists on issues not normally considered to be church related. Finally, such individual attitudes as expectations of individual economic well-being and presidential job approval might be amenable to church influence, though in this case the impetus for that influence is likely to be transmitted strictly through interaction with fellow church members.

THEORETICAL UNDERPINNINGS

Wald, Owen, and Hill (1988) assert that churches provide a medium for a "behavioral contagion" within congregations. The opinions and beliefs of church members are influenced by the general political and social orientation of the church itself (as expressed through sermons, literature, or even decorative materials) as well as the opinions of other church members (1988: 533, 545-546). After controlling for individual traits, they observe a contextual component to individual theological conservatism:

> [T]he evidence suggested that the collective outlook of the church was more politically influential than the worldview of the individual church member. . . . Messages from the pulpit and social interaction with congregants apparently promote a common political outlook among church members. . . . *Individuals do not simply reason through the political implications of their religious views in a vacuum* [emphasis added]. (1988: 545, 546)

Michael MacKuen and Courtney Brown (1987) also argue for a contagion model of contextual influence on attitudes. Transmission of cues depends on personal interaction (discussion) rather than exogenous characteristics of the local environment. Furthermore, short-term politics plays a major role in determining the depth and direction of the contextual influence (1987: 485). This indicates that long-term attitudes such as partisanship should play minor roles in contextual influence in two important respects: The stable political milieu, as measured by partisanship, drives long-term change, not short-term change (recall that Chapter 4 presented findings consistent with this point); and short-term attitudes are likely to be influenced by other short-term forces, meaning that the strength of the contagion depends on the salience of political forces present at any given point in time. Hence attitude change is swift but temporary.

Although these two articles share a common affinity for the influence of contexts on attitudes, there is one subtle difference between their conclusions. Wald, Owen, and Hill stress that church influences work on members through the pulpit, social interaction, and observations of the surrounding environment, but MacKuen and Brown place full weight on social interaction as the key to contextual effects. MacKuen and Brown imply that informal assessments of the church environment, as described by Wald, Owen, and Hill, have little effect on individual beliefs, for there is no direct reinforcement mechanism that connects wall hangings or bumper stickers with specific political attitudes or positions. It remains to be seen whether churches, because of their unique nature as agents of social influence, can produce salient effects on their members through indirect, absorption processes as well as through more direct means such as face-to-face discussions.

ATTITUDES ON PUBLIC POLICY ISSUES

Before discussing in detail the findings of this section, the expectations are worth repeating. It is hypothesized that churches will probably not address directly such issues as defense spending, aid to minorities, or expectations for the economy. This is not to say that such issues are of no concern to all churches. On the contrary, there are definite social and moral components to these issues, and surely there are ministers and priests in South Bend who specifically address such policy areas from time to time. This is precisely why the nature of individual attitudes on these issues is of such interest, and why this section provides a good test for the proposition that indirect contextual effects are less salient than direct attempts to change individual views.

Although ministers may preach about the proliferation of nuclear weapons or the need to help disadvantaged social groups, the level of intrachurch discourse on these matters is probably less than would be found with abortion or public school prayer. Hence these dependent behaviors represent a "middle ground" of issues: On the surface, they should be less salient to the church and its members than issues such as abortion, but more salient than individual economic expectation, which is strictly a personal assessment.

The independent measures used in the models include individual demographic traits and contextual components. The church context in this section is operationalized as the mean attitude of individual church members on the dependent attitude in question.[1] As in Chapter 4, the strategy for modeling involves testing for contextual influences from neighborhood environments as well as churches. In addition, involvement in the church context, as measured by church attendance and group activity, is considered an important filter. Involvement here is more properly thought of as measuring a threshold for contextual effects—citizens need some minimal level of exposure to their social environments in order to receive and process the cues from those environments. Where appropriate, the South Bend sample has been divided by levels of church attendance to better understand the possible contextual influences under study.

Importance of National Defense

South Bend residents were asked whether they considered national defense extremely important, very important, somewhat important, or not important. Responses are coded on a four-point scale, ranging from 1, not important, to 4, extremely important. Results from the regression model showing determinants of this attitude are shown in Table 5.1. A positive coefficient on an independent variable means that the variable is associated with greater individual importance placed on national defense.

Among the individual-level variables, increasing personal income is associated with a reduced importance of national defense, and activity in a veterans group drives a respondent to place heightened importance on national defense. Not surprisingly, an increasingly conservative personal ideology also causes a citizen to find national defense more important. Party identification plays no role, nor does an individual's 1984 presidential vote.[2] With the possible exception of income, the independent variables behave as one would expect.

TABLE 5.1
Estimated 1984 South Bend Attitude Toward Importance of National Defense
(OLS Regression Estimates)

Independent Variable	Coefficient
Intercept	0.15 (1.20)
Individual income	−0.04 (0.02)**
Party identification	−0.00 (0.05)
Ideology self-placement	0.03 (0.02)*
Membership and activity in a veterans group	0.18 (0.07)**
Reagan vote instrument	1.23 (1.20)
Church attendance times mean church attitude on defense	0.00 (0.01)
Mean neighborhood attitude on defense	0.60 (0.35)*
Total number of cases	749
Adjusted R-square	.03

Source: 1984 South Bend study.
Note: Standard errors in parentheses.
    *=Significant at 0.10 level.
    **=Significant at 0.05 level.
    ***=Significant at 0.01 level.

As for the contextual measures, mean neighborhood attitudes on defense significantly affect individual attitudes in a positive, pro-defense direction, but mean church attitudes on defense (interacted with church attendance to introduce a measure of involvement in context) are not significant. Two possible explanations for the significance of the neighborhood measure come to mind. The first is that defense attitudes within the neighborhood are correlated with some other social characteristics, so that residents of a given locale are predisposed to think alike on this issue. The second explanation is that the significant coefficient represents an interaction-and-contagion process that spreads the word on the importance of national defense from resident to resident. Neither explanation is particularly convincing, although some combination of the two might be more plausible. In any case, the model in Table 5.1 shows absolutely no church contextual component to individual attitudes on the importance of defense.

In an attempt to find some church contextual component to defense attitudes, I divide the full South Bend sample into frequent and infrequent church attenders (frequent meaning every week or almost every week) and estimate the national defense model again. Table 5.2 shows that for infrequent church attenders, only mean neighborhood attitude on defense is a significant predictor of individual defense beliefs. For frequent attenders, on the other hand, veterans group activity pushes respondents in a pro-defense direction, and income and

TABLE 5.2
Estimated Importance of National Defense, Frequent and
    Infrequent Church Attenders
        (OLS Regression Estimates)

Independent Variable	Frequent Attenders Coefficient	Infrequent Attenders Coefficient
Intercept	1.87 (1.63)	-1.40 (1.81)
Individual income	-0.05 (0.03)*	-0.03 (0.03)
Party identification	0.02 (0.06)	-0.04 (0.07)
Ideology self-placement	0.04 (0.03)	0.03 (0.03)
Membership and activity in a veterans group	0.23 (0.11)**	0.12 (0.10)
Reagan vote instrument	0.38 (1.58)	2.62 (1.87)
Mean church attitude on defense	-0.22 (0.13)*	-0.09 (0.13)
Mean neighborhood attitude on defense	0.39 (0.45)	0.97 (0.55)*
Total number of cases	454	295
Adjusted R-square	.02	.03

Source: 1984 South Bend study.
Note: Standard errors in parentheses.
        *=Significant at 0.10 level.
        **=Significant at 0.05 level.
        ***=Significant at 0.01 level.

mean church attitudes drive citizens the opposite way. This
means that as churches become more pro-defense on average,
church members are driven to believe that national defense is
less important. On the surface, this is contradictory.
However, similar results for the next dependent attitude begin
to show how the puzzle fits together.

Government Aid to Minorities

Respondents are asked: Do you feel the government should
help improve the position of minorities, that minorities
should help themselves, or is your position somewhere in
between? Responses are coded into a five-point scale, with 1
denoting the belief that government should help minorities to
a great extent, 3 denoting an in-between position, and 5
denoting the view that minorities should help themselves.
Positive coefficients can be interpreted as favoring less
government involvement and more individual initiative on the
part of minorities.

In Table 5.3, party identification and ideology are
significant and positive: Increasing Republican attachments
and conservative viewpoints leads to greater belief in the
"help-yourself" view. White respondents are also more likely
to believe in self-help among minorities. Increasing
educational levels lead individuals to believe that more

TABLE 5.3
Estimated 1984 South Bend Attitude Toward Government Aid to
    Minorities
                (OLS Regression Estimates)

Independent Variable	Coefficient
Intercept	2.48 (0.84)***
Male	-0.11 (0.08)
White	0.82 (0.19)***
Individual education	-0.15 (0.04)***
Age	-0.04 (0.03)
Party identification	0.08 (0.02)***
Ideology self-placement	0.07 (0.02)***
Membership and activity in a minority group	0.16 (0.10)
Jewish	-0.44 (0.37)
Church attendance	-0.01 (0.04)
Percent Reagan vote in neighborhood	-0.94 (0.40)**
Mean neighborhood attitude on government aid to minorities	0.11 (0.24)
Percent Reagan vote in church	1.03 (0.53)**
Church attendance times percent Reagan vote in church	-0.20 (0.14)
Mean church attitude on government aid to minorities	-0.05 (0.08)
Mean church ideology self-placement	0.04 (0.06)
Total number of cases	700
Adjusted R-square	.10

Source: 1984 South Bend study.
Note: Standard errors in parentheses.
    *=Significant at 0.10 level.
    **=Significant at 0.05 level.
    ***=Significant at 0.01 level.

government involvement is necessary. These results are
consistent with the responses one would expect on this
question.
    As for contextual measures, the mean attitudes of church
and neighborhood have no bearing on individual attitudes, but
levels of Reagan voting in both church and neighborhood do
matter. As Reagan voting in a church increases, individuals
are more likely to believe in self-help for minorities, surely
a position consonant with Republican issue positions in 1984.
Neighborhood Reagan voting has the opposite effect: As more
people vote Republican in a neighborhood, residents of that
neighborhood become more disposed to support government aid to
minorities.
    These seemingly contradictory results suggest an
explanation similar to that offered for national defense. It

would appear that some respondents give answers consistent with their surrounding social contexts, though these answers are not necessarily influenced by those contexts. Other respondents, especially those more involved in their contexts, actually send and receive cues that alter both their own positions and those of people around them.

What would be the result of these two processes, if accurate? Uninvolved individuals would show significant effects from contexts, but the effects would represent artifacts of a selection process and not a true contextual influence on behavior. Involved individuals, on the other hand, would not show the neighborhood effects (a detached level of context) but may still show influences from churches, where their heightened level of personal involvement makes them more open to influence, thus providing an impetus to the behavioral contagion processes within the church environment.

Table 5.4 divides respondents again by church attendance to find evidence supporting these suppositions. Infrequent church attenders are influenced by church and neighborhood levels of Reagan voting, but as in Table 5.3, the effects work at cross-purposes. Frequent attenders show no inclination to be affected by levels of voting or by mean attitudes within church and neighborhood. But frequent attenders are affected by the mean ideological tenor of their churches. Recall from Table 5.2, which looked at defense positions sorted by church attendance, that frequent attenders were influenced by two principal factors: activity in a veterans group (an additional context) and mean church attitudes on defense. Infrequent attenders showed a significant correlation only with mean neighborhood attitudes. The contextual effects for frequent churchgoers are small in magnitude *but consistent in direction*. The contextual effects for infrequent churchgoers are not consistent, probably because this group has less frequent interaction with others in the church environment.

Expectations for the Economy

To assess expectations for the nation's economy in the future, respondents are asked if they expect the economy to get better, get worse, or stay about the same. Answers are coded into a three-level scale (1, will get worse; 3, stay about the same; 5, will get better). Hence a positive coefficient in Table 5.5 denotes greater optimism in the country's economic future.

Both individual Reagan votes and increasing levels of neighborhood Reagan voting are positively associated with optimistic economic expectations. Education is negatively related to economic expectations; well-educated citizens are more likely to regard present prosperity as temporary or economic downturns as inevitable. Finally, the mean position of fellow churchgoers on future economic expectations is positively related to optimistic forecasts, though the magnitude of the coefficient is quite small.

TABLE 5.4
Estimated Attitude Toward Government Aid to Minorities,
   Frequent and Infrequent Church Attenders
               (OLS Regression Estimates)

Independent Variable	Frequent Attenders Coefficient	Infrequent Attenders Coefficient
Intercept	2.97 (1.09)***	1.18 (1.34)
Male	0.05 (0.11)	-0.33 (0.13)**
White	0.65 (0.26)**	0.78 (0.32)**
Individual education	-0.17 (0.05)***	-0.11 (0.06)*
Age	-0.03 (0.04)	-0.03 (0.05)
Party identification	0.06 (0.03)**	0.08 (0.03)**
Ideology self-placement	0.08 (0.03)***	0.07 (0.04)*
Membership and activity in a minority group	0.11 (0.14)	0.12 (0.14)
Percent Reagan vote in neighborhood	-0.81 (0.51)	-1.13 (0.65)*
Mean neighborhood attitude on government aid to minorities	-0.13 (0.31)	0.61 (0.39)
Percent Reagan vote in church	0.03 (0.28)	0.74 (0.30)**
Mean church attitude on government aid to minorities	-0.06 (0.11)	-0.02 (0.12)
Mean church ideology self-placement	0.13 (0.08)*	-0.02 (0.08)
Total number of cases	431	269
Adjusted R-square	.09	.12

Source: 1984 South Bend study.
Note: Standard errors in parentheses.
   *=Significant at 0.10 level.
   **=Significant at 0.05 level.
   ***=Significant at 0.01 level.

Tentative Conclusions

These three dependent measures can be characterized as "middle-level" attitudes. Though there may be a specific position espoused by the church as an institution, there is not likely to be a strong impetus from the pulpit or within the congregation to direct members' personal views. Thus the church effect, if any, is likely to be minor. It turns out that a minor effect does exist, especially among frequent churchgoers, and a systematic interpretation of the church effect is becoming apparent. Individuals involved in church contexts become less susceptible to effects from neighborhood contexts, because the proximity of the interaction with fellow churchgoers is a stronger influence for change than is the more diffuse assessment and reconciliation of attitudes with

TABLE 5.5
Estimated 1984 South Bend Expectations for the National Economy
        (OLS Regression Estimates)

Independent Variable	Coefficient
Intercept	4.55 (1.48)***
Individual education	-0.07 (0.04)**
Party identification	0.10 (0.06)
Reagan vote instrument	2.61 (1.64)*
Percent Reagan vote in neighborhood	1.33 (0.56)**
Church attendance times mean church attitude on economy	0.02 (0.01)*
Church attendance times percent Reagan vote in church	-0.01 (0.06)
Total number of cases	811
Adjusted R-square	.10

Source: 1984 South Bend study.
Note: Standard errors in parentheses.
      *=Significant at 0.10 level.
      **=Significant at 0.05 level.
      ***=Significant at 0.01 level.

neighbors (though personal interaction with neighbors may also come into play for some citizens).

INDIVIDUAL ASSESSMENTS: ECONOMIC EXPECTATIONS AND PRESIDENTIAL APPROVAL

The driving forces behind presidential performance evaluations and personal expectations for the economy are thought to be individual factors. If there is a church influence on these dependent measures, that influence is likely to be spread through interactions with other churchgoers. It may also be argued that the theological values of the church itself, as expressed through sermons or other communications from clergy and church elites, promote a particular view of the world that may predispose church members to take an optimistic or pessimistic position on the economy. Such a process cannot be directly measured with the South Bend data, but its effects might be uncovered through group mean variables in the course of modeling responses on these dependent measures. Such an effect appears to have occurred with expectations for the national economic future in the previous section.

Personal Economic Expectations

To assess this attitude, respondents are asked: Looking ahead to next year, do you think that a year from now you (and

TABLE 5.6
Estimated 1984 South Bend Expectations for Future Personal
     Economic Situation
                    (OLS Regression Estimates)

Independent Variable	Coefficient
Intercept	2.66 (0.85)***
Expectation for national economy instrument	0.13 (0.33)
Party identification	0.07 (0.06)
Individual income	-0.01 (0.03)
Male	0.23 (0.08)***
White	-0.14 (0.18)
Age	-0.20 (0.03)***
Ideology self-placement	0.03 (0.02)
Reagan vote instrument	0.87 (1.77)
Church attendance times mean church attitude on personal economic situation	-0.01 (0.01)
Percent Reagan vote in church	-0.23 (0.18)
Percent Reagan vote in neighborhood	0.43 (0.34)
Total number of cases	772
Adjusted R-square	.16

Source: 1984 South Bend study.
Note: Standard errors in parentheses.
     *=Significant at 0.10 level.
     **=Significant at 0.05 level.
     ***=Significant at 0.01 level.

your family living here) will be better off financially, or
worse off, or just about the same as now? Answers are coded
into the same three-level scale used for the national economy
question.[3]

     The only significant predictors of individual economic
expectations in Table 5.6 are age and race; whites and older
citizens tend to be more pessimistic about their fortunes in
the coming year. Personal income does not make a difference,
nor does Reagan voting, and the assessments of personal
fortunes by fellow churchgoers also have a negligible (and
statistically insignificant) effect. Substantively, these
results suggest that survey questions calling for an
evaluation of other individuals (national economic future)
elicit responses that display a systematic bias toward the
prevailing views of a social context; questions concerning
individual future situations provoke individually based
responses with no systematic contextual influence.

Presidential Job Approval

     Prior to the 1984 election, respondents are asked if they
approve or disapprove of Ronald Reagan's performance as

TABLE 5.7
Estimated 1984 South Bend Presidential Job Approval
(OLS Regression Estimates)

Independent Variable	Coefficient
Intercept	-1.63 (0.89)*
Individual education	-0.07 (0.03)**
Individual income	0.03 (0.03)
Male	0.13 (0.08)*
White	-0.12 (0.18)
Age	-0.11 (0.03)***
Pays attention to campaign	0.04 (0.08)
Index of political activity	0.02 (0.04)
Party identification	0.07 (0.06)
Ideology self-placement	0.08 (0.02)***
Reagan vote instrument	7.38 (1.53)***
Catholic	0.08 (0.08)
Mean church attitude on Reagan job approval	0.05 (0.06)
Mean neighborhood attitude on Reagan job approval	-0.18 (0.18)
Total number of cases	551
Adjusted R-square	.52

Source: 1984 South Bend study.
Note: Standard errors in parentheses.
    *=Significant at 0.10 level.
    **=Significant at 0.05 level.
    ***=Significant at 0.01 level.

president; they are further probed as to the strength of their approval or disapproval. Answers are coded on a four-point scale (1, strong disapproval, to 4, strong approval). Positive coefficients in Table 5.7 indicate increasing approval of Reagan's performance.

Presidential job approval should be tied to presidential voting, but other factors also play a role. As expected, Table 5.7 shows that a citizen likely to vote for Reagan also believes that Reagan is performing well in office. Males are likely to approve of the president, and increasing conservatism is a significant predictor as well. Increasing education drives assessments of performance downward, and older citizens also are less likely to approve of Reagan's performance. Neither contextual measure, for church or neighborhood mean job approval, is significant, which fits well with the theoretical framework discussed above.

What Have We Learned So Far?

For the two dependent measures modeled in this section, no significant contextual influences, either from churches or from neighborhoods, are discovered. This finding lends credence to the argument that church contextual cues require some degree of involvement and interaction in order to become salient political signals for churchgoers. Further, in the absence of direct cues from friends or ministers regarding these dependent measures, cues that I argue are more likely to exist for the first set of issues modeled here, individual citizens appear to rely on their own personal judgment and expertise to structure their responses to attitudinal questions. Although a discussion partner-level model might well unearth strong influences within discussion pairs, modeling at the level of church produces no contextual effect on these individual attitudes.

ATTITUDES ON ISSUES SALIENT TO THE CHURCH: ABORTION AND SCHOOL PRAYER

Though this chapter has ascribed to school prayer and abortion the highest levels of church-generated contextual cues, it should not be assumed that churches are necessarily teeming with activity or discussion on these two issues. Certainly with the political salience of abortion on the rise, there may well be high levels of activity and discussion on both sides of the issue within churches. School prayer, on the other hand, is not nearly as "hot" an issue, at least not in South Bend in 1984, as far as can be discerned.[4] Nevertheless, prayer in public schools takes on significance for many denominations and devout worshipers as a symbol either of moral and ethical decline in the nation and its young people or of the religious freedom that is a bedrock principle in the United States. Thus these two issues present the best case for church contextual influences, with all the ingredients of a behavioral contagion process working to structure the views of church members.

Attitudes on Abortion

One systematic attempt to derive the foundations of abortion attitudes from social and cultural, as well as individual, factors has been undertaken by Eric Plutzer (1986). Among the relevant factors unearthed by Plutzer and other researchers are education, income, and attitudes on sexual behavior (Granberg and Granberg 1980; Harris and Mills 1985); age (Cutler et al. 1980); and church attendance and strength of religious conviction (Granberg and Granberg 1980; Plutzer 1986). Plutzer finds that interactions between particular denominations and church attendance may be an important intervening factor; however, no such significant relationships could be found in this research.

Based on existing knowledge about the determinants of attitudes toward abortion, two separate models for abortion attitudes are estimated. The first model (Table 5.8) looks at all respondents; the second (Table 5.9) divides respondents into frequent and infrequent church attenders. Abortion attitudes are coded on a seven-point scale (0 to 6), with increasing values on the scale denoting increasingly pro-life (anti-abortion) attitudes. This scale is constructed from

TABLE 5.8
Estimated 1984 South Bend Attitude Toward Abortion
                (OLS Regression Estimates)

Independent Variable	Coefficient
Intercept	-0.84 (0.93)
Individual education	-0.13 (0.07)*
Individual income	-0.08 (0.06)
Party identification	0.07 (0.04)*
Ideology self-placement	0.14 (0.04)***
Catholic	1.10 (0.20)***
Evangelical Protestant	0.90 (0.23)***
Jewish	-0.46 (0.75)
Index of church activity	0.08 (0.02)***
Church attendance times mean church attitude on abortion	0.07 (0.02)***
Mean church ideology	0.08 (0.11)
Mean neighborhood attitude on abortion	0.23 (0.24)
Percent Reagan vote in neighborhood	1.03 (0.81)
Total number of cases	648
Adjusted R-square	.21

Source: 1984 South Bend study.
Note: Standard errors in parentheses.
    *=Significant at 0.10 level.
    **=Significant at 0.05 level.
    ***=Significant at 0.01 level.

responses to six questions concerning the legality of abortion in specific situations:

— If a woman is married and wants no more children;

— If a woman is unmarried and does not want to marry the father;

— If a family has low income and cannot afford any more children;

— If there is a strong chance that there is a serious defect in the fetus;

— If a woman became pregnant as a result of rape;

— If a woman's own health is endangered by the pregnancy.

Thus an individual who believes that abortion should be illegal in all six situations is coded as a 6 on the 0-to-6 scale, a strong anti-abortion, pro-life advocate; an individual who believes abortion should be legal in all circumstances listed would be coded as a 0. Although 10 percent of respondents in the South Bend sample are strongly pro-choice (scale score = 0), almost 40 percent are strongly opposed to abortion regardless of circumstance (scale score = 6).[5]

Table 5.8, which does not differentiate respondents by church attendance, reveals that church activity is positively associated with pro-life attitudes, as are Republican party identification and conservative ideology. Not surprisingly, Catholics and Evangelicals are more likely to be pro-life. The mean attitude of an individual's church on abortion, interacted with church attendance, is also significant—as citizens attend increasingly pro-life churches, they take on increasingly pro-life views.

When the South Bend sample is divided into frequent and infrequent church attenders in Table 5.9, a curious thing happens to the church contextual effect found in the previous table: It disappears. Among frequent attenders, Catholics and Evangelical Protestants are again found to be strongly pro-life due to their religious adherence. This is a crucial point: Denomination alone accounts for the church effect among frequent attenders, not the views of other people in the church. Party identification, ideology, and church group activity still matter, but only denominations are significant among church-related variables. Also, two neighborhood contextual measures are significant among frequent attenders. As neighborhoods become increasingly pro-life on average, residents become more pro-life themselves. Increasing levels of Republican voting in the neighborhood also drive residents to the pro-life end of the scale.

Infrequent attenders are not influenced by any context. Increasing education pushes infrequent attenders toward a pro-choice position, while Catholic and Evangelical adherents and a personal conservative ideology are positively related to pro-life views. Infrequent attenders are not susceptible to neighborhood effects; indeed, the signs on the two neighborhood measures are the opposite of those found for frequent attenders.

The model for frequent attenders suggests that belonging to certain denominations determines an individual's abortion attitudes to such an extent that no additional influence is forthcoming from other churchgoers. It also suggests that despite the potential for transmission of cues within churches, individuals make up their own minds on abortion, and hence are less susceptible to such cues.

The neighborhood effects are most curious, since neighborhoods have only been found to matter in some cases for *infrequent* attenders earlier in this chapter. An attempt to differentiate between Catholics (whose neighborhoods more closely match patterns and measures found in their churches) and non-Catholics on mean neighborhood abortion attitudes finds that the neighborhood effect does not go away, though its magnitude is smaller for non-Catholics.[6] Reagan voting is at least consistent with a pro-life attitude, and perhaps the contrast between the 1984 presidential candidates' abortion positions heightens the salience of neighbors' vote intentions. But this line of reasoning runs counter to the theory that if any context should affect abortion attitudes,

TABLE 5.9
Estimated Attitude Toward Abortion, Frequent and Infrequent Church Attenders
(OLS Regression Estimates)

Independent Variable	Frequent Attenders Coefficient	Infrequent Attenders Coefficient
Intercept	-2.01 (1.28)	1.95 (1.32)
Individual education	-0.14 (0.09)	-0.17 (0.10)*
Individual income	-0.12 (0.08)	-0.06 (0.08)
Party identification	0.15 (0.05)***	0.00 (0.05)
Ideology self-placement	0.13 (0.06)**	0.14 (0.06)**
Catholic	1.70 (0.29)***	0.72 (0.27)***
Evangelical Protestant	1.52 (0.32)***	0.54 (0.31)*
Membership and activity in a church-related group	0.19 (0.11)*	0.09 (0.13)
Mean church attitude on abortion	0.08 (0.11)	0.00 (0.10)
Mean church ideology	0.10 (0.15)	0.17 (0.14)
Mean neighborhood attitude on abortion	0.63 (0.32)**	-0.31 (0.35)
Percent Reagan vote in neighborhood	2.48 (1.10)**	-1.20 (1.12)
Total number of cases	383	265
Adjusted R-square	.15	.06

Source: 1984 South Bend study.
Note: Standard errors in parentheses.
    *=Significant at 0.10 level.
    **=Significant at 0.05 level.
    ***=Significant at 0.01 level.

the church context is the most likely suspect.

A resolution to this problem would have to consider the salience of abortion as a political issue in 1984 rather than as a moral issue at some other point in time. If individual abortion attitudes are structured largely by short-term forces, which are made salient only in the context of the campaign season, then whatever church interest there is in the issue (an interest likely to remain more or less constant over time, though perhaps also heightened in an election year) may be overwhelmed by political considerations in the short run. Granted, this explanation still does not rescue the original theory expounded here, but it may account for the unexpected results of Table 5.9.

Attitudes on Prayer in Public Schools

Support for prayer in public schools is modeled using the same strategy as with abortion. One model (Table 5.10) looks at the entire sample, and the second (Table 5.11) sorts by

TABLE 5.10
Estimated 1984 South Bend Attitude Toward Prayer in Public Schools
(OLS Regression Estimates)

Independent Variable	Coefficient
Intercept	0.53 (0.32)*
Individual education	-0.13 (0.03)***
Ideology self-placement	0.03 (0.02)*
Reagan vote instrument	1.38 (0.42)***
Catholic	0.45 (0.14)***
Mainline Protestant	0.42 (0.15)***
Evangelical Protestant	0.57 (0.15)***
Church attendance	0.07 (0.03)***
Mean church attitude on school prayer	0.23 (0.08)***
Mean church ideology	-0.03 (0.04)
Total number of cases	740
Adjusted R-square	.10

Source: 1984 South Bend study.
Note: Standard errors in parentheses.
    *=Significant at 0.10 level.
    **=Significant at 0.05 level.
    ***=Significant at 0.01 level.

church attendance.   Respondents are asked for their opinions on this issue with a two-part question: Some people think it is all right for the public schools to start each day with a prayer.   Others feel that religion does not belong in the public schools but should be taken care of by the family and the church.   Have you been interested enough in this to favor one side over the other?   If yes, which do you think—schools should be allowed to start each day with a prayer, or religion does not belong in the schools?

Answers to this question are coded in two ways.   First, there is a three-level scale (1, no prayer in schools; 2, no opinion; 3, favors school prayer); then for a second set of models, the no-opinion group is omitted, hence a logistic model is estimated on the dichotomous dependent measure.   This logit model also is divided by church attendance (Tables 5.12 and 5.13).   In both sets of models, a positive coefficient denotes increasing support for allowing prayer in public schools.

To test for the effects of church context, Tables 5.10 and 5.11 include a variable measuring the mean church attitude on prayer in public schools.   This contextual variable is a significant predictor in Table 5.10 and drives respondents in a pro-prayer direction.   Recall that the mean attitude of the church on abortion was also significant in the abortion model not sorted by attendance.   In addition to the church context measure, several other independent measures are positively associated with increased support for public school prayer.

TABLE 5.11
**Estimated 1984 South Bend Attitude Toward Prayer in Public
Schools, Frequent and Infrequent Church Attenders**
(OLS Regression Estimates)

Independent Variable	Frequent Attenders Coefficient	Infrequent Attenders Coefficient
Intercept	1.13 (0.46)**	0.74 (0.47)
Individual education	-0.13 (0.03)***	-0.12 (0.05)***
Ideology self-placement	0.05 (0.02)**	0.00 (0.03)
Reagan vote instrument	1.89 (0.54)***	0.93 (0.70)
Catholic	0.03 (0.23)	0.68 (0.19)***
Mainline Protestant	-0.01 (0.24)	0.62 (0.20)***
Evangelical Protestant	0.19 (0.24)	0.71 (0.21)***
Mean church attitude on school prayer	0.25 (0.11)**	0.15 (0.13)
Mean church ideology	-0.11 (0.06)*	0.05 (0.06)
Total number of cases	445	295
Adjusted R-square	.10	.09

Source: 1984 South Bend study.
Note: Standard errors in parentheses.
    *=Significant at 0.10 level.
    **=Significant at 0.05 level.
    ***=Significant at 0.01 level.

These include conservative personal ideology, Reagan voting,
increasing church attendance, and the denominational
categories mainline Protestant, Evangelical Protestant, and
Catholic.   Higher levels of education are associated with
opposition to prayer in public schools.

Table 5.11 presents the same school prayer model for
frequent and infrequent church attenders. The denominational
categories are the only significant predictors for infrequent
attenders, with the exception of education, which maintains
its significance and negative sign for both frequent and
infrequent attenders. These findings are consistent with the
theory presented so far.

For frequent attenders, the church mean attitude on
school prayer maintains its significance and continues to
drive respondents in a pro-school prayer direction.   This
result confirms the theory that issues with moral dimensions
and church interests (at both the institutional and personal
levels) are highly amenable to the behavioral contagion
processes described by Wald, Owen, and Hill, and MacKuen and
Brown. Reagan voting, education, and ideology are significant
measures and behave in expected ways.   The mean church
ideology is also significant and negative (the more
conservative a church, the more individual members are opposed
to school prayer).

Finally, denominational categories are *not* significant
for frequent attenders.   This result is contrary to the
results for frequent attenders on abortion, where the

TABLE 5.12
Estimated 1984 South Bend Attitude Toward Prayer in Public
Schools, Responses Collapsed to Yes/No Only
(Logit Estimates)

Independent Variable	Coefficient
Intercept	-4.16 (0.94)***
Individual education	-0.35 (0.07)***
Ideology self-placement	0.10 (0.05)*
Reagan vote instrument	3.67 (1.17)***
Catholic	1.25 (0.40)***
Mainline Protestant	1.20 (0.41)***
Evangelical Protestant	1.55 (0.43)***
Church attendance	0.17 (0.07)**
Mean church attitude on school prayer	0.65 (0.23)***
Mean church ideology	-0.05 (0.13)
Total number of cases	655
Percent of cases correctly predicted	69.5
Model chi-square	83.78 with 9 df

Source: 1984 South Bend study.
Note: Standard errors in parentheses.
    *=Significant at 0.10 level.
    **=Significant at 0.05 level.
    ***=Significant at 0.01 level.

denominational variables superseded the church contextual measures.

Tables 5.12 and 5.13 utilize the alternative, dichotomous coding scheme for attitudes toward public school prayer. The estimated logit models allow for the use of probability traces to assess differences between frequent and infrequent attenders. Table 5.12 looks at the entire sample, and the results match (in terms of signs and significance levels) the results for the entire sample (including respondents with no opinion) in Table 5.10. Mean church attitudes on school prayer still drive individual attitudes.

Table 5.13 divides the logit model by attendance, and once again the results, in terms of significance levels and signs, exactly match Table 5.11. Most importantly, the contextual measure for mean church attitude on school prayer is significant among frequent attenders and not significant for infrequent attenders. And unlike the abortion model, denominational adherence does not matter for frequent attenders. That is, denominations do not supersede contextual forces in driving school prayer attitudes.

Figure 5.1 traces the probability of favoring public school prayer. Three traces are displayed, representing the probability for all respondents (from Table 5.12) and the traces for frequent and infrequent attenders (from Table 5.13). As with the graphs in Chapter 4, these traces are

TABLE 5.13
Estimated 1984 South Bend Attitude Toward Prayer in Public Schools, Responses Collapsed to Yes/No Only, Frequent and Infrequent Church Attenders
(Logit Estimates)

Independent Variable	Frequent Attenders Coefficient	Infrequent Attenders Coefficient
Intercept	-2.26 (1.31)*	-3.63 (1.41)***
Individual education	-0.38 (0.09)***	-0.34 (0.12)***
Ideology self-placement	0.16 (0.06)**	0.09 (0.08)
Reagan vote instrument	4.51 (1.50)***	2.11 (1.79)
Index of church activity	0.17 (0.13)	-0.14 (0.17)
Evangelical Protestant	0.51 (0.68)	1.56 (0.56)***
Catholic	0.18 (0.65)	1.63 (0.53)***
Mainline Protestant	0.03 (0.67)	1.58 (0.53)***
Mean church attitude on school prayer	0.63 (0.30)**	0.55 (0.34)
Mean church ideology	-0.29 (0.17)*	0.20 (0.19)
Total number of cases	435	270
Percent of cases correctly predicted	70.8	68.5
Model chi-square	53.04 with 9 df	37.47 with 9 df

Source: 1984 South Bend study.
Note: Standard errors in parentheses.
    *=Significant at 0.10 level.
    **=Significant at 0.05 level.
    ***=Significant at 0.01 level.

calculated holding all other variables constant and allowing the mean church attitude on school prayer to vary from opposition to full support. Although the three traces look quite similar, frequent attenders show the greatest propensity to favor school prayer. Figure 5.2 shows the difference between frequent and infrequent attenders to be roughly 0.1 on a zero-to-one scale. Considering that so many other individual-level variables predict school prayer attitudes, this difference is rather sizable.

SUMMARY AND CONCLUSIONS

The results of this chapter confirm much of the theory presented at the outset, and yet they can also be categorized as idiosyncratic. Without explicitly testing for levels of interpersonal interaction, I find several consistent results:

    — Church context significantly affects attitudes on
    issues that have an explicit moral or religious
    dimension—abortion and school prayer, for example.

FIGURE 5.1
**Predicted 1984 Support for School Prayer, Responses Collapsed
   to Yes/No Only, Frequent and Infrequent Church Attenders**
(Mean church attitude on school prayer varying)

LEGEND

All respondents	————————
Frequent attenders	- - - - - - - -
Infrequent attenders	··············

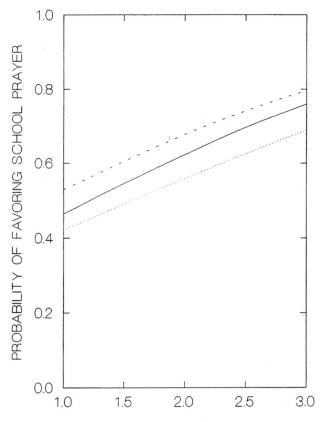

MEAN CHURCH ATTITUDE TOWARD SCHOOL PRAYER

FIGURE 5.2
Probability Difference, 1984 Support for School Prayer, Frequent and Infrequent Church Attenders

(Probability of support for school prayer,
frequent attenders, minus probability of support
for school prayer, infrequent attenders)

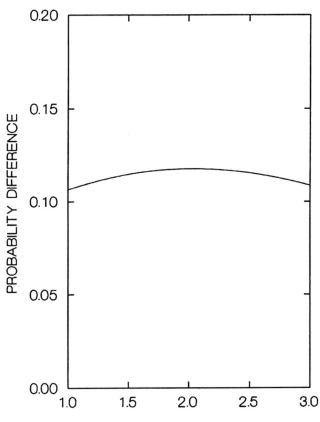

— Short-term political forces may mitigate the behavioral contagion at work that must drive the contextual influences within churches.

— For issues that have no obvious church dimension (national defense, aid to minorities), or attitudes that are largely determined by individuals alone (presidential job approval, personal economic future), no church contextual influence is found.

A second set of findings regarding the relative influence of denominations on abortion and school prayer reveals some trends that may have been less predictable:

— Among frequent attenders, denominations are important predictors on abortion attitudes, but they are not statistically significant predictors in the school prayer models.

— In those same frequent-attender models, church context matters for school prayer attitudes but not for abortion attitudes.

These two findings are clearly related: For individuals who are deeply involved in their church contexts, denomination matters over church context when short-term forces drive the attitude in question (abortion, a politically salient issue in 1984), and church context matters over denomination when the attitude in question is less politically salient (school prayer) and is structured over an indeterminate period of time.

Extensions of the findings here might bring in interaction with discussion partners to test the strength of contextual effects in churches. Such a test is undertaken with abortion attitudes in Chapter 7. Regardless of those findings, the results in this chapter, determined without the presence of any explicit measure of the moral character of churches or the content of cues within churches, still present evidence of a systematic ordering of contextual influence within churches and further demonstrate that by controlling for involvement in the church context, the systematic nature of the results does not vary.

NOTES

1. The construction of group mean variables for this chapter follows the same procedure described in Chapter 1.

2. Because the 1984 vote is correlated with several other variables in this and the other models in this chapter, an instrumental variable is used instead of the actual dichotomous vote measure. The instrumental variable for vote represents the predicted probability of a Reagan vote, as determined by a full model estimating Reagan vote; by using this method, the correlated error among the independent variables is removed, hence the interpretation of coefficients and significance levels is straightforward.

3. Because expectations for personal economic future are related to expectations for the national economy (simple correlation of 0.37), an instrumental variable for the national economic assessment is used rather than the straight measure. It turns out that this instrument is not significant in the final model.

4. Prayer in public schools was on the national agenda in 1984. President Reagan spoke favorably of a constitutional amendment allowing public school prayer at the National Prayer Day Breakfast, and a plank in the Republican party platform also advocated passage of the amendment. Despite strong Evangelical support for President Reagan, there was little attention given by either candidate to such issues during the fall campaign (Wald 1992: 235-236).

5. This attitude probably does not reflect that of the U.S. public as a whole. Roughly 40 percent of South Bend respondents fall in the middle of the six-point scale (scores 2, 3, 4), which is not surprising. The large number of strong pro-life respondents is atypical. Note, however, that effective modeling of determinants of abortion attitudes does not depend on the distribution of views; the statistical results are not corrupted by the data.

6. Model results are not reported.

Chapter 6

Church Contexts and
Individual Self-Evaluations

So far in this book it has been assumed that citizens interact
with their surroundings, their contexts, in ways that allow
political messages to be shared and interpreted. And so far
we have found evidence to support the contention that not all
contexts have equal weight when it comes to influencing
attitudes. And of course, for some attitudes context simply
does not matter at all. An indicator that would allow us to
assess just how attuned any individual is to any particular
context would greatly enhance the ability to predict which
contexts will be salient and on what specific issues. In
short, one needs a way to answer the question of how citizens
perceive and evaluate their social surroundings. What
indicators, what evidence do people use to judge their
neighbors, their coworkers, their fellow churchgoers,
themselves? And if one can measure these judgments, do they
provide a clue as to how important a specific social context
will be in affecting individual attitudes and behaviors?

It is commonly accepted that one primary purpose of
churches and religions is to impart meaning and direction to
individual lives. This chapter starts from that assumption
and proceeds to examine how individual perceptions of
neighbors and fellow churchgoers affect individual attitudes
and beliefs. The analysis starts by modeling these
evaluations themselves: Are evaluations of one's personal
situation and happiness affected by religious affiliation, or
by the similar evaluations given by fellow church members?
What political meanings can be derived from such
relationships?

Churches and neighborhoods in South Bend are again the
focus for this chapter, and appropriate contextual measures
are constructed to test for the presence of contextual
influences. Moreover, many of the independent measures in
this chapter, as well as all the dependent measures, consist
of subjective assessments by the South Bend respondents. So
rather than relying on objective measurements of contexts (for
example, the mean educational level of a neighborhood), this
chapter focuses on how individuals make such assessments
(asking how educated one's neighbors are).

CHURCHES AND SELF-EVALUATIONS: PRELIMINARY HYPOTHESES

The motivating belief behind investigating the source of individuals' self-evaluations of their surroundings is that perceptions of such relationships, especially those with neighbors, may be affected by observation and information gathered from fellow churchgoers. Moreover, the level of individual involvement in the church should have an impact on the information-gathering process. Thus different behavioral outcomes are posited, depending on individual levels of involvement in church contexts.

It has been established that churches often are important sources of political cues, and high levels of involvement often correspond to higher levels of agreement with fellow churchgoers. This does not necessarily mean that for the most committed, the church stands above other contexts in affecting attitudes and actions. Some researchers have made this assertion, however. Kenneth Wald argues:

> Although the point should not be overstated, a strong sense of collective religious identity, with its associated political messages, may override the other sources of political cues available to the church members. Instead of picking up political orientations from the newspaper, neighbors, coworkers, or other secondary organizations, the individual may imbibe loyalties from the church members and leaders who are the principal partners in social interaction. (1992: 113)

Based on Wald's argument, one would expect to find that self-evaluations are strongly related to the feelings and self-evaluations of fellow churchgoers.

For citizens not involved actively in their church contexts, there are two obvious scenarios. First, some other social context (the neighborhood is explicitly considered in this chapter, but workplaces or other group attachments are likely alternatives) may offer more salient cues. Alternatively, some citizens may have little grounding or attachment to any social context; thus, effectively alienated from potential social sources of political influence, they should not exhibit any inclination to conform to or be influenced by what their friends and neighbors think.

Pulling these tentative hypotheses together, I propose that an individual's perception of his or her standing relative to neighbors depends on several factors:

— Attitudes toward those neighbors;

— Individual demographic and political characteristics and attitudes;

— Majority or minority status within the neighborhood context, based on class, race, or religion;

- Attitudes of others in the same neighborhood; and

- Attitudes of others in the church.

DEPENDENT MEASURES AND MODELING STRATEGIES

Three separate individual self-evaluations are examined:

- Individual satisfaction with the neighborhood;

- A subjective comparison of family interest in politics with the interest of neighboring families; and

- A subjective comparison of family political activity with the political activity of neighbors.

Once I have analyzed the determinants of these three indicators, the chapter concludes with a reexamination of the school prayer model from Chapter 5, incorporating a new filter variable and two of the independent measures examined in this chapter.

The independent measures used in the regression models to follow combine individual demographic traits with contextual components. As in previous chapters, the strategy for modeling involves the consideration of and testing for contextual influences from neighborhood environments as well as churches. And as in previous chapters, where appropriate, the sample has been divided by levels of church attendance and group involvement to test the effects of different levels of involvement.

NEIGHBORHOOD SATISFACTION

How satisfied are people with their neighborhoods? The responses of South Bend residents are coded on a four-point scale, with 1 meaning very dissatisfied and 4 meaning very satisfied with the neighborhood. These responses provide a concise summary of individual feelings and opinions with regard to neighbors; further, the question itself has no direct or obvious linkage to individual political views or the political views of neighbors. Thus one can test the extent to which satisfaction depends on the political as well as the social character of one's immediate surroundings.

A wide range of independent variables are introduced as possible predictors of satisfaction levels. These include: whether the individual plans to move or stay in the neighborhood, the quality of neighborhood schools and streets, the perceived friendliness and helpfulness of neighbors, and self-reported comparisons of the neighborhood's economic well-being and educational level in relation to those of other neighborhoods. In addition, some explicitly political questions are included as independent variables: whether politics is discussed with neighbors and how interested in politics the family is, relative to neighbors (also a self-reported comparison). Finally, two questions that tap into a religious component of satisfaction have been included. The first is a self-reported comparison of family religion compared with that of neighbors: Is your religion the same as your neighbors, different, or very different? Second, for each individual's church, a mean level of satisfaction with neighborhoods is computed; in other words, one can measure how satisfied or dissatisfied one's fellow churchgoers are with their neighborhood surroundings.

The relevance of these independent measures should be clear. Good schools and streets, friendly neighbors, a desire to stay put, and a belief that the present neighborhood is better off than other locations—all these factors should lead, prima facie, to high levels of satisfaction. As for the religious measures, if individuals perceive themselves to differ from their neighbors, two things may occur: They may withdraw from the neighborhood environment and tie themselves more closely to the church, and they may feel less satisfied with their present surroundings, since they perceive a dissonance with their neighbors.

For political discussion and relative interest in politics, the interpretation is less clear. Those citizens more interested in political affairs could be less satisfied with their neighborhood. In fact, their political interest may be sparked by some unfavorable condition or situation. Talking with neighbors about politics, on the other hand, may lead to greater satisfaction. A citizen who actively engages her neighbors may emerge from that discussion with a sense that her neighbors share her concerns. Hence, the citizen feels a bit more secure in her current surroundings.

Table 6.1 reports the results of an OLS regression estimating individual satisfaction with the neighborhood. The results support the preliminary hypotheses—all independent measures are statistically significant indicators of satisfaction. Three findings merit further elaboration. First, a perception that one's family is different from neighbors in terms of religious beliefs is negatively related to neighborhood satisfaction; families are less satisfied and more uncomfortable when they do not reside among members of the same faith. Second, family political interest also is negatively related to satisfaction. When a family sees itself as more interested in politics than its neighbors, the family is less satisfied with the neighborhood. Indeed, perhaps the dissatisfaction drives the increased interest in politics, not vice versa. Finally, the contextual variable measuring the mean satisfaction of fellow churchgoers is significant and positive. Apparently, members of the same church do think alike in terms of their feelings about the quality of their residential areas.

One caveat to the last finding is important: Catholic church memberships are organized geographically, meaning that there is a relatively high correlation between neighborhood and church for the contextual measures of satisfaction (Pearson's $r = .53$). This has a potentially corrupting effect on the interpretation of the church contextual measure of satisfaction.[1] Accordingly, Table 6.2 introduces the church contextual measure of neighborhood satisfaction for non-Catholics only (alternative model 1). Table 6.2 also displays a model (alternative model 2) that includes mean church levels

TABLE 6.1
Estimated Satisfaction with Neighborhood
                 (OLS Regression Estimates)

Independent Variable	Coefficient
Intercept	2.38 (0.21)***
Planning to move (1) or stay (0)	-0.25 (0.04)***
Relative quality of neighborhood's schools	0.09 (0.03)***
Relative quality of neighborhood's streets	0.06 (0.03)**
Friendliness of neighbors	0.10 (0.03)***
Helpfulness of neighbors	0.21 (0.03)***
Family's interest in politics compared to neighbors	-0.08 (0.03)***
Neighborhood's education compared to other neighborhoods	0.12 (0.04)***
Own neighborhood better off compared to other neighborhoods	0.18 (0.04)***
Family's religion different from neighbors	-0.06 (0.02)***
Discusses politics with neighbors	0.04 (0.02)*
Mean church level of satisfaction with neighborhood	0.24 (0.06)***
Total number of cases	1165
Adjusted R-square	.23

Source: 1984 South Bend study.
Note: Standard errors in parentheses.
    *=Significant at 0.10 level.
    **=Significant at 0.05 level.
    ***=Significant at 0.01 level.

of neighborhood satisfaction (for Catholics and non-Catholics together) and an interaction term assessing the joint impact of family religious difference and mean church satisfaction. This model tests the hypothesis that when an individual believes his family's religion to be different from that of neighbors, the overall satisfaction of fellow church members should have less effect on individual satisfaction. That is, the individual is cross-pressured, and the perception of a difference in religious orientations reduces satisfaction, relative to the prevailing attitudes of the church.

The first thing to note about the alternative models estimated in Table 6.2 is that none of the variables from Table 6.1 have changed in sign or statistical significance (with one exception, covered below). Thus changes to the specification of the contextual measures have not affected the basic findings on satisfaction. In the first alternative model, the new variable mean church satisfaction for non-Catholics only is still a significant and positive factor (more satisfied with neighborhood). However, the magnitude of the estimated coefficient has dropped to .02 from .24, and the

TABLE 6.2
Estimated Satisfaction with Neighborhood, Alternative Model
   Specifications
            (OLS Regression Estimates)

Independent Variable	Alternative Model 1 Coefficient	Alternative Model 2 Coefficient
Intercept	3.17 (0.09)***	2.24 (0.56)***
Planning to move	-0.26 (0.04)***	-0.25 (0.04)***
Relative quality of neighborhood schools	0.09 (0.03)***	0.09 (0.03)***
Relative quality of neighborhood's streets	0.06 (0.03)**	0.06 (0.03)**
Friendliness of neighbors	0.11 (0.03)***	0.10 (0.03)***
Helpfulness of neighbors	0.21 (0.03)***	0.21 (0.03)***
Family's interest in politics compared to neighbors'	-0.08 (0.03)***	-0.08 (0.03)***
Neighborhood's education compared to other neighborhoods'	0.13 (0.04)***	0.12 (0.04)***
Own neighborhood better off compared to other neighborhoods	0.18 (0.04)***	0.18 (0.04)***
Family's religion different from neighbors'	-0.06 (0.02)***	-0.01 (0.24)
Discusses politics with neighbors	0.04 (0.02)*	0.04 (0.02)*
Mean church satisfaction with neighborhood, non-Catholics only	0.02 (0.01)*	---
Mean church level of satisfaction with neighborhood	---	0.28 (0.17)*
Family's religion different times mean church satisfaction	---	-0.02 (0.07)
Total number of cases	1165	1165
Adjusted R-square	.21	.23

Source: 1984 South Bend study.
Note: Standard errors in parentheses.
         *=Significant at 0.10 level.
         **=Significant at 0.05 level.
         ***=Significant at 0.01 level.

estimate is statistically far less robust than before. Hence
mean church satisfaction levels appear to be relatively minor
factors in individual determinations of satisfaction, at least
when controlling for the dual church-neighborhood position of
Catholics.

   Results from the second model in Table 6.2 show that the
interactive measure (perceived religious difference from

neighbors times mean church satisfaction) is not a significant factor. Its effect on the model is to reduce the crispness of the estimate for mean church satisfaction (the two variables are highly correlated, not surprisingly), and to completely eliminate the statistical significance of perceived family religious difference from neighbors (again, a high correlation is the likely culprit). Clearly, there is no evidence for a straightforward interactive effect between perceived dissonant religious belief and mean church levels of satisfaction.

FAMILY INTEREST IN POLITICS

Another South Bend survey question asks for an evaluation of family interest in politics compared with that of neighboring families. Answers are coded into a three-level scale: -1 indicates that one's family is less interested; 0 indicates similar levels of interest; and 1 denotes greater interest in politics than neighboring families.

Table 6.1 has revealed that neighborhood satisfaction is inversely related to family interest in politics: The more satisfied a family is, the less that family cares about politics relative to neighbors. Accordingly, satisfaction is included as an independent measure through an instrumental variable to account for the interdependence of the two measures. Other individual-level variables used in this analysis include age and gender; a self-reported evaluation of the family's educational level compared to the education of neighbors; family political views compared to the views of neighbors, also self-reported; self-reported frequency of political discussion with neighbors; attention to the 1984 campaign; frequent voluntary group activity; and a dichotomous variable measuring whether the respondent is a strong partisan of either party.

Two contextual measures are also specified: the mean response of an individual's church to the dependent measure—in other words, the amount of political interest one's fellow church members have relative to their neighbors—as well as the mean response of an individual's neighborhood to the political interest question. These contextual measures attempt to assess which context, if any, an individual agrees with in terms of relative political interest. Finally, church attendance and church-connected group activity are included as assessments of involvement in the life and work of the church. With the exception of satisfaction with neighborhood, all the above independent measures are expected to be positively related to an individual perception of greater political interest than one's neighbors.

In Table 6.3, I find once again that most of the variables that do not deal with church or neighborhood context are statistically significant, with signs in the expected direction. Measures of church activity are not significant, however. Further, the mean response of neighbors has no effect.

The church context appears to play a role in determining individual responses to relative interest in politics. The more interested fellow churchgoers are in politics, relative to their neighbors, the more interested individuals say they

TABLE 6.3
Estimated Family Interest in Politics Compared with Other
Families in Same Neighborhood
(OLS Regression Estimates)

Independent Variable	Coefficient
Intercept	-0.66 (0.31)**
Satisfaction with neighborhood instrument	-0.07 (0.03)***
Age	0.01 (0.01)
Male	0.09 (0.04)***
Family more educated than neighbors	0.16 (0.03)***
Family political views different from neighbors'	0.06 (0.02)***
Discusses politics with neighbors	0.08 (0.02)***
Active in 3 or more groups	0.10 (0.04)***
Strong partisan	0.16 (0.04)***
Pays attention to campaign	0.24 (0.04)***
Church attendance	0.01 (0.01)
Church-connected group activity	0.01 (0.02)
Mean church level of political interest relative to neighbors	0.14 (0.04)***
Mean neighborhood level of political interest relative to neighbors	-0.02 (0.10)
Total number of cases	936
Adjusted R-square	.19

Source: 1984 South Bend study.
Note: Standard errors in parentheses.
    *=Significant at 0.10 level.
    **=Significant at 0.05 level.
    ***=Significant at 0.01 level.

are in politics. This could mean two things. Either individual responses correlate with the responses of fellow churchgoers, with no causality implied, or the attitude of the church toward politics, measured by the sum of political interest responses, creates a climate of political interest that touches other churchgoers who may not share such interests in the first place—in other words, a causal relationship.

Taking the basic model a bit further may clarify which of these scenarios is closer to reality. The models in Table 6.4 report estimates calculated separately for Catholics and non-Catholics. One might expect that for Catholics, the church context would not be significant. Since Catholics tend to live among other Catholics, more so than their Protestant counterparts, the church's level of relative political interest should not have a great impact on individual

TABLE 6.4
Estimated Family Interest in Politics Compared with Other Families in Same Neighborhood, Catholics and Non-Catholics
(OLS Regression Estimates)

Independent Variable	Catholics Coefficient	Non-Catholics Coefficient
Intercept	-0.78 (0.40)**	-0.74 (0.19)***
Satisfaction with neighborhood instrument	-0.12 (0.04)***	-0.03 (0.03)
Age	0.02 (0.02)	0.01 (0.02)
Male	0.10 (0.05)**	0.07 (0.05)
Family more educated than neighbors	0.14 (0.05)***	0.18 (0.05)***
Family political views different from neighbors'	0.09 (0.03)***	0.03 (0.03)
Discusses politics with neighbors	0.06 (0.03)**	0.09 (0.03)***
Active in 3 or more groups	0.17 (0.06)***	0.04 (0.05)
Strong partisan	0.14 (0.05)***	0.18 (0.05)***
Pays attention to campaign	0.27 (0.06)***	0.21 (0.05)***
Church attendance	0.01 (0.02)	0.01 (0.02)
Church-connected group activity	-0.02 (0.03)	0.01 (0.03)
Mean church level of political interest relative to neighbors	0.18 (0.11)*	0.13 (0.04)***
Total number of cases	446	490
Adjusted R-square	.20	.19

Source: 1984 South Bend study.
Note: Standard errors in parentheses.
*=Significant at 0.10 level.
**=Significant at 0.05 level.
***=Significant at 0.01 level.

determinations. Instead, church context is a significant predictor for both Catholics and non-Catholics.

Moreover, the satisfaction instrument is now a significant influence on relative family political interest only for Catholics. Recall from the results in Table 6.2 that mean church satisfaction for non-Catholics reduces the effect of that contextual measure on individual satisfaction. Non-Catholic feelings of satisfaction are only modestly influenced by the mean satisfaction of fellow churchgoers. The results from both sets of models indicate that non-Catholics are affected differently by church and neighborhood, a situation that does not arise in the shared church-neighborhood situation Catholics face.

TABLE 6.5
**Estimated Family Interest in Politics Compared with Other
Families in Same Neighborhood, Frequent and Infrequent
Church Attenders**
(OLS Regression Estimates)

Independent Variable	Frequent Attenders Coefficient	Infrequent Attenders Coefficient
Intercept	-0.77 (0.38)**	-0.37 (0.51)
Satisfaction with neighborhood instrument	-0.09 (0.03)***	-0.03 (0.04)
Age	0.02 (0.02)	0.01 (0.02)
Male	0.11 (0.04)***	0.04 (0.06)
Family more educated than neighbors	0.18 (0.04)***	0.13 (0.06)**
Family political views different from neighbors'	0.03 (0.03)	0.10 (0.04)***
Discusses politics with neighbors	0.07 (0.03)***	0.09 (0.04)**
Active in 3 or more groups	0.15 (0.05)***	0.03 (0.07)
Strong partisan	0.16 (0.04)***	0.18 (0.06)***
Pays attention to campaign	0.24 (0.04)***	0.23 (0.06)***
Mean church level of political interest relative to neighbors	0.15 (0.05)***	0.14 (0.07)**
Total number of cases	580	356
Adjusted R-square	.22	.15

Source: 1984 South Bend study.
Note: Standard errors in parentheses.
  *=Significant at 0.10 level.
  **=Significant at 0.05 level.
  ***=Significant at 0.01 level.

Table 6.5 resurrects the hypothesis that church
involvement has an impact on church contextual influence; no
such impact was found in Table 6.3. The sample is divided
into frequent (every week or nearly every week) and infrequent
church attenders, and separate models are estimated for each
group. Once again, the church contextual measure for mean
political interest is significant and similar in magnitude for
both frequent and infrequent attenders. Further, neighborhood
satisfaction is significant for frequent attenders only.
Finally, the assessment of family political views relative to
those of neighbors is significant only for infrequent
attenders.
    These findings, coupled with those from Table 6.4,
suggest a pattern, albeit a subtle one. The assessment of
family political views relative to those of neighbors is
significant for Catholics and infrequent church attenders—two

sets of individuals who have stronger ties to neighbors than to the church or whose church and neighborhood contexts overlap. Frequent attenders and non-Catholics—who participate in other social contexts or at least attend churches in other residential areas—do not appear to mind holding views that are different from their neighbors'.

Although this sorting scheme fits this particular case, some other results do not. The satisfaction instruments, for example, are significant for Catholics and frequent attenders. Other variables have the same effect regardless of how the sample is divided.

The crux of the problem is the question of what social groups or contexts, if any, provide an identifiable and persuasive set of political cues for those individuals embedded in contexts. These models give no definitive answer to that question. At this point, only two things can be stated with some confidence:

— There is some relationship between the perceived levels of political interest of the group (church mean) and the individual.

— Ties to neighborhood point to one means of sorting out social groups that behave in different ways.

Table 6.6 offers a final attempt to sort out which individuals might be more inclined to follow the cues of their churches as opposed to those of their neighbors or some other social group. The filter used here is the question asking for an assessment of family religion relative to neighbors. The first column in the table represents citizens who either cannot make a judgment or judge their religious preferences to be about the same as those of their neighbors. The second column represents individuals who report their family's religious preference to be different or very different from the religions of their neighbors. These latter two categories account for about one-fourth of the total sample.

Table 6.6 shows that the magnitude and significance of the church contextual measure of relative political interest are nearly identical for both groups. Thus the relationship between fellow churchgoers and individual church members does not differ for those individuals who perceive a difference in religious preference between themselves and neighbors. Perhaps the most interesting finding of this model is that satisfaction with neighborhood is a powerful negative (less interest) influence on political interest for the different/very different religion group. This means that when individuals in the different/very different category are less satisfied with their neighborhoods, they are far more likely to take an interest in politics; in contrast, for the can't judge/about the same group, satisfaction with neighborhood is not a statistically significant predictor of relative political interest. Clearly there is some connection between perceptions of being different from one's neighbors and the resulting evaluations of neighbors.

TABLE 6.6
Estimated Family Interest in Politics Compared with Other
Families in Same Neighborhood, Sorted by Family's
Perceived Religious Difference (Collapsed)
(OLS Regression Estimates)

Independent Variable	Religion Same/Can't Judge Coefficient	Religion Different Coefficient
Intercept	-0.66 (0.34)*	-0.92 (0.70)
Satisfaction with neighborhood instrument	-0.04 (0.03)	-0.17 (0.06)***
Age	0.02 (0.01)	0.02 (0.03)
Male	0.09 (0.04)**	0.12 (0.08)
Family more educated than neighbors	0.17 (0.04)***	0.10 (0.07)
Family political views different from neighbors'	0.06 (0.03)**	0.03 (0.04)
Discusses politics with neighbors	0.09 (0.02)***	0.07 (0.05)
Active in 3 or more groups	0.09 (0.04)**	0.16 (0.09)*
Strong partisan	0.20 (0.04)***	0.04 (0.08)
Pays attention to campaign	0.23 (0.04)***	0.28 (0.08)***
Church attendance	0.01 (0.01)	0.01 (0.03)
Mean church level of political interest relative to neighbors	0.14 (0.05)***	0.15 (0.07)**
Mean neighborhood level of political interest relative to neighbors	-0.07 (0.11)	0.19 (0.22)
Total number of cases	724	212
Adjusted R-square	.21	.15

Source: 1984 South Bend study.
Note: Standard errors in parentheses.
       *=Significant at 0.10 level.
       **=Significant at 0.05 level.
       ***=Significant at 0.01 level.

FAMILY POLITICAL ACTIVITY

As opposed to an interest in political affairs, which
implies no need or desire to become involved, political
activity requires an effort beyond simple observation or
reflection. Political activity, then, is fundamentally
different from interest, and thus I investigate it to
determine what causes individuals to declare their families
more or less politically active than their neighbors. Once
again, the variable is measured on a three-level scale,
identical to the scale measuring relative political interest.

TABLE 6.7
Estimated Family Political Activity Compared with Other Families in Same Neighborhood
(OLS Regression Estimates)

Independent Variable	Coefficient
Intercept	-0.84 (0.19)***
Satisfaction with neighborhood instrument	-0.03 (0.04)
Family more educated than neighbors	0.10 (0.05)**
Discusses politics with neighbors	0.08 (0.03)***
Active in politics	0.15 (0.02)***
Strong partisan	0.13 (0.05)**
Pays attention to campaign	0.20 (0.05)***
Church attendance	-0.00 (0.02)
Church-connected group activity	0.03 (0.03)
Mean church level of political activity relative to neighbors	0.02 (0.04)
Mean neighborhood level of political activity relative to neighbors	0.04 (0.09)
Total number of cases	558
Adjusted R-square	.23

Source: 1984 South Bend study.
Note: Standard errors in parentheses.
 *=Significant at 0.10 level.
 **=Significant at 0.05 level.
 ***=Significant at 0.01 level.

Table 6.7 shows that contextual variables measuring the mean responses of fellow church members and neighbors, respectively, are not significant predictors of relative political activity. This indicates, in support of much of the literature on political activity (Zipp and Smith 1979; Giles and Dantico 1982), that contextual influences do not play a major role in what is essentially a personal decision to participate in politics.

Despite this contrary evidence, Tables 6.8 and 6.9 subdivide the basic model in two ways. First, as with political interest, individuals who perceive a difference between their religion and their neighbors' religion are considered separately. This tests the argument that a perception of being different from one's neighbors promotes a heightened level of political activity. Second, church attendance is again used as a sorting measure; the question is whether frequent church attendance is a proxy for greater involvement in many activities, including political ones.

For those individuals who see their family's religion as similar to that of their neighbors (or cannot make that comparison), the model parameters in Table 6.8 behave exactly as they do in the full model of Table 6.7. However, those

TABLE 6.8
Estimated Family Political Activity Compared with Other
   Families in Same Neighborhood, Sorted by Family's
   Perceived Religious Difference (Collapsed)
         (OLS Regression Estimates)

Independent Variable	Religion Same/Can't Judge Coefficient	Religion Different Coefficient
Intercept	-1.13 (0.41)***	-0.79 (0.21)***
Satisfaction with neighborhood		
instrument	-0.03 (0.08)	-0.03 (0.04)
Family more educated than		
neighbors	0.01 (0.11)	0.13 (0.05)**
Discusses politics with		
neighbors	0.10 (0.07)	0.08 (0.03)**
Active in politics	0.11 (0.05)**	0.16 (0.02)***
Strong partisan	0.04 (0.12)	0.15 (0.06)**
Pays attention to		
campaign	0.20 (0.12)*	0.20 (0.06)***
Church attendance	0.02 (0.05)	-0.00 (0.02)
Mean church level of political		
activity relative to		
neighbors	0.07 (0.08)	0.02 (0.04)
Mean neighborhood level of		
political activity relative		
to neighbors	0.19 (0.20)	0.00 (0.01)
Total number of cases	126	432
Adjusted R-square	.13	.25

Source: 1984 South Bend study.
Note: Standard errors in parentheses.
   *=Significant at 0.10 level.
   **=Significant at 0.05 level.
   ***=Significant at 0.01 level.

individuals who perceive their religion to be different show
very few significant coefficients at all. The variable
"active in politics," an objective measure incorporating
responses to questions about various forms of political
activity, and attention to the campaign are the only
significant predictors for those who see their religion as
different from their neighbors'. What is most important to
note about these models is that the contextual measures are
still not significant determinants of relative family
political activity.
      Sorting on church attendance does not rescue the
contextual measures in the models of Table 6.9. Frequent
attenders behave much as they do in the full model, with all
variables except strong partisanship remaining significant.
For infrequent church attenders, political activity, strong
partisanship, and attention to the campaign all predict
responses to the question of relative political activity.
There is no doubt that the models for relative political

TABLE 6.9
Estimated Family Political Activity Compared with Other Families in Same Neighborhood, Frequent and Infrequent Church Attenders
(OLS Regression Estimates)

Independent Variable	Frequent Attenders Coefficient	Infrequent Attenders Coefficient
Intercept	-0.83 (0.23)***	-0.84 (0.29)***
Satisfaction with neighborhood instrument	-0.01 (0.05)	-0.05 (0.06)
Family more educated than neighbors	0.15 (0.06)**	0.04 (0.08)
Discusses politics with neighbors	0.09 (0.04)**	0.06 (0.05)
Active in politics	0.14 (0.03)***	0.15 (0.03)***
Strong partisan	0.06 (0.07)	0.22 (0.09)**
Pays attention to campaign	0.17 (0.07)***	0.24 (0.08)***
Mean church level of political activity relative to neighbors	0.01 (0.05)	0.04 (0.06)
Mean neighborhood level of political activity relative to neighbors	0.02 (0.10)	0.06 (0.15)
Total number of cases	349	209
Adjusted R-square	.20	.27

Source: 1984 South Bend study.
Note: Standard errors in parentheses.
*=Significant at 0.10 level.
**=Significant at 0.05 level.
***=Significant at 0.01 level.

activity are the most straightforward to interpret, even though they do not support arguments favoring church contextual influences on self-evaluations.

A SECOND LOOK AT SCHOOL PRAYER

Having investigated the relationships between self-evaluations and church contexts, I now attempt to link these findings with analysis of the school prayer model (dichotomous measure) from Chapter 5. This is done to demonstrate that the measures of individual self-evaluations, and their relationship to the perceptions of fellow churchgoers, are important filters for contextual influences from the church on other attitudes and behaviors. If this is true, then I should find strengthened ties between church context and individual actions, in the form of coefficients of higher magnitude and greater explanatory power, in the school prayer logit model whose results are displayed in Table 6.10.

TABLE 6.10
Estimated Support for Prayer in Public Schools, Responses
  Collapsed to Yes/No Only, Sorted by Family's Perceived
  Religious Difference (Collapsed)
(Logit Estimates)

Independent Variable	Religion Same/Can't Judge Coefficient	Religion Different Coefficient
Intercept	-1.87 (2.37)	-8.16 (5.06)*
Mean church attitude on school prayer	0.50 (0.27)*	0.75 (0.42)*
Individual education	-0.35 (0.08)***	-0.40 (0.18)**
Ideology self-placement	0.12 (0.05)**	0.17 (0.12)
Reagan vote instrument	3.51 (1.29)***	4.34 (2.73)
Index of church activity	0.02 (0.02)	0.08 (0.05)*
Evangelical Protestant	0.98 (0.60)*	1.75 (0.67)***
Catholic	0.92 (0.58)	1.76 (0.65)***
Mainline Protestant	0.80 (0.59)	1.52 (0.74)**
Mean church ideology	-0.14 (0.14)	0.21 (0.28)
Satisfaction with neighborhood instrument	-0.04 (0.15)	-0.05 (0.28)
Mean church level of satisfaction with neighborhood	-0.20 (0.32)	-0.12 (0.65)
Total number of cases	537	163
Percent of cases correctly predicted	70.0	76.7
Model chi-square	48.77 with 12 df	50.81 with 12 df

Source: 1984 South Bend study.
Note: Standard errors in parentheses.
     *=Significant at 0.10 level.
     **=Significant at 0.05 level.
     ***=Significant at 0.01 level.

The filter variable used is the perception of family religious difference. As with models presented in Tables 6.6 and 6.8, responses have been collapsed to two categories: those who cannot guess at any difference or who believe that their religion is the same as their neighbors', and those who find their religion different or very different from their neighbors'. Further, the school prayer model from Chapter 5 now also includes independent variables for individual satisfaction with the neighborhood and the mean satisfaction of fellow churchgoers.

In Chapter 5, mean church attitudes toward school prayer were found to be significant predictors of individual attitudes toward school prayer. The magnitude of the church context coefficient in Chapter 5 was 0.65, indicating that the attitudes of fellow churchgoers could boost the probability of individual support for school prayer by a magnitude of 0.2 (see Figure 5.1). Compare this to the entries in Table 6.10. Those individuals who do not perceive a difference in

FIGURE 6.1
Predicted Probability of Support for School Prayer, Responses Collapsed to Yes/No Only, Sorted by Family's Perceived Religious Difference (Collapsed)

LEGEND

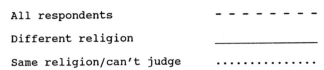

All respondents	– – – – – – – –
Different religion	————————
Same religion/can't judge	· · · · · · · · · · · · · ·

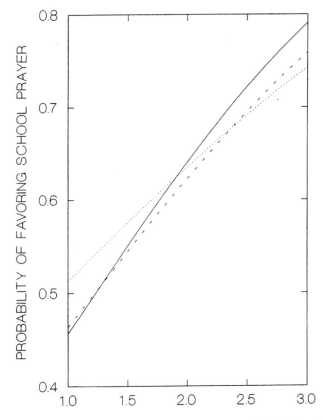

religious preference within their neighborhoods are still significantly influenced by the church's mean school prayer attitude, but the magnitude is reduced to 0.50. For the group that does perceive differences in religion, the magnitude of the church contextual coefficient is 0.75.

Displaying this result in graphic form makes the difference between the two subgroups of Table 6.10 slightly more apparent. Figure 6.1 shows the difference between the two groups examined in Table 6.10 (the logit function curve for all respondents is also included for reference).   In substantive terms, the figure shows that when all other factors are held constant, a perception of religious preference differing from that of neighbors tends to strengthen the impact of the church context, though the amplification of contextual influence is not dramatic. Although there is a sizable difference in magnitude between the church context coefficients, other independent measures drive school prayer attitudes more strongly than either of the church context measures, such that when those other independent measures are held constant, church context accounts for relatively little extra variance. Yet Figure 6.1 still supports the basic finding of magnified church contextual influence.

Although none of the additional independent variables in Table 6.10, such as neighborhood satisfaction and mean church satisfaction, has a significant effect on school prayer attitudes, sorting on perceived religious difference does produce a strengthened contextual effect from the church. Based on the results reported in Table 6.10 and Figure 6.1, it appears that individual self-perceptions of religious difference have important implications for the salience of church environments.   When a difference between family religious preference and the preference of neighbors is sensed, the church context becomes a stronger determinant of individual attitude toward prayer in public schools. Further application of this type of analysis to other contextual models may provide important clues as to which social contexts offer the most salient political cues on different political attitudes and behaviors.

SUMMARY AND CONCLUSIONS

Although most researchers have utilized the South Bend study to derive objective measures of neighborhood and church contexts, this chapter has relied primarily on the self-reported perceptions, evaluations, and conclusions of the respondents themselves. Some central conclusions are clear:

— The perceptions of individuals are significantly related to the perceptions of fellow churchgoers (recall that this is an objective measure—the sum of subjective perceptions), *when perceptions themselves are the objects under study.*

— When a variable measuring a perceived comparison of *activity* is utilized as the dependent measure, the church contextual influence disappears.

— Contact with the church environment, considered to play a crucial mediating role for contextual effects, never achieves statistical significance in any of the models presented.

— Only minor differences are noted when respondents are sorted on church attendance, though these differences do support the hypothesized importance of attendance as a proxy for individual receptiveness to political cues emanating from the church environment.

The importance of perceptions, rather than objective measures generated by researchers, stands out as one of the most significant findings uncovered in this chapter. Other models run with objective measures of some independent variables[2] do not produce significant results; evidently, perceptions matter more than reality for respondents in the South Bend sample.

A second result deserves further consideration. A consistent link between church activity and the presence of church contextual influences is almost nowhere to be found in this chapter. Why? Perhaps the answer lies again in the dynamic nature of contextual processes: Socialization to church norms occurs over a period of time, and it is plausible that churchgoers become aware of their fellow members' feelings over time, such that greater or lesser attendance matters little when individual perceptions and attitudes are measured in a cross-sectional analysis. A research design that tracks church attenders over time would be more likely to demonstrate the salience of attendance.

The school prayer model offers a further test of the salience of perceptions. With some of the perception questions included as independent variables (satisfaction, mean church satisfaction) and as filters (perceived religious difference), I find that sorting on perceived religious difference causes the church contextual influence (significant in Chapter 5) to be *magnified* for those individuals who consider their family's religion to differ from that of neighbors. This is the final and perhaps most important result from this chapter: Individual perceptions of standing relative to neighbors can be utilized to identify those citizens for whom the church (or some other alternative) context may have more important consequences for political attitudes and actions than does the neighborhood (or another) context.

Finally, some results that test the intertwining nature of church-versus-neighborhood ties, especially among Catholics, suggest that extensions of this chapter should explicitly consider the location of all churches attended. That is, can some of the ties between church and neighborhood be untangled if it is known whether individuals attend churches in or outside their residential areas? A full assessment of this question remains to be done in South Bend or some other community.

NOTES

1.   High levels of correlation between an included independent variable—in this case, mean church satisfaction with the neighborhood—and a relevant, excluded independent variable such as non-Catholic religious adherence make the interpretation of the included variable's coefficient difficult if not impossible.

2.   For example, instead of utilizing the self-reported question of whether an individual is more or less educated than his or her neighbors, a variable that measures the difference between individual reported education and the mean neighborhood education is incorporated into the model. These results are not formally reported.

Chapter 7

The Political Influence of Church Discussion Partners

One of the unique features of the South Bend study is its section on political discussion partners. Indeed, much of the existing literature generated from the South Bend project focuses on the role of political discussion partners in influencing political attitudes and actions. Huckfeldt and Sprague (1987, 1988) and Kenny (1989) have found that discussion partners exert significant and reciprocal influences on each other on such items as party identification, vote choice, and attitude questions such as abortion. Moreover, the degree of influence varies with several intervening characteristics of the discussion pair, including frequency of interaction, frequency of agreement or disagreement, and accuracy of perceptions concerning the political behavior of the discussion partner (Huckfeldt and Sprague 1987, 1988; Kenny 1989; Kenny and Gilbert 1988).

This chapter applies and further tests what is known about the political influence of discussion partners by specifying another intervening factor: the presence or absence of a shared church environment.[1] The central research question for this chapter is, to what extent do political discussion partners from the same church influence each other's political attitudes and behaviors? The focus is not on whether any influence occurs in same-church discussion pairs as opposed to different-church pairs—existing research offers persuasive evidence that influence does take place, and there is no a priori reason to suspect that selecting on shared church environment should alter that result for either group of discussion pairs. Rather, the important question is whether the reciprocal relationship between discussion partners is stronger when both partners attend the same church. Sharing a common environment—church, home, work—adds a common element or base of information to a discussion pair that is not present in pairs who have no contexts in common. If the local congregation matters for individual political behavior, as the three previous chapters have argued, then this common environment to which both partners are exposed, albeit not necessarily at the same level or with the same fervor, should produce effects on behavior distinguishable from that of the larger, undifferentiated set of discussion partners. The contrast between those pairs attending the same church and other pairs not similarly situated is the principal object of study in this chapter.

To the question of whether influence in same-church pairs is stronger than that in different-church pairs, either a positive or a negative answer offers insight into the political influence of churches. Little or no discernible difference between the influence exerted in same-church pairs and different-church pairs eliminates only the idea that going to the same church amplifies the shared contextual influences; it says nothing about whether such influences exist at all. On the other hand, if a shared church environment amplifies contextual effects within discussion pairs, then there must be something unique or different about the church environment that drives the amplification of influence.

What factors might account for the amplification of contextual effects within the church environment? First, church attendance is an obvious measure of the degree of participation in the life of the church, though by no means a perfect measure. Second, discussion pairs within a church are receiving signals not only from each other but from other common sources as well—through sermons, services, social interaction with other churchgoers, or participation in other church-related activities. Thus same-church pairs will have a broad range of shared experiences and signals, some of which may impact their political discussions.

Furthermore, the nature of the signals from the church environment differs in one significant respect from similar common signals that may reach discussion pairs who only live or work together, for example. Churches are manifestly concerned with influencing the behavior and worldviews of their members, not to mention attitudes on social and moral issues. In general, increasing exposure to the attitudes and cues of one's church serves to reinforce those attitudes and norms over time (Wald 1992: 113). Hence the potential political content of cues from the religious environment would seem to be greater than those from work or neighborhood environments. Taken together, the above factors suggest that a church is a potentially powerful force in influencing individual political behavior, either through direct appeals or through the conduit of a political discussion partner who hears, repeats, and reinforces church influences.

In the above discussion, one obvious potential variable has yet to be mentioned—denomination. No doubt denomination will have an impact on the processes of social influence described above. Some religious and denominational groups require of their members a large commitment in terms of time, money, and emotion, while others are more lax and casual. With the data at hand, it is difficult to say much about personal religious sentiments or the degree of commitment felt toward the church; attendance does not fully capture either concept. Further, the relatively small number of cases present in this section of the South Bend data set does not allow for rigorous statistical testing of models for all major denominations.

I therefore argue here that denominational differences are reflected by changes in the magnitude of influence among discussion pairs (something that will be examined in the analysis to follow), but that the mechanisms of influence are essentially the same regardless of denomination. This nondenominational approach departs from the approach of previous chapters and from the dominant practices in the study of religious characteristics and political behavior, which almost always stress the unique effects of denominations on their members. This is not to deny the existence of those effects; instead, the point is to identify commonalities across denominations. Differences among denominations are less salient than the common ways in which political attitudes are shaped and influenced by same-church discussion partners. In one instance, differences across denominations will be explored to ascertain their magnitude and importance for the basic findings herein.

Finally, there are expectations regarding what behaviors and attitudes will most likely respond to influence from discussion partners in a common church environment. The obvious choices within church contexts are attitudes on issues with strong moral or social components—abortion attitudes, for example. The idea of the congregation as a moral community, described most recently by Wald, Owen, and Hill (1988), exemplifies the ways in which contextual factors within the church can cause the operation of a behavioral contagion on congregation members. On the other hand, partisanship is an attitude with several components, including religious ones. Prior research has shown that when religion influences partisanship, the nature of the relationship is often based on class, ethnicity, or social structure rather than religious belief (Fee 1976; Leege and Welch 1989). Finally, vote choice and political participation are motivated by a wide range of factors, many of them transitory and specific to the particular election involved.

It seems clear that expectations of how shared church environments affect the interplay between discussion partners will vary with the dependent behavior under study. Abortion attitudes are hypothesized to be susceptible to amplified influence by discussion partners in shared church environments, but partisanship will probably not exhibit amplifications of the same magnitudes. A short-term decision such as voting should be highly susceptible to influence from the discussion partner, though as with partisanship, the potential amplification from shared church environment is at present an unanswered empirical question. Finally, political participation, as measured by turnout, should not be highly susceptible to church contextual influences. The lack of contextual impact on participation has been a consistent theme so far in my analysis, and I hypothesize that a strong contextual component is unlikely to turn up in this chapter either.

PERSONAL INFLUENCE AND RELIGIOUS EFFECTS

Since the promising findings of the Columbia sociologists in the 1940s and 1950s, personal influence has not been forcefully pursued as an avenue to explain individual political behavior. Consequently, no systematic approach to the concept has developed, and there is relatively little in the literature regarding personal influence.   For this research, personal influence is defined as the consequence of political discussion between discussion partners, assuming that the influence is reciprocal: Each side of the pair influences the other.

Any discussion of personal influence must begin with the path-breaking work of Bernard Berelson, Paul Lazarsfeld, and several collaborators from Columbia University.   In *The People's Choice* (Lazarsfeld, Berelson, and Gaudet 1948), the authors begin to move away from the notion of a two-step communications flow, arguing instead that "above and beyond opinion leadership are the mutual interactions of group members which reinforce the vague feelings of each individual" (1948: xxiii).   *Personal Influence* (Katz and Lazarsfeld 1955) pursues this theme and finds "that individuals are influenced by quite different kinds of people on different sorts of things" (1955:   97).   Networks   of   opinion-leading relationships, in concert with a more indirect process of influence termed "social absorption," and generally located *within*, not between, social and cultural groups, are the focus of *Voting* (Berelson, Lazarsfeld, and McPhee 1954).   The end result   of   all   these   processes   is   "the   development   of homogenous political preferences within small groups and along lines of close social ties connecting them" (1954: 122).

It is worth recalling how the original empirical findings of the Columbia researchers leads to the development of a theory of personal influence.   William McPhee (1963) argues that political discussion reveals to an individual that his or her beliefs are either in agreement or not with those of the discussion partner.   If there is agreement, the attitudes under discussion are positively reinforced.   If there is disagreement, the individual engages in a reconsideration of his or her own views, then seeks out additional information in order to resolve the dissonance.   Most important to McPhee's formalization is the idea that the environment in which the individual searches for information is biased in favor of the social structure; hence the modification of beliefs that is likely to result is also biased in the direction typical of the microenvironment.   The consequences of social interaction depend on three factors:

— Attention to the interaction, which is necessary for information to be processed;

— Motivation to learn; and

— Interaction patterns, which determine with whom an individual interacts as well as the frequency of the interaction and reinforcement.

Empirical evidence that confirms much of this theory has been produced by Huckfeldt (1986), Huckfeldt and Sprague (1987, 1988), and Kenny (1989).

The world of personal influence networks described above may be diagrammed in the following manner:

where R denotes a respondent, D the discussion partner, and Z_R and Z_D exogenous factors that also influence each member of the discussion pair.   Note again that respondents and discussants are hypothesized to simultaneously influence each other.

Where does the church fit into this world of discussion partners and reciprocal influences?   In line with Gerhard Lenski's assertion of an individual-level component to religious influence, a second schematic diagram of personal influence produces a framework whose workings can be explored through the unique structure of the South Bend data:

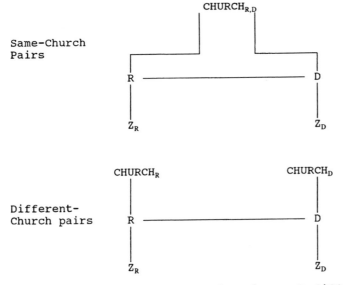

Although both same-church pairs and different-church pairs influence each other, the same-church pairs have an additional factor operating on both sides of the discussion pair.   The magnitude and mechanisms of the shared church environment concern us most in this chapter.

SOUTH BEND DATA STRUCTURE AND NEW METHODS OF PROBING SURVEY RESPONDENTS

As described in Chapter 1, part of the third wave of interviews in South Bend asked respondents to name up to three individuals with whom they talked about events of the past election year.   A battery of social network questions was asked regarding the social and political characteristics of each discussant, including the family relationship (if any) between the respondent and discussant.

Following the third wave, a fourth wave of interviews was conducted with approximately 930 of the named discussants, focusing primarily on discussants who are not immediate family members. These discussants were asked standard postelection questions concerning vote choice, partisanship, and political activities and opinions. In addition, discussants also named three discussion partners, allowing for investigation of reciprocity within main respondents' discussion networks.

The full set of 934 discussion pairs has been divided into two groups, those pairs who belong to the same church and those pairs who do not. A pair is classified as same church if both respondent and discussant report belonging to the same specific church; respondents and discussants both reporting no church membership are classified as different church. Note that classification is based on shared congregation or parish, not shared religious preference: If both members of a discussion pair profess to be Catholics but attend different parishes, the pair is classified as different church. This division results in 220 same-church pairs, approximately 23 percent of the total sample of pairs. Of these 220 pairs, 92 pairs (42 percent) represent spouses.

In the analysis that follows, controls for spouses are introduced into the models; in almost all cases, none of the control variables achieves statistical significance. This does not mean that spouses do not influence each other, but rather that spouse pairs and nonspouse pairs appear to operate in a similar manner. Thus for the bulk of the analysis, little differentiation is made between spouses and nonspouses in either the same-church or different-church groups.

Since the theory of personal influence holds that each discussion partner's partisanship affects the other's, the regression estimation method used must allow for this simultaneity. The standard ordinary least squares (OLS) estimation technique cannot be utilized, hence a two-stage least squares (2SLS) estimation is used to provide consistent estimates and allow for the simultaneous influence on the dependent variable. For each dependent variable tested, two separate systems of equations are estimated, one for discussion partners attending the same church, one for partners attending different churches.

It is important to note that the set of 934 discussion pairs utilized here *do not* necessarily represent reciprocal discussion pairs; that is, respondents named their discussants (the basis for the discussion pair coming from the respondents' end), but discussants did not necessarily name the respondents who named them. This has implications and effects in the analysis to follow.

OVERVIEW OF SAME-CHURCH PAIRS

A brief description of the same-church discussion pairs, compared with their different-church counterparts, reveals important differences that may influence later results. For instance, same-church pairs are more frequent church attenders—a mean attendance score of 4.24 versus 3.37 (on a one-to-five scale). That statistically significant difference implies that amplified effects may be built in for same-church pairs: Attending more often might make discussion partners more likely to choose each other in the first place, and regardless of the selection process, more frequent attendance obviously means more exposure to the same environment.

Same-church pairs are more likely to be Catholic than the sample as a whole (48 percent versus 35 percent), and they hold more conservative (pro-life) positions than different-church pairs. Same-church pairs also report more frequent political discussion, perhaps because of more opportunities due to higher attendance—35 percent have political discussions often or very often versus 29 percent of different-church pairs. One final difference of note is the length of the relationship between the discussion pairs. Same-church pairs have known each other longer than different-church pairs. When the sample is divided by spouses as well, it turns out that same-church spouse pairs have the longest relationships; same-church nonspouse pairs still have longer relationships than different-church pairs.

On demographic variables such as years of education, income, and age, same-church and different-church discussion partners are statistically indistinguishable. This finding is as important as the differences described above, for if the demographic profiles of the two sets are the same, then it can be said with some confidence that the differences between the sets are behaviorally induced. The fact that same-church pairs attend church more frequently and have more frequent political exchanges lends initial support to the hypothesis that shared church environment amplifies personal influence. The greater length of relationship between same-church pairs, spouses or not, also supports the belief that common church environments can operate as behavioral contagions for their members.

Objects to Be Studied

My hypotheses concerning religious environments as amplifiers of personal influence are tested for four separate dependent variables: party identification, attitudes toward abortion, 1984 presidential vote choice, and voter turnout. The rationale behind choosing this varied group is that each variable represents something different about an individual's political actions and attitudes. In addition, these differing measures should *not* be equally susceptible to influence from either the discussion partner or the church itself. Thus the range of dependent behaviors and attitudes tests the hypothesis that short-term behaviors, such as vote choice, and attitudes on social issues with which the church is concerned, such as abortion, are most likely to induce amplified influence in the common church environment.

PARTY IDENTIFICATION

Since the 1960 publication of *The American Voter*, party identification has been accorded a primary role in the study and understanding of individual electoral behavior.   Party identification was found by the authors of *The American Voter* to be very stable over time, grounded in individual political experiences and past behaviors as well as individual-level factors, and susceptible to change usually during major social upheavals (Campbell, et al. 1960).   More recent research has shown partisanship to be far more responsive to short-term and other political forces than was previously thought (Markus and Converse 1979; Fiorina 1981; Franklin and Jackson 1983; Mackuen, Erikson, and Stimson 1989, 1992).

Religion has traditionally been accorded a secondary role in the literature on partisanship, especially when researchers focus on national samples of individuals with little regard for local or regional contexts.   When local or regional subcultures constitute the level of analysis, however, religious affiliation together with other measures of culture such as racial and ethnic ancestry are found to explain partisanship and partisan change very well (Lieske 1988a, 1988b; Leege, Lieske, and Wald 1989).

The models tested here for partisanship contain a series of individual-level variables commonly thought to influence party identification.   These variables are similar to those utilized in previous chapters: race, age, educational level, income, union membership, ideology, political activity, and dichotomous variables for high-status occupations (professionals, managers) and low-status occupations (cleaning worker, private household worker).   Dichotomous variables for Catholic and Protestant religious preference and for church attendance are also tested.   Finally, three variables characterizing the length of the relationship between discussion partners are included: length of time the discussion partners have known each other (as reported by the respondent in the pair), length of the relationship for nonspouses only, and a variable categorizing the discussion partners as coworkers but not spouses.[2]

Most importantly, the partisanship models contain instrumental variables measuring the influence of one side of the discussion pair on the other.   For this and all subsequent dependent variables, results from the two-stage estimations on same-church and different-church pairs are compared both in table form and with the aid of graphs showing relationships of interest.[3]

Table 7.1 presents results from the estimation of party identification for same-church discussion pairs.   Partisanship is measured on the usual seven-point scale, with 0 denoting a strong Democrat and 6 a strong Republican; hence a positive coefficient indicates influence in a Republican direction.   As discussed above, the simultaneous nature of the respondent-discussant relationship means that two-stage least squares is the preferred method of estimation.

As expected, the instrumental variables representing the influence of one discussion partner's party identification on the others are statistically significant and positively related.   Among other individual-level variables, individual ideology, education, and Protestant church affiliation are significant predictors for both respondents and discussants. For respondents, the length of the relationship with the discussant has a positive (Republican) effect on partisanship.

TABLE 7.1
Estimated Party Identification, Same-Church Pairs
(2SLS Estimates)

Independent Variable	Respondent Coefficient	Discussant Coefficient
Intercept	-1.71 (0.94)*	0.09 (0.81)
Respondent partisanship instrument		0.36 (0.12)***
Discussant partisanship instrument	0.51 (0.13)***	
Race	0.61 (0.72)	---
Age	-0.05 (0.10)	-0.07 (0.10)
Member of labor union	-0.29 (0.26)	-0.00 (0.30)
Education	0.23 (0.12)*	0.22 (0.12)*
Income	0.07 (0.09)	0.13 (0.09)
Ideology self-placement	0.27 (0.07)***	0.33 (0.08)***
Professional/manager	0.10 (0.31)	-0.19 (0.31)
Cleaning/household worker	-0.37 (0.28)	-0.12 (0.33)
Political activity	0.06 (0.17)	-0.10 (0.11)
Catholic	0.52 (0.47)	0.23 (0.51)
Protestant	1.08 (0.47)**	0.88 (0.51)*
Church attendance	-0.08 (0.11)	-0.06 (0.10)
Time known discussion partner	0.18 (0.10)*	-0.06 (0.10)
Non-spouse time known discussion partner	-0.08 (0.05)	-0.02 (0.06)
Total number of cases	208	208
Adjusted R-square	.47	.41

Source: 1984 South Bend study.
Note: Standard errors in parentheses.
   *=Significant at 0.10 level.
   **=Significant at 0.05 level.
   ***=Significant at 0.01 level.

It should be recalled that this particular variable measures effects for spouses only.

What are the implications of the results from Table 7.1? Put simply, the model is a respectable estimation of influences on partisanship—significant variables behave in the expected manner and direction of effect—with the added bonus that discussion partner partisanship also plays a role in determining the dependent measure.

Again in Table 7.2, the instrumental variables for the partisanship of the discussion partner are positively related and statistically robust. The magnitude of the coefficients for the different-church pairs is smaller than for same-church pairs when comparing respondents to respondents (0.51 versus 0.36) and discussants to discussants (0.36 versus 0.32). Further, the effect of discussant partisanship on respondent

TABLE 7.2
Estimated Party Identification, Different-Church Pairs
(2SLS Estimates)

Independent Variable	Respondent Coefficient	Discussant Coefficient
Intercept	-1.41 (0.49)***	-0.94 (0.54)*
Respondent partisanship instrument		0.32 (0.07)***
Discussant partisanship instrument	0.36 (0.06)***	
Race	1.01 (0.35)***	0.68 (0.36)*
Age	0.11 (0.06)*	-0.08 (0.06)
Member of labor union	-0.52 (0.17)***	-0.86 (0.16)***
Education	0.18 (0.07)***	0.15 (0.07)**
Income	0.10 (0.06)*	0.16 (0.05)***
Ideology self-placement	0.34 (0.04)***	0.37 (0.04)***
Professional/manager	-0.00 (0.20)	-0.38 (0.19)**
Cleaning/household worker	0.18 (0.19)	-0.14 (0.21)
Political activity	-0.09 (0.07)	-0.08 (0.06)
Catholic	-0.03 (0.27)	-0.15 (0.27)
Protestant	0.58 (0.25)**	0.59 (0.26)**
Church attendance	0.07 (0.05)	0.00 (0.05)
Time known discussion partner	-0.16 (0.07)**	0.09 (0.06)
Non-spouse time known discussion partner	0.06 (0.05)	0.01 (0.05)
Non-spouse co-worker	-0.05 (0.24)	0.29 (0.23)
Total number of cases	679	679
Adjusted R-square	.34	.36

Source: 1984 South Bend study.
Note: Standard errors in parentheses.
    *=Significant at 0.10 level.
    **=Significant at 0.05 level.
    ***=Significant at 0.01 level.

is greater than vice versa, also consistent with past findings and present expectations (Kenny and Gilbert 1988). Since respondents name their discussion partners, but those discussion partners do not necessarily name the individuals who named them, the effect of discussant on respondent is likely to exhibit a greater magnitude than the reverse.

As for the individual-level variables, the significant variables from the same-church pairs—education, ideology, Protestant belief, and time known among spouses (respondents only)—maintain their significance and signs in Table 7.2, with one exception. For the time known among spouses variable, the effect is reversed in Table 7.2. Different-church pairs also show significance on several other variables that did not achieve significance with same-church pairs. Among these are race, union membership, and income (both respondent and discussant), age (respondent only), and professional occupational status (discussant only). Given the greater number of cases available for different-church pairs, it is not surprising that more statistically significant variables are found. Finally, there are no surprises in Table 7.2 in terms of direction of effects, with the exception of the switch on time known among spouses, which will be discussed later.

To show more clearly how the models for same-church and different-church pairs relate to each other, the predicted party identification for one side of the discussion pair is plotted against the predicted partisanship for the other side. Using the estimated coefficients and mean values of the independent variables in the two models, the plots compare predicted partisanship for same-church versus different-church pairs. Each plot (plots for the other dependent behaviors are derived in the same manner) shows the predicted value of the dependent variable (vertical axis) against the range of predicted values of that same variable for the other member of the discussion pair (horizontal axis). The results are displayed in Figures 7.1 and 7.2.

Figure 7.1 shows respondents, same-church (solid line) versus different-church (dotted line), and Figure 7.2 shows discussants divided in the same manner. Recall that the coefficient on the partisanship instrument was 0.51 for same-church respondents and 0.36 for different-church respondents (Tables 7.1 and 7.2); this difference is reflected by the steeper gradient for the line representing same-church respondents. The magnitude of the gap never exceeds one point in either direction on the seven-point partisanship scale. This is not a dramatic difference, yet the meaning is clear. The plot for respondents in Figure 7.1 shows an amplification effect from a shared church environment; when the discussion partner's partisanship is strong Democrat or strong Republican, then if all other factors are held constant, a same-church respondent will have more of a tendency to be Democratic or Republican than will a different-church respondent.

In Figure 7.2, again only a small difference in magnitude between same-church and different-church discussants is detected. But this time there is no amplification of influence; the two lines are nearly parallel throughout the entire range of predicted respondent partisanship, meaning that same-church discussants are always somewhat more likely to be Republican than are different-church discussants, at all values for predicted respondent partisanship.

The tentative conclusion from Figures 7.1 and 7.2 is that partisanship is susceptible to influences from discussion partners regardless of shared or different churches (witness the significant coefficients on all instrumental variables from Tables 7.1 and 7.2), and selecting on those partners who share a common church environment produces a boost to the magnitude of the influence for same-church respondents but not for discussants.

FIGURE 7.1
**Predicted   Respondent   Partisanship,   Same-Church   versus
    Different-Church Pairs**

LEGEND

Same-church respondents

Different-church respondents   - - - - - - - -

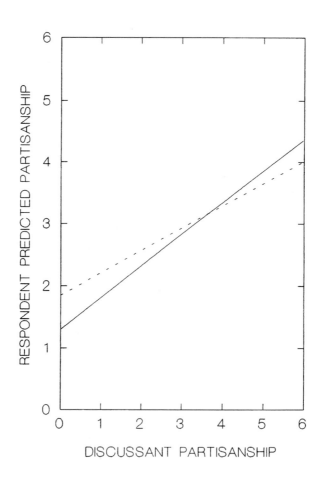

FIGURE 7.2
Predicted Discussant Partisanship, Same-Church versus Different-Church Pairs

LEGEND

Same-church discussants   _____

Different-church discussants   - - - - - - - -

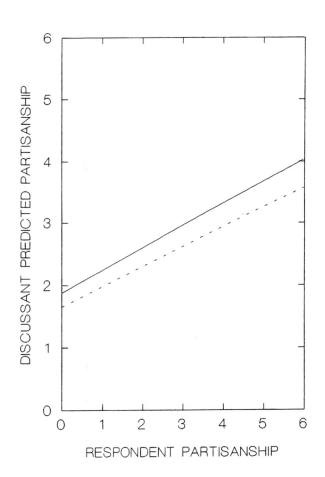

ATTITUDES TOWARD ABORTION

As a highly explosive political and social issue, abortion seems to be more the kind of issue that churches and church leaders would find of interest to their congregations. Thus much attention has been paid to the determinants of individual abortion attitudes, as the literature review in Chapter 5 indicates.

For the South Bend discussion pairs, both respondents' and discussants' attitudes toward abortion are measured on the same scale utilized in Chapter 5, ranging from 0 (strong pro-choice) to 6 (strong pro-life). Once again, two-stage least squares estimation is employed to test models predicting abortion attitudes from the predicted abortion position of the other half of the discussion pair as well as a series of demographic variables. And once again, plots of predicted attitudes are produced to facilitate comparison between same-church and different-church respondents and discussants.

Table 7.3 shows the estimated model for same-church discussion pairs. The respondent abortion instrument significantly affects discussant abortion attitudes, but not vice versa. Contrast this to Table 7.4, which shows nearly identical and significant coefficients on both instrumental variables. Further, church attendance is significant and positive for all sets of individuals, with nearly identical magnitude on the attendance coefficients. Variables interacting church attendance with Catholic and Protestant religious affiliation (not reported) did not produce significant results. Increasing church attendance thus appears to exert a steadily increasing pro-life influence, regardless of church environment or denomination (at least as measured here), though the earlier finding that same-church pairs attend services more frequently may mean a stronger influence for that group.

A second set of variables to note in Tables 7.3 and 7.4 are variables for 1984 presidential vote, the discussion partner's 1984 presidential vote, and partisanship. None is significant in any permutation of the model. It was hypothesized that the choice between Reagan and Mondale, with their different policy positions on abortion, might influence individual attitudes, or at least vary with them. Instead, abortion attitudes appear to be long-term beliefs, and individual-level factors seem to take precedence over short-term decisions such as vote choice.

Figures 7.3 and 7.4 graphically depict predicted abortion attitudes for respondents and discussants, respectively, same-church versus different-church. In Figure 7.3, same-church and different-church respondents are not distinguishable except at extremely low predicted values for discussant abortion attitudes (off the seven-point scale, in fact).

In Figure 7.4, however, same-church discussants show a definite amplified effect versus their different-church counterparts, primarily due to the magnitude of the respondent abortion instrument (0.41 to 0.27). As respondents move to the upper (pro-life) end of the abortion scale in Figure 7.4, the gap between same-church and different-church discussants becomes noticeable and dramatic—approximately one point in magnitude.

TABLE 7.3
Estimated Attitude Toward Abortion, Same-Church Pairs
(2SLS Estimates)

Independent Variable	Respondent Coefficient	Discussant Coefficient
Intercept	-1.08 (1.69)	0.02 (1.16)
Respondent abortion instrument		0.41 (0.17)**
Discussant abortion instrument	0.19 (0.16)	
Party identification	0.05 (0.14)	0.10 (0.12)
1984 presidential vote	0.06 (0.62)	-0.11 (0.46)
Discussion partner's 1984 presidential vote	0.32 (0.39)	-0.68 (0.48)
Race	0.06 (1.27)	---
Age	-0.31 (0.15)**	-0.10 (0.15)
Member of labor union	0.17 (0.36)	-0.28 (0.44)
Education	-0.27 (0.18)	-0.23 (0.18)
Income	0.05 (0.11)	0.05 (0.13)
Ideology self-placement	0.27 (0.09)***	0.28 (0.10)***
Professional/manager	0.23 (0.47)	0.09 (0.44)
Cleaning/household worker	1.10 (0.38)***	-0.17 (0.49)
Political activity	-0.07 (0.21)	-0.32 (0.16)**
Catholic	0.79 (0.81)	0.68 (0.76)
Protestant	0.85 (0.72)	-0.20 (0.74)
Church attendance	0.45 (0.17)***	0.41 (0.15)***
Time known discussion partner	0.06 (0.14)	0.05 (0.14)
Nonspouse time known partner	0.00 (0.08)	-0.03 (0.08)
Total number of cases	133	133
Adjusted R-square	.28	.29

Source: 1984 South Bend study.
Note: Standard errors in parentheses.
*   *=Significant at 0.10 level.*
*   **=Significant at 0.05 level.*
*   ***=Significant at 0.01 level.*

The key puzzle in estimating the abortion models is why, for same-church pairs, respondent-on-discussant influence is greater than discussant-on-respondent influence. The consistency of the greater magnitude of discussant-on-respondent influence is a hallmark of other research utilizing this data, though accuracy of perceptions concerning the discussion partner's beliefs and partisanship may mitigate or even completely close the gap (Kenny and Gilbert 1988; Kenny 1989). It may be the case that with abortion, respondents are more predisposed to press their points of view on their discussion partners; abortion as an issue offers little in the

TABLE 7.4
Estimated Attitude Toward Abortion, Different-Church Pairs
(2SLS Estimates)

Independent Variable	Respondent Coefficient	Discussant Coefficient
Intercept	0.43 (0.72)	-0.32 (0.80)
Respondent abortion instrument		0.27 (0.12)**
Discussant abortion instrument	0.26 (0.09)***	
Party identification	-0.01 (0.06)	0.01 (0.07)
1984 presidential vote	0.19 (0.27)	0.19 (0.31)
Discussion partner's 1984 presidential vote	0.14 (0.20)	0.23 (0.21)
Race	0.25 (0.52)	-0.79 (0.54)
Age	0.06 (0.08)	-0.01 (0.08)
Member of labor union	-0.23 (0.22)	-0.10 (0.22)
Education	-0.29 (0.09)***	0.01 (0.10)
Income	0.02 (0.07)	-0.13 (0.07)*
Ideology self-placement	0.08 (0.05)	0.07 (0.06)
Professional/manager	0.09 (0.26)	-0.42 (0.25)*
Cleaning/household worker	0.20 (0.24)	-0.07 (0.29)
Political activity	0.00 (0.09)	-0.01 (0.08)
Catholic	0.61 (0.37)*	1.31 (0.37)***
Protestant	0.33 (0.35)	0.52 (0.36)
Church attendance	0.41 (0.07)***	0.43 (0.08)***
Time known discussion partner	-0.19 (0.09)**	0.14 (0.10)
Nonspouse time known partner	-0.05 (0.07)	-0.04 (0.07)
Nonspouse coworker	-0.14 (0.28)	0.65 (0.29)**
Total number of cases	421	421
Adjusted R-square	.20	.23

Source: 1984 South Bend study.
Note: Standard errors in parentheses.
    *=Significant at 0.10 level.
    **=Significant at 0.05 level.
    ***=Significant at 0.01 level.

way of a middle-ground position, and this may be reflected in more vehement disagreement during discussion. An empirical test that controlled for disagreement within discussion pairs (not reported) offered no conclusive answers.

There is perhaps another explanation for these results. For same-church pairs (Table 7.3), dichotomous variables for Catholic and Protestant adherence are not significant, but in different-church pairs (Table 7.4), being Catholic is a significant factor in determining abortion attitudes for both respondents and discussants. Recall from Chapter 5 that the

FIGURE 7.3
Predicted Respondent Attitude Toward Abortion, Same-Church versus Different-Church Pairs

LEGEND

Same-church respondents _____

Different-church respondents – – – – – – – –

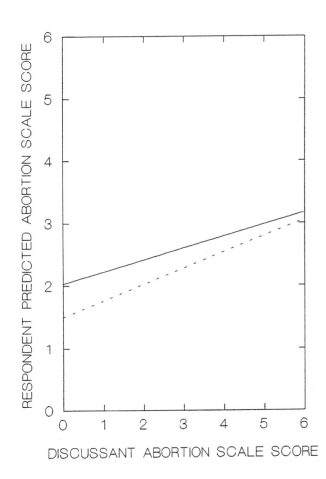

FIGURE 7.4
Predicted Discussant Attitude Toward Abortion, Same-Church versus Different-Church Pairs

LEGEND

Same-church discussants _____

Different-church discussants – – – – – – – –

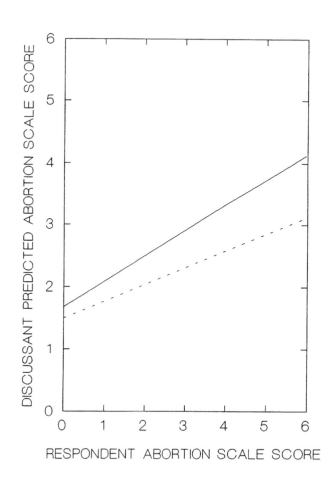

church contextual influence on individual abortion attitudes disappears when one controls for church attendance. These findings suggest that the variance in abortion attitudes within churches is low. Church members who attend frequently and interact with a discussion partner (specifically, a discussant) in the congregation show no contextual effect or denominational effect because, over time, their attitudes and those of their coreligionists converge. Without that common ground, presumably developed over time, infrequent attenders are influenced by other factors (including their denominational affiliations), and different-church discussion partners bring the distinct perspectives of their own churches, such that there is room to affect the views of the other partner. Shared church environment appears to reduce disagreement over the abortion issue; reduced disagreement has negative implications for modeling techniques based on explaining variance, as evidenced by the results in Tables 7.3 and 7.4.

PRESIDENTIAL VOTING

Vote choice in the 1984 presidential election is coded 1 if a Reagan vote, 0 if a Mondale vote. All other vote choices and nonvoters are excluded. With a dichotomous dependent variable, the two-stage least squares estimation technique gives way to a logit model. The logit model is also estimated using a two-stage procedure, in which predicted respondent and discussant probabilities of choosing Reagan or Mondale (based only on exogenous factors) are estimated and then used in the second-stage logit models to produce the coefficients in Tables 7.5 and 7.6.

Along with partisanship, voting is one of the most-studied political behaviors in U.S. politics. Several competing theories of voting behavior exist;[4] they differ primarily on the relative strengths accorded to long-term factors (prior voting behavior, partisanship, demographics), group attachments, and short-term forces (economic trends, rational calculus of voting). Without denigrating any of those approaches, the theory of personal and contextual influence argues that some truth exists in each. Contextual forces are not mere add-ons to recognized important individual characteristics, but rather affect how those individual variables come to determine a vote choice. Thus voting must necessarily be a short-term decision, since each election is unique and the confluence of social and individual factors is never identical. Accordingly, churches and other groups and institutions may be expected to play a significant role, and the atmosphere of a presidential race surely permeates the discussion pair. Voting is therefore a good test for amplification effects of shared church environments.

It is hypothesized that vote choice is definitely susceptible to short-term influences, from both discussion partners and other contexts, hence the amplification effect from shared church environments should arise here. In fact, comparing Tables 7.5 and 7.6, the predicted vote instruments are positively related, significant, and sizable for all groups. Most importantly, the coefficients on the vote

TABLE 7.5
Estimated 1984 Presidential Vote, Same-Church Pairs
(Two-Stage Logit Estimates)

Independent Variable	Respondent Coefficient	Discussant Coefficient
Intercept	-10.09 (4.72)**	-8.19 (2.93)***
Respondent predicted vote		7.97 (2.90)***
Discussant predicted vote	11.36 (5.40)**	
Party identification	2.62 (0.64)***	0.86 (0.17)***
Age	0.13 (0.36)	0.16 (0.21)
Member of labor union	-1.94 (1.24)	-0.88 (0.63)
Education	-0.97 (0.48)**	0.34 (0.27)
Income	0.70 (0.36)*	-0.18 (0.21)
Ideology self-placement	-0.18 (0.23)	0.10 (0.14)
Professional/manager	0.93 (1.17)	-0.74 (0.65)
Cleaning/household worker	0.43 (1.00)	-0.32 (0.69)
Political activity	0.44 (0.81)	-0.22 (0.28)
Catholic	-5.40 (2.15)**	1.82 (1.15)
Protestant	-3.58 (1.96)*	1.85 (1.12)*
Church attendance	-0.06 (0.40)	-0.27 (0.20)
Time known discussion partner	0.51 (0.39)	0.06 (0.22)
Nonspouse time known partner	0.29 (0.20)	0.06 (0.11)
Total number of cases	186	186
Percent of cases correctly predicted	93.5	89.2
Model chi-square	136.15 with 15 df	103.67 with 15 df

Source: 1984 South Bend study.
Note: Standard errors in parentheses.
        *=Significant at 0.10 level.
        **=Significant at 0.05 level.
        ***=Significant at 0.01 level.

instruments in the same-church models are two to three times larger than those in the different-church models. This indicates that although discussion partners in both shared and different church environments influence each other's vote, those in shared church environments exert a greater influence. Figures 7.5 and 7.6 demonstrate this amplification effect more clearly.

Figures 7.5 and 7.6 produce strong evidence to support the amplification hypothesis. They indicate that once a discussion partner is more likely than not to vote for Reagan (probability of Reagan vote greater than 0.5), a same-church discussion partner has a higher probability of voting for Reagan than a different-church counterpart. The tipping point

TABLE 7.6
Estimated 1984 Presidential Vote, Different-Church Pairs
(Two-Stage Logit Estimates)

Independent Variable	Respondent Coefficient	Discussant Coefficient
Intercept	-6.86 (1.51)***	-6.78 (1.44)***
Respondent predicted vote		4.36 (1.69)***
Discussant predicted vote	4.32 (1.57)***	
Party identification	1.00 (0.09)***	1.01 (0.09)***
Race	1.94 (0.99)**	-0.19 (0.70)
Age	-0.23 (0.12)**	-0.29 (0.12)**
Member of labor union	-1.20 (0.31)***	-0.59 (0.31)*
Education	0.01 (0.14)	0.07 (0.15)
Income	0.11 (0.11)	0.16 (0.11)
Ideology self-placement	0.15 (0.08)**	0.27 (0.08)***
Professional/manager	0.16 (0.39)	-0.67 (0.38)*
Cleaning/household worker	-0.45 (0.36)	-0.50 (0.43)
Political activity	0.14 (0.14)	-0.09 (0.13)
Catholic	0.27 (0.54)	0.44 (0.57)
Protestant	0.20 (0.51)	0.45 (0.56)
Church attendance	0.05 (0.10)	0.18 (0.11)*
Time known discussion partner	-0.16 (0.13)	0.31 (0.13)**
Nonspouse time known partner	0.25 (0.10)***	-0.16 (0.10)*
Nonspouse coworker	-0.93 (0.45)**	0.26 (0.45)
Total number of cases	603	603
Percent of cases correctly predicted	85.7	88.7
Model chi-square	348.62 with 17 df	367.65 with 17 df

Source: 1984 South Bend study.
Note: Standard errors in parentheses.
  *=Significant at 0.10 level.
  **=Significant at 0.05 level.
  ***=Significant at 0.01 level.

at which this occurs is just over 0.5 on the horizontal axis (measuring discussant probability) for respondents, and slightly less than 0.5 for discussants.

Looking further, at the lower ends of Figures 7.5 and 7.6, another amplification effect is seen: Once a discussion partner is more likely than not to vote for Mondale (probability of Reagan vote *less* than 0.5), a same-church discussion partner has a higher probability of voting Democratic than a different-church counterpart. Thus Figures 7.5 and 7.6 demonstrate the same amplification effect within

FIGURE 7.5
Predicted Respondent 1984 Presidential Vote, Same-Church versus Different-Church Pairs

LEGEND

Same-church respondents   _____

Different-church respondents   - - - - - - - -

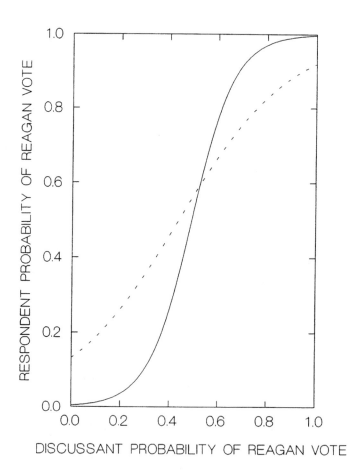

DISCUSSANT PROBABILITY OF REAGAN VOTE

FIGURE 7.6
Predicted Discussant 1984 Presidential Vote, Same-Church versus Different-Church Pairs

LEGEND

Same-church discussants

Different-church discussants – – – – – – – –

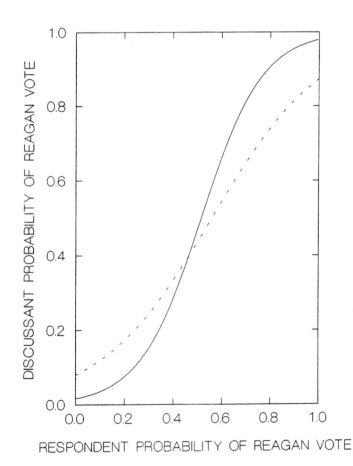

same-church pairs: Same-church pairs are more likely to vote *together*, either both for Reagan or both for Mondale, than different-church pairs. All other things being equal, a shared church context does not guarantee that both sides of the discussion pair will agree on the same candidate, but the chances rise significantly as one discussion partner becomes more and more likely to vote for one particular candidate.

Several other findings in Tables 7.5 and 7.6 are worth noting. Party identification predicts vote choice for all groups. Several other individual variables predict vote, and all significant variables exhibit expected signs. Different-church discussants show church attendance to be positively related to Reagan voting. In shared church environments, respondents are less likely to vote Republican if either Catholic or Protestant, while Protestant discussants show greater likelihood of voting Republican. These puzzling results invite further exploration of denominational differences, to be taken up later.

The final variables of interest for vote choice are those measuring the length of the relationship between respondent and discussant. As discussed earlier, since spouses have known each other for longer periods of time, a separate control variable for nonspouses has been used in this and preceding models. For same-church pairs, the length of the relationship does not appear to matter. In the different-church models, the length of the relationship has a positive effect for discussant spouses and a negative (though not significant) one for respondent spouses. For nonspouses, those findings are exactly reversed—respondent nonspouses with longer relationships are more likely Reagan voters, while discussant nonspouses are less likely Reagan voters under similar circumstances. In addition, different-church respondents who report their discussion partners to be coworkers but not spouses are negatively influenced by that relationship.

These results for length-of-relationship variables suggest explanations that could cut several ways, depending on the dependent behavior in question. On the one hand, other research suggests that individuals move closer to each other on attitudes over time, especially if those individuals find themselves in the minority (Finifter 1974; Putnam 1966); this would explain why time known is rarely significant for nonspouses in either the partisanship or abortion models. As I argued with abortion attitudes, length of relationship (perhaps in concert with frequency of interaction or exposure to church context) eliminates some of the variance in attitudes. On the other hand, voting is subject to short-term pressures and thus time known would become significant, because the past history does not fully determine the present choice. Perhaps there is some middle ground on the length of the relationship: Up to a certain point (which would certainly vary with spouses versus nonspouses, and frequency of interaction as well), individuals still have much to learn about and from each other; after some period of time, perceptions of the other discussion partner become more or less fixed on a broad range of issues and attitudes, and no more influence is to be found. Certainly the cross-sectional methods employed here cannot fully explore this question; they merely demonstrate the dynamic processes at work in the discussion pair.

Finally, in shared church environments, rarely is any relationship between length of time known and the measured criterion behaviors found. Based on the higher rates of attendance and frequency of interaction found with same-church pairs, it can be speculated that common church environments overcome time constraints on the relationship more quickly—by providing frequent common stimuli that reach both members of the discussion pair and attempt to influence their thoughts and actions. Whatever the exact causes, the nature of the length of relationship appears important enough to merit a more complete treatment and empirical test than can be offered here.

TURNOUT

Turnout is included as a dependent variable because it measures one aspect of political participation. There is reason to suspect that turnout is individually determined and not strongly susceptible to contextual influences; for example, Zipp and Smith (1979) find that social context is not relevant for forms of participation that are low involvement, low information (such as voting). And specific empirical tests of possible social influences on voting have generally yielded negative results (Huckfeldt 1979; Giles and Dantico 1982; Leighley 1989). A much larger body of research has identified individual characteristics related to participation. Among these are education, income, work status, and age (Wolfinger and Rosenstone 1980; Abramson, Aldrich, and Rohde 1987).

Religious groups have been known to influence political participation by their members. For example, some sects urge their members to withdraw from worldly activities such as politics (Wald 1992). Thus church contextual influences on participation may be negative, in the sense that one discussion partner's lack of participation induces the other partner to also remain on the sidelines come election day.

Once again the dependent variable is coded 1 if the respondent/discussant voted in the 1984 general election, 0 otherwise. Turnout should respond to such individual factors as education, income, and degree of involvement in political activities. Whether the presence of a shared church environment should magnify the likelihood of turnout is an open question. Given existing results, it is probable that selecting on shared church environment may yield a negative amplification of turnout (i.e., not voting influences the discussion partner not to vote), but is unlikely to positively amplify turnout probabilities.

Tables 7.7 and 7.8 present the logit models, estimated in the same manner as those for vote choice. For different-church pairs, the demographic variables all correlate with higher turnout, as expected; this is not true for same-church pairs, which yield the particularly puzzling result that union membership is positively related to turnout for respondents but negatively related for discussants. *The instrumental variables have no significant impact on turnout*, save for the

TABLE 7.7
Estimated 1984 Turnout, Same-Church Pairs
(Two-Stage Logit Estimates)

Independent Variable	Respondent Coefficient	Discussant Coefficient
Intercept	-13.96 (4.92)***	-12.50 (6.75)*
Respondent predicted turnout		16.29 (10.4)
Discussant predicted turnout	13.65 (7.11)*	
Party identification	-0.11 (0.18)	-0.06 (0.18)
Age	0.42 (0.31)	0.89 (0.37)**
Member of labor union	1.50 (0.87)*	-1.83 (0.73)**
Education	1.53 (0.53)***	0.02 (0.39)
Income	0.28 (0.30)	0.27 (0.31)
Ideology self-placement	0.04 (0.18)	-0.22 (0.19)
Professional/manager	-1.11 (1.02)	0.47 (1.32)
Cleaning/household worker	-0.34 (0.79)	-1.59 (0.70)**
Political activity	1.26 (0.94)	0.63 (0.42)
Catholic	1.21 (1.28)	1.90 (1.07)*
Protestant	1.15 (1.32)	3.19 (1.23)***
Church attendance	-0.01 (0.27)	0.32 (0.30)
Time known discussion partner	0.08 (0.30)	-0.35 (0.39)
Nonspouse time known partner	0.01 (0.17)	0.07 (0.17)
Total number of cases	208	208
Percent of cases correctly predicted	94.2	93.8
Model chi-square	31.01 with 15 df	47.18 with 15 df

Source: 1984 South Bend study.
Note: Standard errors in parentheses.
  *=Significant at 0.10 level.
  **=Significant at 0.05 level.
  ***=Significant at 0.01 level.

effect of same-church discussants on same-church respondents.
    Figures 7.7 and 7.8 show strong effects from shared church environments on turnout among respondents. The lone significant coefficient (same-church discussant instrument) produces the amplification of turnout for same-church respondents in Figure 7.7. The amplification is most marked at the lower end of the figure. When a discussant has only a 30 percent or less probability of voting, the difference in turnout between same-church and different-church respondents is dramatic. Different-church respondents are still probable voters regardless of the intentions of their discussants. But same-church respondents are far more likely to abstain from

TABLE 7.8
Estimated 1984 Turnout, Different-Church Pairs
(Two-Stage Logit Estimates)

Independent Variable	Respondent Coefficient	Discussant Coefficient
Intercept	-5.81 (3.22)*	-10.01 (4.00)**
Respondent predicted turnout		9.65 (6.01)
Discussant predicted turnout	5.12 (4.66)	
Party identification	-0.01 (0.07)	0.05 (0.09)
Age	0.29 (0.12)**	0.45 (0.13)***
Member of labor union	0.06 (0.34)	0.22 (0.36)
Education	0.81 (0.19)***	0.82 (0.22)***
Income	0.41 (0.16)***	0.29 (0.15)*
Ideology self-placement	-0.17 (0.09)*	0.10 (0.09)
Professional/manager	-0.95 (0.43)**	-1.14 (0.43)***
Cleaning/household worker	-0.01 (0.39)	0.68 (0.47)
Political activity	0.66 (0.28)**	2.29 (0.60)***
Catholic	-1.20 (0.56)**	0.12 (0.60)
Protestant	-0.55 (0.53)	-0.38 (0.57)
Church attendance	0.36 (0.11)***	0.16 (0.12)
Time known discussion partner	0.27 (0.14)*	0.32 (0.17)*
Nonspouse time known partner	0.10 (0.11)	-0.28 (0.14)**
Nonspouse coworker	-0.11 (0.46)	0.54 (0.57)
Total number of cases	679	679
Percent of cases correctly predicted	91.0	91.3
Model chi-square	77.95 with 16 df	82.14 with 16 df

Source: 1984 South Bend study.
Note: Standard errors in parentheses.
   *=Significant at 0.10 level.
   **=Significant at 0.05 level.
   ***=Significant at 0.01 level.

participating when their discussants also abstain. At the
high end of the figure, all voters become nearly certain
participators.

For discussants in Figure 7.8, shared church environment
produces a similar, though less dramatic, amplification among
nonvoters. Once again, when the discussion partner has less
than 30 percent likelihood of voting, same-church discussants
have a voting probability of less than 0.05, compared with a
probability range of 0.1 to 0.5 for different-church
discussants. At the upper end, the results tend to support
the existing research findings of little contextual influence.

FIGURE 7.7
Predicted Respondent 1984 Turnout, Same-Church versus Different-Church Pairs

LEGEND

Same-church respondents   _____

Different-church respondents   - - - - - - - -

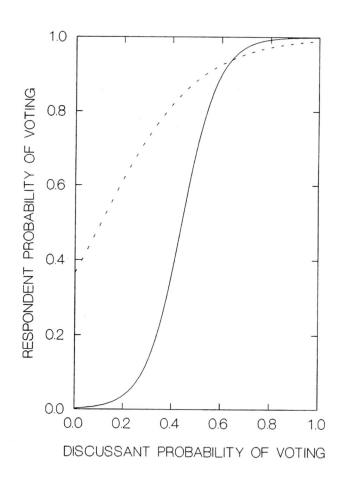

FIGURE 7.8
Predicted Discussant 1984 Turnout, Same-Church versus Different-Church Pairs

LEGEND

Same-church discussants   _____

Different-church discussants   - - - - - - - -

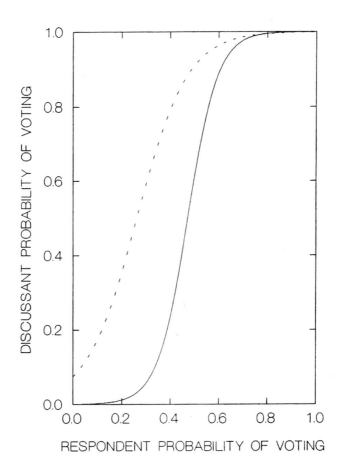

EXTENSIONS: A TEST OF DENOMINATIONAL EFFECTS ON VOTING

Recall from the analysis of vote choice that in shared church environments, respondents are less likely to vote Republican if they are either Catholic or Protestant, but Protestant discussants show greater likelihood of voting Republican. Vote choice is now broken down one step further. Same-church pairs, in which an amplification effect was found earlier, are divided into three categories—Catholic discussion pairs (89 out of the 193 pairs with reported votes for both partners), mainline Protestant pairs (49), and Evangelical Protestant pairs (37).[5]

Table 7.9 breaks down the voting behavior of discussion pairs, showing the degree of agreement between discussion partners. Evangelical pairs agree on vote choice 92 percent of the time, slightly higher than mainliners. Catholics show the least agreement, though 74 percent is still rather high. All different-church pairs show only 68 percent agreement, which again points out the amplification effect of shared church environment. The differentiation among the same-church religious groupings is sufficient to warrant estimation of two-stage logit models for Evangelicals, mainline Protestants, and Catholics. Plots based on those models are shown in Figures 7.9 and 7.10. Note that Figures 7.9 and 7.10 plot only same-church discussion pairs, in an attempt to decompose the same-church curves by denominational groupings.

With small sample sizes, logit estimates become more unstable, and standard errors tend toward infinity (Hanushek and Jackson 1977); this produces coefficients of sizable magnitude, though the plots still produce sensible results. Figure 7.9 shows a dramatic difference between Catholics and both Protestant groups. When separated out from the entire sample of same-church pairs, Catholic respondents show no

TABLE 7.9
Percent of Discussion Pairs Agreeing on 1984 Presidential Vote Choice

Pair Type/Denomination	% Both Mondale	% Both Reagan	% Both Agree	N
All pairs	31.0	40.5	71.5	814
All different-church pairs	30.1	38.2	68.3	621
All same-church pairs	33.7	48.2	81.9	193
Same-church Evangelicals	10.8	81.1	91.9	37
Same-church mainliners	28.6	61.2	89.8	49
Other same-church pairs	27.8	50.0	77.8	18
Same-church Catholics	47.2	27.0	74.2	89

Source: 1984 South Bend study.

FIGURE 7.9
Predicted Respondent 1984 Presidential Vote, Same-Church
Pairs, for Catholics, Mainline Protestants, and
Evangelical Protestants

LEGEND

All same-church respondents _____

Same-church Catholic
    respondents   ....

Same-church Evangelical
    respondents   - - - - - - - - - - - - -

Same-church mainline
    Protestant respondents   __ __ __ __ __ __ __ __

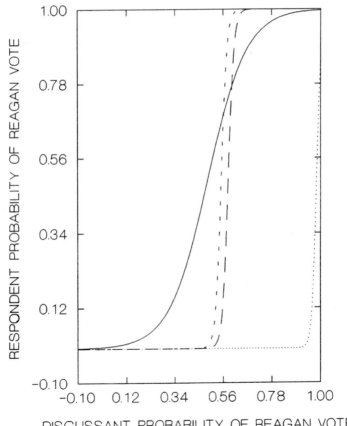

FIGURE 7.10
Predicted Discussant 1984 Presidential Vote, Same-Church Pairs, for Catholics, Mainline Protestants, and Evangelical Protestants

LEGEND

All same-church respondents   _____

Same-church Catholic
    respondents   ....

Same-church Evangelical
    respondents   — — — — — — — — — —

Same-church mainline
    Protestant respondents   — — — — — — — —

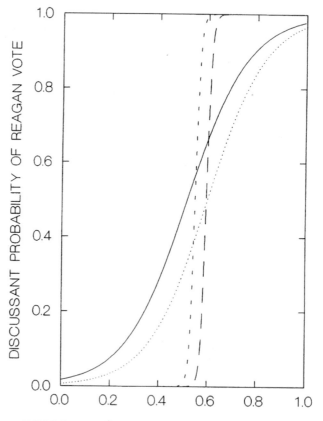

propensity to vote Republican until their discussion partners are nearly certain to do so.   In contrast, mainline and Evangelical Protestants show an extremely steep rise in probability of Reagan vote once the discussion partner's probability exceeds 0.5.   For Evangelical respondents, the tipping point occurs slightly sooner than for mainliners.   The two Protestant groups, though hardly separable from each other, must be providing the impetus for the aggregate behavior of the same-church respondents—in this case, a dramatic distinction based on religious affiliation appears.

Figure 7.10 traces same-church discussants.   Once again, Evangelicals and mainliners become probable Reagan voters faster than the entire sample; this time, Catholic discussants fall consistently below the line for the entire sample.   The magnitude of the gap between Catholics and all same-church discussants is about 0.05 to 0.1 percentage points through the range of the graph.   A visual comparison of same-church Catholic discussants in Figure 7.10 with different-church discussants in Figure 7.6 shows Catholics still more probable Reagan voters at high levels of respondent probability than different-church discussants.   Thus, for discussants, the amplification effect works for all religious groups tested, though again Protestant groups show the greatest strength from shared church environments.

Two explanations for the steep Protestant curves in Figures 7.9 and 7.10 come to mind.   First, given the fact that Evangelical and mainline pairs are nearly all clustered at either end of the scale (recall the 90 percent agreement rates from Table 7.9), the logistic curve fitted to that data must show this dramatic rise—both partners must exhibit high probabilities of voting for the same candidate.   This fact confirms the hypothesis that shared church environment amplifies agreement on vote choice within discussion pairs. Catholics are distributed across the range of predicted probabilities, hence the gradual curve exhibited in Figure 7.10.

A second tentative conclusion to be reached from Figures 7.9 and 7.10 is that because Protestant churches tend to be more heterogeneous environments, the presence of a discussion partner in that shared church environment brings a sharpened focus to the political signals from the church, the discussion partner, or both.   Since it is known that there is frequent contact, with political content, between respondent and discussant, the heterogeneity of the Protestant church is reduced, at least in the eyes of that discussion pair.   In contrast, the Protestant worshiper who does not have a political discussion partner in the same church has no means of sorting out the dissonance, hence the church becomes a competitor, rather than a compatriot, with the discussion partner.

Catholic discussion partners should more closely reflect the plot for the entire group, the results of Figure 7.9 notwithstanding.   Two Catholics from different parishes would likely have a greater common store of experience than two Protestants from different congregations, but again the shared church environment should amplify the effects of the discussion partner.   A further test of Catholics broken down along ethnic lines (not reported) failed to yield significantly different results from those portrayed in Figure 7.9.

SUMMARY AND CONCLUSIONS

All the preliminary hypotheses appear to have been confirmed by the empirical analysis in this chapter:

— Shared church contexts amplify personal influence for voting.

— Shared church contexts provide smaller or inconsequential amplification for party identification and abortion attitudes.

— Shared church contexts have a differentiating effect on turnout in the sense that lack of participation by one discussion partner seems to influence lack of participation by the other partner.

— Differentiating same-church pairs into Catholics, Evangelicals, and mainliners alters the magnitude but not the significance of the amplifications on voting behavior.

This last result seems to provide further confirmation that the mechanisms of church contextual influence do not vary across religions. Although it is now accepted that for political socialization and learning, churches can be treated much the same as other social groups (Wald 1992), it may prove fruitful in some cases to treat all churches alike, regardless of denomination, in future church contextual research.

Recalling the point made by McPhee, and later Huckfeldt and Sprague, that discussion partners search for more information in contexts that are informationally biased, it becomes apparent that the amplification effects shown in this research are further evidence of that informational bias. Since both discussion partners are searching the same context in not one but two ways—separately and through the other partner—they must pick up on the prevailing climate of the church environment, and they appear to do so much more efficiently and accurately than do different-church partners, who have no such help when it comes to searching and interpreting the myriad cues encountered.

Possible extensions of the analysis in this chapter fall into two categories, depending on whether the focus is contextual effects or religious influences. Those interested in exploring personal influence would break the analysis down along the attention-motivation-interaction trail specified by McPhee (1963) and Sprague (1982). A parallel line of research would test whether discussion partners in common work environments show similar amplification effects.

Religion and politics scholars might well ask what the effects of further differentiation among denominations would be. A second interesting subplot concerns Catholics who attend different parishes: Do they behave more like other different-church pairs (as defined here), or can they be grouped with same-church pairs in certain circumstances? Finally, because the 1984 election saw so many otherwise Democratic voting blocs shifting to the Republican side, an exploration of 1980 voting among discussion pairs (reporting a relationship that predates 1980) might not produce the same results. Nevertheless, the basic findings in this chapter are clear: *Repeated exposure to one's church environment, combined with political discussion with a partner who also is exposed to that same church environment, amplifies the salience of that political discussion partner for the respondent in question.*

NOTES

1. Before proceeding further, a clarification of terms is in order. The terms *respondent* and *discussant* refer to specific halves of a discussion pair; these terms are more fully explained in the section on the structure of the South Bend data set. The term *discussion partner* refers to one member of the discussion pair; this is a generic term that is used when there is no distinction made or implied between respondent and discussant. *Same-church* and *different-church* refer to discussion pairs in which either both members attend the same specific church or attend different churches.

2. With this coding scheme, the first variable, time known discussion partner, measures the influence for *spouses only*; separating the effect of length of relationship for spouses and nonspouses allows for more precise assessment of this factor's impact on the discussion pair.

3. The two-stage procedure estimates a predicted partisanship value for each member of the discussion pair in the first stage (ignoring for the moment the influence from the other individual), then uses that predicted value in the final, reported estimation to test the reciprocal influence.

4. For a neat summary of three schools of thought and a fourth, culture-based paradigm, see the excellent theme essay by Leege, Lieske, and Wald (1989, especially pages 35-47).

5. A third category for nontraditional Protestants, including Jehovah's Witnesses and Mormons, yielded only four same-church pairs and is not used for analysis.

Chapter 8

Conclusions:
The Political Relevance
of Churches as Contexts

The preceding chapters have examined the impact of church contexts on a wide array of attitudes and behaviors. Taken as a whole, the findings clearly support the initial hypothesis that churches are significant sources of political cues, and that churches do affect the political actions and beliefs of their members. The empirical results further imply that the traditional operationalization of religious identification in mass behavior research—dichotomous variables identifying and testing specific denominations for which a unique causal influence on some dependent behavior is posited—is inadequate as a complete explanation for the effects of religion on political behavior.

Throughout the book, I have emphasized church over context in discussing hypotheses and empirical findings. In this closing chapter I wish to divide things more equally between church and context, in an effort to show where this research fits into our understanding of mass political behavior and its individual and social determinants. I do not wish to simply repeat the findings and implications discussed at the end of each empirical chapter, but rather to animate those points on a more general level and suggest directions for future research. If there is an overriding lesson to be gleaned from my analysis, it is that more research into churches as political contexts is long overdue.

COUNTY-LEVEL RELIGIOUS CONTEXTUAL INFLUENCES

Locating county-level determinants of individual political behavior is an inherently arduous task. Probably very few citizens are aware of the religious composition of their counties. In fact, probably very few county officials are aware of the religious composition of their domain. Thus, defining a county as a relevant contextual unit, from an individual point of view, requires a leap of faith that might lead one to conclude that any empirical findings should be considered tenuous at best.

And yet, defining a county religious context as the macro distribution of denominational adherents within counties produces significant empirical results.   County religious contexts have selective importance for voting behavior, affecting decisions in 1960 and 1980 but not in 1976. Partisanship, however, is influenced by a nonreligious county measure (levels of Republican voting in counties); county religious contexts have no consistent impact. For turnout and attention to public affairs, county religious contexts hardly matter at all.   Finally, abortion attitudes do show significant influence from the county environment: Weak religious concentrations lead to more tolerant positions for mainline Protestants and Catholics; Evangelical Protestants strengthen their opposition to abortion when living among high concentrations of other Evangelicals.

Regardless of what one thinks of the county as a relevant contextual unit, all these worthwhile results must somehow be explained by both skeptics and believers in contextual effects. So let us assume for a moment that there is a causal link at work that connects county religious concentrations directly with individual actions. How are citizens perceiving their county environments in ways that would explain the link?

A critical assumption made by nearly all students of contextual processes is that individuals search their social environments as part of an information-gathering process. How would such a search process reveal information about how many religious adherents live in a particular area?   There are several visible manifestations of relative religious strength that come to mind: Churches that sponsor charitable programs or social causes would attract attention; local interest groups may be church based or church directed; proselytizing activities bring people from different religious backgrounds face to face; prominent local citizens might certainly include members of the clergy; and a local ecumenical organization such as a council of churches may tally and publicize actual church membership totals in a given area.

Add to these potential sources the anecdotal cues shared through interaction at work, in the neighborhood, at grocery stores or recreational sites, and it becomes clear that there are many sources through which an individual can acquire some knowledge about the religious makeup of the local environment. The best-case example would be a county or locality in which one religion dominates, in both public and private life. No resident of or visitor to Salt Lake City could fail to notice the pervasive influence of the Church of Jesus Christ of Latter-Day Saints, or Mormons; on a smaller scale and in different ways, residents of many major U.S. cities (New York, Boston, St. Louis) can perceive that the Roman Catholic Church and its leaders are important and influential players in the political and social issues of the local community. It is possible, however, that county residents may form a false impression of relative religious strength if one particular church or denomination receives extensive attention through local media or word of mouth—attention that far exceeds its numerical strength.

The models and discussion in Chapter 3 pursue this issue of how perceptions gathered from a variety of sources might affect political decisions and beliefs. Suffice it to say that the nature of the influence depends on perceptions of minority or majority status as well as the dependent behavior under study. The sheer volume of evidence from Chapter 3 alone is persuasive; clearly some ties exist between county environments and citizens, too many to be dismissed on methodological or theoretical grounds.

The most encouraging implication of these findings is that if one can develop a plausible theory explaining how county religious concentrations affect political behavior, then one can generalize beyond just the religious nature of counties. If citizens can scan an environment for cues to relative religious strengths, they can surely perceive cues about the relative strengths of other political or social groups. This implies that the average citizen is more sophisticated and aware than most contemporary students of political behavior would concede. Although all students of political attitudes seek out the determinants of those attitudes and behavior, few would characterize their subjects of study as extremely knowledgeable and aware of surroundings.[1] Elisabeth Noelle-Neumann probably makes the strongest case for conceiving of the citizen as a prescient and shrewd judge of public opinion. In *The Spiral of Silence* (1977), Noelle-Neumann spells out a theory that assumes that people possess a sophisticated information-gathering apparatus that they utilize to guide their behavior. Absent a convincing explanation of why her findings (and mine) do not mean what we think they mean, perhaps the assumption that people cannot form complex political ideas needs some strengthening of its own.

CHURCHES, POLITICAL ATTITUDES, AND POLITICAL BEHAVIORS

Chapters 4 and 5 show the congregation to be a significant source of influence for some political behaviors and attitudes. The fact that not all attitudes or behaviors are significantly driven by congregational factors demonstrates that the significant findings are not easily explained away as the result of a biased or purposive selection process. Further, those individuals who do not attend church on a regular basis appear to be minimally affected by the church context.

Chapter 4 demonstrates that churches, regardless of denomination, exert a consistent and significant impact on the voting preferences of their members. Such a result strongly endorses the notion that considering churches in a blind, nondenominational manner does not preclude the discovery of salient contextual effects. Attendance and involvement also lead to a consistent intensity of church contextual influence, which also strengthens the argument for a common mechanism to contextual influences across denominations. The behavioral contagion process must be the driving force behind context. All the evidence in Chapters 4 and 5 points to interaction within the church being crucial.

Moreover, examining political behaviors and attitudes leads to an understanding of the role of time and intensity in a political context. For issues that are of immediate concern to churchgoers and politically active citizens—for example, whom to vote for or what position to take on abortion—church contexts take on added salience. But for issues lacking any immediate political relevance—school prayer—or that clearly must develop over an extended period of time—party identification, the willingness to participate in politics—the church loses most or all of its relevance. Contextual effects are dynamic in nature, and more sophisticated survey instruments will be required in the future to unravel the full structure of this dynamic process.

Chapters 4 and 5 also attempt to address cross-pressures among different social contexts. In operationalizing church and neighborhood as the two contexts, I again must confront the question of whether or how a neighborhood constitutes a relevant context. Again, some information search process must take place in the neighborhood through direct and indirect means. But the church has an advantage over the neighborhood in that churches are definable, discrete units, whereas neighborhoods can be defined in whatever manner a citizen (or a researcher gathering data) chooses. Further, social scientists continue to note the privatization of life in the United States, as individuals grow more remote from one another and interact less frequently outside the office and within the residential environment. It is not surprising, therefore, that neighborhoods have limited impact on the political views of residents.

How the neighborhood or another relevant context is defined determines whether a cross-pressure situation (one context pulls a citizen one way, another pulls in a different direction) exists. The results in Chapters 4 and 5 suggest that churches can sometimes be more powerful than neighborhoods as determinants of behavior, but the question of how cross-pressured citizens make up their minds, or how they sort and choose among multiple contexts, requires a more complex framework. The limited research into this question has yielded some promising results. A recent paper suggests that when more than one context is considered, a definite ordering of salience appears. Specifically, for issues such as party identification, an individual's friends are most salient, followed by an individual's church and then neighborhood (Bowler and Gilbert 1992: 20-21). Further, the *clarity* of political cues from whatever source appears to matter less than does the *frequency* of contact, particularly contact with friends (Bowler and Gilbert 1992: 21).

The best possible scenario for resolving the problem of multiple contexts is to construct a data set that allows for multiple contexts to be measured and evaluated. The obvious next choice among potentially salient political environments is the workplace. South Bend respondents did give their places of work, but the aggregation of this information does not yield enough usable units.[2] Still, it makes intuitive sense to consider the workplace as an interactive environment teeming with political cues.

SELF-EVALUATIONS: HOW CITIZENS VIEW THE WORLD AROUND THEM

Chapter 6 brings some relevant findings to the question of how contexts are defined. I find here that however a citizen chooses to define his or her neighborhood, an important influence on behavior is the individual *perception* of the neighborhood's characteristics, not the objective characteristics themselves. Moreover, the opinions of fellow churchgoers about their neighborhoods (not considering whether churchgoers live in the same neighborhood) affect individual perceptions. And a feeling that one's faith is not the same as the faith of the person next door makes an individual more uneasy about where he or she resides.

These findings demonstrate that churches do affect how their members perceive the world. Most importantly, when these perception variables are used as filters, church contextual influences are heightened when citizens perceive their religious faiths as different from those of their neighbors. Individual perceptions of standing relative to neighbors can be utilized to identify those citizens for whom the church (or some alternative) context may have more important consequences for political attitudes and actions than does the neighborhood context. Failure to identify these underlying biases in the minds of citizens will imperil efforts to identify and measure relevant social contexts.

The logical extension of the Chapter 6 findings, as I note at the end of the chapter, is to identify all church locations, so that a researcher can specify who attends church close to home and who does not. This information would also inform a study of cross-pressured citizens and their behavior when confronted with contrary cues across contexts.

Moreover, the importance of perceptions in determining attitudes and (indirectly) contextual sources of political cues again brings us into sharp disagreement with the idea that citizens know little about politics or their surroundings. In the most extreme case, it would be possible for all of a citizen's knowledge about politics—and about his or her friends and their political views—to be dead wrong. Yet this citizen could still be influenced by the political context. Which is more relevant, a person's (mistaken) belief that his best friend is a Republican, or the fact (perhaps uncovered by a researcher) that the best friend is actually a Democrat?

Consider how such incorrect perceptions might be developed in the first place. Perhaps the best friend is a so-called Reagan Democrat, a Democratic partisan who has voted for Ronald Reagan and George Bush in recent presidential elections. When the best friend talks politics with our hypothetical Mr. Wrong, the best friend probably discusses his voting history, not his partisan ties; even if party identification is raised, its very existence is likely to be downplayed: "Oh, I don't pay any attention to party. I just vote for the best candidate." Given this situation, when Mr. Wrong is quizzed about his best friend's views, Mr. Wrong might well say that his best friend is a good Republican. And if this belief is what guides Mr. Wrong's own choices, is it right to say that Mr. Wrong is incorrect? Clearly, individual responses to survey questions cannot be treated like test answers by researchers. What people believe is far more important than what is true or what can be derived by disinterested survey analysts. This is the best lesson that can be derived from Chapter 6.

POLITICAL DISCUSSION PARTNERS

Chapter 7 contributes to the burgeoning literature on the influence of political discussion partners by identifying dependent behaviors for which common or shared contexts amplify personal influence within discussion dyads. Discussion partners attending the same church exert stronger influences on each other's vote choice and partisan identification than do discussion partners attending different churches. The findings on abortion attitudes and turnout are less clear; on abortion there is no consistent effect among same-church discussion partners, and it appears that turnout is hardly affected at all.

The causal determinants at work here are obvious, but the question of self-selection bias is also strongly raised. The empirical findings offer a convincing rejoinder to any lingering self-selection adherents. One in three respondents incorrectly identified the partisanship of their partners (from the researcher's point of view). Respondents and discussants disagreed on vote choice a significant percentage of the time. Other research (recall Wald, Owen, and Hill 1988) shows that a bare majority of individuals choose churches whose theology is consistent with their own; if people are not choosing churches on the basis of religious factors, it is not plausible to suggest that they choose churches for political factors. Undoubtedly self-selection is a factor in some discussion pairs, particularly among spouses. But the fact that amplified influences are found even when a spousal relationship is controlled for is compelling evidence that self-selection does not account for the behavior of discussion partners.

The findings of Chapter 7 have much to say about how discussion partners interact in general. It remains to be seen whether other shared social contexts produce amplified effects among discussion partners, or whether churches are unique in this regard. I surmise that other contexts, specifically the workplace, would reveal similar patterns.

However, I also claim that the patterns of influence engendered by shared church contexts would still be unique, even after multiple contexts are analyzed. Churches are simply not like all other institutions and groups. The principal reason for this is the otherworldly component inherent in the very concept of religion. This element has been the missing component of my analysis throughout the book, and it is perhaps appropriate that in the pursuit of final, conclusive thoughts, we should turn at last to God.

A SEARCH FOR RELIGION IN CHURCH POLITICAL CONTEXTS

This book has been concerned with religion and religious environments, yet there has been next to nothing written about religious beliefs. The main reason for this relative silence is that neither the National Election Studies data utilized here nor the South Bend data address questions of individual beliefs or practices beyond those measures utilized herein. Some would see this as a critical missing link in an explanation of how religious environments affect individuals politically. I agree with part of that criticism: There is a missing link, but its absence is not critical. This assertion warrants some elaboration.

Throughout the book I have attempted to understand churches as political contexts; accordingly, I have defined the South Bend churches in terms of their politics—how their members vote, where their partisan loyalties lie, what the group as a whole thinks about abortion and school prayer, and so on. Would the incorporation of some contextual measures of theological orientation alter the significance of the contextual measures now included? This is an empirical question that needs to be pursued in future research.

Such empirical research is becoming possible; in recent years, specific questions about religious beliefs and practices have been incorporated into the National Election Studies. There are now survey items that probe for the importance of religion in a person's life; views on the Bible; frequency of prayer; denomination, using a revised and updated response list; the faith in which a person was raised; frequency of watching or listening to religious programs; whether the respondent considers himself or herself to be born again; and questions about the topics that might be discussed within the church (Leege, Kellstedt, and Wald 1990). The initial analysis of political phenomena using these new measures has been promising, and surely the presence of rich new sources of information will spur new ideas and new directions for research.

Another nearly pristine source for investigation is the newest phenomenon on the U.S. religious landscape, the megachurch. Megachurches deliver religion in a thoroughly contemporary manner: using modern music; providing amenities such as child care, food, and in some cases health clubs; and downplaying the theological message, replacing it with practical wisdom and self-help advice (R. Niebuhr 1991: 1). Some megachurches have gone so far as to hold services in shopping malls, bringing their message to the public instead of waiting for the public to come to them (Schmickle 1992: 1). The Reverend Lyle Schaller, a United Methodist minister and church consultant, says that megachurches represent one of the "most significant changes taking place in American Protestantism in the second half of the 20th century" (R. Niebuhr 1991: 1). Who knows what would turn up in an investigation of the salience of megachurches as political contexts?

New Directions

What might any of these new directions reveal about the connections between spirituality, church environments, and individual political attitudes and beliefs? Regardless of how new research might alter our existing perceptions, this book still contributes to the body of background knowledge necessary to pursue new avenues. If church congregations operate in the ways I have described here, then the theological and spiritual orientation of the church is already part of the analysis, as an unmeasured influence on the church contextual measures that are included. Citizens are affected by the political views of their fellow churchgoers, whose own views are in part determined by the theological and spiritual character of the same institution. If and when we can quantify, measure, and incorporate those theological and spiritual qualities into empirical analysis, then our understanding of churches and church contexts will be heightened.

But an analysis without such measures is clearly not handicapped in its ability to explain and understand the nature of churches as political contexts. In many respects, it is fitting that spiritual beliefs should not yield easily to the social scientist's urge to quantify abstract ideas. Faith, too, must be part of our worldview.

NOTES

1. On this point, I speak from experience. I vividly recall my first conference presentation on this subject, which was greeted with a simple question from the first panel discussant: "People don't care about politics. Why bother?"

2. In fact, the workplace in the South Bend data with the most respondents had only 39. In contrast, there are nine churches surveyed with more respondents (the highest was 92).

Appendix

Variable Coding Schemes

The specific coding schemes for all variables used in the book are found here. Chapter 3 utilizes data from three different years of the National Election Studies; coding for variables across years is identical unless otherwise noted. Chapters 4 through 7 utilize data from the South Bend community study. For the South Bend data, variable coding schemes are listed only under the *first* chapter in which they are introduced; the coding for Chapters 5 through 7 includes variables used in those chapters for the first time. Coding schemes for dependent variables and many of the independent variables are also discussed throughout the text.

CHAPTER 3 VARIABLES AND CODING SCHEMES

Presidential vote: coded 1 if a Republican vote (Nixon, Ford, Reagan), 0 if a Democratic vote; 1980 votes for Anderson are excluded

Party identification: 7-point scale, from 0 (strong Democrat) to 6 (strong Republican)

Education: For 1960 and 1976, 4-point scale, 1 = less than high school, 2 = high school graduate, 3 = post-high school, 4 = college graduate or above; for 1980, 5-point scale, same as above, except 4 = college graduate, 5 = post-college or professional degree

Income: annual household income in thousands of dollars, scaled from 2 ($2,000 or less) to 10 ($10,000 or more), except 1980, when top level of scale is 22 ($22,000 or more)

Male: 1 if male, 0 if female

Nonwhite respondent: 1 if self-identified as race other than white, 0 if white

Percent [religion] in county: percent of [religion] in respondent's county of residence; measured as number of church members divided by total county population

[Religion] X percent [religion] in county: interaction, measuring the effect of one religion's county concentration on members of a specific religion; for example, "Catholic X percent Catholic in county" measures the effect of Catholic county concentration on Catholics only

Mainline Protestant: 1 if a member of a mainline Protestant denomination, 0 otherwise; groups included: Episcopalian, Lutheran, Methodist, Presbyterian

Evangelical Protestant: 1 if a member of an Evangelical Protestant denomination, 0 otherwise; groups included: Assemblies of God, Baptist, Church of the Brethren, Church of Christ, Disciples of Christ, Pentecostals, nondenominational Christian, Seventh-Day Adventist

Catholic: 1 if a Catholic, 0 otherwise

Church attendance: 5-point scale, 1 = almost never attends to 5 = attends every week

[Religion] X church attendance: interaction, measuring the effect of church attendance on the specific religion named

Interest in campaign: 1 if paid "a great deal" or "some" attention, 0 otherwise

Pluralist county: county in which no single religion has more than 35 percent of residents

[Religion] X pluralist county: interaction, measuring the effect of pluralist county environment on the specific religion named

CHAPTER 4 VARIABLES AND CODING SCHEMES

Party identification: 7-point scale, from 0 (strong Democrat) to 6 (strong Republican) (same as Chapter 3 coding)

Individual education: 5-point scale; same as Chapter 3, 1980 coding

Individual income: scaled from 0.75 ($7,500 or less) to 6 ($60,000 or more)

Male: 1 if male, 0 if female

Lifelong resident: 1 if resided in South Bend for 30 or more years, 0 otherwise

White: 1 if self-identified as white, 0 otherwise

Neighborhood mean party identification: mean party identification of other respondents in neighborhood (excluding self)

Neighborhood mean education: mean education of other respondents in neighborhood (excluding self)

Church mean party identification: mean party identification of other respondents in church (excluding self)

Church mean education: mean education of other respondents in church (excluding self)

Catholic density: percent Catholic in respondent's neighborhood (excluding self)

Protestant density: percent Protestant in respondent's neighborhood (excluding self)

Mainline Protestant: 1 if a member of a mainline Protestant denomination, 0 otherwise; groups included: Episcopalian, Lutheran, Methodist, Presbyterian

Evangelical Protestant: 1 if a member of an Evangelical Protestant denomination, 0 otherwise; groups included: Assemblies of God, Baptist, Church of the Brethren, Church of Christ, Disciples of Christ, Pentecostals, nondenominational Christian, Seventh-Day Adventist

Catholic: 1 if a Catholic, 0 otherwise

Church attendance: 5-point scale, same as Chapter 3 coding

Catholic/church attendance: interaction, Catholic times church attendance

Church-connected group activity: 0 = nonmember of a church-connected group, 1 = nonactive member, 2 = active member

Index of church activity: interaction, church attendance times church-connected group activity

Attention to campaign: 1 if paid "a great deal" or "some" attention, 0 otherwise

Active in a neighborhood group: active member of a neighborhood group

Pluralist neighborhood: neighborhood in which no single religion has more than 35 percent of residents

Duopolistic neighborhood: neighborhood in which two religions combine to have more than 50 percent of residents

Hegemonic neighborhood: neighborhood in which one religion has more than 60 percent of residents

Monopolistic neighborhood: neighborhood in which one religion
has more than 75 percent of residents

CHAPTER 5 VARIABLES AND CODING SCHEMES

Membership and activity in a veterans/minority group: 0 if a
nonmember of a veterans/minority group, 1 if a nonactive
member, 2 if an active member

Reagan vote instrument: predicted probability of voting for
Reagan, calculated from Reagan voting model in Chapter 4
(Table 4.5)

Jewish: 1 if Jewish, 0 otherwise

Age: age in years

Political activity: scaled from 0 to 4, based on positive
responses to several types of political activities
engaged in during the campaign, e.g., making phone calls
or canvassing for a candidate, distributing bumper
stickers, or placing lawn signs

CHAPTER 6 VARIABLES AND CODING SCHEMES

Satisfaction with neighborhood: 4-point scale, 1 = very
dissatisfied, 2 = somewhat dissatisfied, 3 = somewhat
satisfied, 4 = very satisfied

Planning to move or stay: 1 if planning to move, 0 if planning
to stay in current home

Relative quality of neighborhood schools/streets: both coded
on 3-point scale, 1 = better than other neighborhoods, 0
= about the same, -1 = worse than other neighborhoods

Friendliness/helpfulness of neighbors: 3-point scale, 1 = very
friendly or helpful, 0 = somewhat, -1 = not friendly or
helpful

Family's interest in politics, family's political activity
relative to neighbors': 3-point scale, -1 = less
interested or active than neighbors, 0 = about the same,
1 = more interested or active

Neighborhood's education compared to other neighborhoods': 3-
point scale, 1 = more educated than other neighborhoods,
0 = about the same, -1 = less educated

Own neighborhood better off than other neighborhoods: 3-point
scale, same logic as above

Family's religion different from neighbors': 4-point scale, 1
= can't say, 2 = about the same, 3 = different, 4 = very
different

Discusses politics with neighbors: self-reported, 4-point scale from 1 = never to 4 = very often

Mean church/neighborhood level of satisfaction with neighborhood: contextual variable; sum of other neighborhood residents or churchgoers on satisfaction question

Mean church/neighborhood level of political interest or activity relative to neighbors: contextual variable; same logic as above, on political interest and political activity questions

Family more educated than neighbors: 3-point scale, self-reported measure, 1 = more educated, 0 = about the same, -1 = less educated

Family political views different from neighbors: 4-point scale, self-reported measure, from 1 = can't say to 4 = very different

Active in 3 or more groups: active in 3 or more groups (of any kind)

Strong partisan: strong Democrat (party identification = 0) or strong Republican (party identification = 6) partisan on 7-point partisanship scale

Family perceived religious difference (collapsed): "Can't say" and "about the same" recoded to 0, "different" and "very different" recoded to 1

CHAPTER 7 VARIABLES AND CODING SCHEMES

Member of labor union: 1 if a union member, 0 otherwise

Professional/manager: 1 if occupation is professional, technical, managerial, or administrative; 0 otherwise

Cleaning/household worker: 1 if occupation is cleaning, service, or private household job; 0 otherwise

Time known discussion partner: length of time discussion pairs have known each other, as reported by respondent; scaled from 1 (less than 5 years) to 6 (40 years or more)

Nonspouse time known: same variable as above, measured only for nonspouses

Nonspouse coworker: 1 if discussion partners are not spouses and are coworkers, 0 otherwise; reported by respondent

Bibliography

Abramson, Paul R., John H. Aldrich, and David W. Rhode. 1987. *Change and Continuity in the 1984 Elections*. Washington, D.C.: CQ Press.

Anderson, Charles. 1973. "Religious Communality and Party Preference." In Benjamin Beit-Hallahmi, *Research in Religious Behavior*. Monterey, Calif.: Brooks Cole.

Anderson, Donald. 1966. "Ascetic Protestantism and Political Preference." *Review of Religious Research* 7: 167-171.

Bellah, Robert, Richard Madsen, William M. Sullivan, Ann Swidler, and Steven M. Tipton. 1985. *Habits of the Heart: Individualism and Commitment in American Life*. New York: Harper & Row.

Berelson, Bernard R., Paul F. Lazarsfeld, and William M. McPhee. 1954. *Voting: A Study of Opinion Formation in a Presidential Election*. Chicago: University of Chicago Press.

Bochel, J. M., and D. T. Denver. 1970. "Religion and Voting: A Critical Review and a New Analysis." *Political Studies* 18: 205-219.

Bowler, Shaun, and Christopher P. Gilbert. 1992. "Partisan Change in Neighborhoods and Churches." Presented at the annual meeting of the Western Political Science Association, San Francisco.

Boyd, Lawrence, and Gudmund Iverson. 1979. *Contextual Analysis: Concepts and Statistical Techniques*. Belmont, California: Wadsworth Publishing.

Brace, Paul, and Barbara Hinckley. 1991. "The Structure of Presidential Approval: Constraints within and across Presidencies." *Journal of Politics* 53: 993-1017.

Brintnall, Michael. 1991. "Organized Sections in APSA: A Status Report." *PS: Political Science & Politics* 24 (3): 559-563.

Brown, Courtney. 1981. "Group Membership and the Social Environment: Multiple Influences on Political Attitudes and Behaviors." Unpublished Ph.D. dissertation, Washington University in St. Louis.

Campbell, Angus, Philip Converse, Warren Miller, and Donald Stokes. 1960. *The American Voter*. New York: Wiley.

_____. 1966. *Elections and the Political Order.* New York: Wiley.

Converse, Philip. 1966. "Religion and Politics: The 1960 Election." In Campbell, Converse, Miller, and Stokes, *Elections and the Political Order.* New York: Wiley.

Cox, Kevin R. 1974. "The Spatial Structuring of Information Flow and Partisan Attitudes." In Mattei Dogan and Stein Rokkan, *Social Ecology.* Cambridge, Mass.: M.I.T. Press, pp. 157-186.

Cutler, S., S. A. Lentz, M. J. Muha, and R. N. Riler. 1980. "Aging and Conservatism: Cohort Changes in Attitudes Towards Legalized Abortion." *Journal of Gerontology* 35: 115-123.

Durkheim, Emile. 1951. *Suicide.* Translated by John A. Spaulding and George Simpson. New York: Free Press. Originally published in 1896.

Fee, Joan L. 1976. "Party Identification among American Catholics." *Ethnicity* 3: 53-69.

Finifter, Ada. 1974. "The Friendship Group as a Protective Environment for Political Deviants." *American Political Science Review* 68: 607-625.

Fiorina, Morris P. 1981. *Retrospective Voting in American National Elections.* New Haven: Yale University Press.

Franklin, Charles H., and John E. Jackson. 1983. "The Dynamics of Party Identification." *American Political Science Review* 77: 957-973.

Gaustad, Edwin. 1976. *Historical Atlas of Religion in America.* New York: Harper & Row.

Gilbert, Christopher P. 1989a. "The Political Influence of Church Discussion Partners." Presented at the annual meeting of the American Political Science Association, Atlanta.

_____. 1989b. "Voting, Party Identification, and Church Political Environments: A Contextual Analysis." Presented at the annual meeting of the Midwest Political Science Association, Chicago.

_____. 1990. "Religious Environments and Individual Self-Evaluations." Presented at the annual meeting of the Midwest Political Science Association, Chicago.

_____. 1991. "Neighborhoods, Religious Environments, and Partisan Behavior." *Political Geography Quarterly* 10: 110-131.

Gilbert, Christopher P., and Brent A. Hendry. 1989. "Neighborhood Religious Environments and Partisan Behavior: A Contextual Analysis." Presented at the annual meeting of the Western Political Science Association, Salt Lake City.

Giles, Michael W., and Marilyn K. Dantico. 1982. "Political Participation and the Neighborhood Social Context Revisited." *American Journal of Political Science* 26: 144-150.

Glock, Charles Y., and Rodney Stark. 1965. *Religion and Society in Tension.* Chicago: Rand McNally.

Granberg, Donald, and Beth William Granberg. 1980. "Abortion Attitudes, 1965-1980: Trends and Determinants." *Family Planning Perspectives* 12: 250-261.

Greeley, Andrew. 1985. *American Catholics Since the Council: An Unauthorized Report.* Chicago: Thomas More.

Guth, James L., Ted G. Jelen, Lyman A. Kellstedt, Corwin E. Smidt, and Kenneth D. Wald. 1988. "The Politics of Religion in America." *American Politics Quarterly* 16: 357-397.

Hanushek, Eric, and John E. Jackson. 1977. *Statistical Models for Social Scientists*. New York: Academic.

Hargrove, Barbara. 1979. *The Sociology of Religion: Classical and Contemporary Approaches*. Arlington Heights, Ill.: Harlan Davidson.

Harris, Richard J., and Edgar W. Mills. 1985. "Religion, Values and Attitudes Toward Abortion." *Journal for the Scientific Study of Religion* 24: 137-154.

Hauser, Robert M. 1974. "Contextual Analysis Revisited." *Sociological Methods and Research* 2 (February): 365-375.

Huckfeldt, Robert. 1979. "Political Participation and the Neighborhood Social Context." *American Journal of Political Science* 23: 579-592.

_____. 1986. *Politics in Context: Assimilation and Conflict in Urban Neighborhoods*. New York: Agathon Press.

Huckfeldt, Robert, Eric Plutzer, and John Sprague. 1990. "Alternative Contexts of Political Behavior." Presented at the annual meeting of the Midwest Political Science Association, Chicago.

Huckfeldt, Robert, and John Sprague. 1987. "Networks in Context: The Social Flow of Political Information." *American Political Science Review* 81: 1197-1216.

_____. 1988. "Choice, Social Structure, and Political Information: the Informational Coercion of Minorities." *American Journal of Political Science* 32: 467-482.

_____. 1991. "Discussant Effects on Vote Choice: Intimacy, Structure, and Interdependence." *Journal of Politics* 53: 122-158.

_____. 1992. "Citizens, Contexts, and Democratic Politics." Unpublished paper (review essay of recent research on contextual effects).

Iverson, Gudmund. 1989. "Absolute and Relative Individual Effects in Contextual Analysis." *Historical Methods* 22: 21-25.

Jelen, Ted G. 1990. "Political Christianity: A Contextual Analysis." Presented at the annual meeting of the American Political Science Association, San Francisco.

Johnson, Benton. 1964. "Ascetic Protestantism and Political Preference in the Deep South." *American Journal of Sociology* 69 (4): 359-366.

Johnson, Benton, and Richard H. White. 1967. "Protestantism, Political Preference, and the Nature of Religious Influence: Comment on Anderson's Paper." *Review of Religious Research* 9: 28-35.

Katz, Elihu, and Paul Lazarsfeld. 1955. *Personal Influence*. Glencoe, Ill.: Free Press.

Kellstedt, Lyman. 1989a. "The Meaning and Measurement of Evangelicalism: Problems and Prospects." In Ted G. Jelen, editor, *Religion and American Political Behavior*. New York: Praeger.

_____. 1989b. "Religion and Partisan Realignment." Presented at the annual meeting of the Midwest Political Science Association, Chicago.

Kellstedt, Lyman, and Mark A. Noll. 1990. "Religion, Voting for President, and Party Identification, 1948-1984." In Mark A. Noll, editor, *Religion and American Politics: From the Colonial Period to the 1980s*. New York: Oxford University Press.

Kenny, Christopher B. 1989. "The Consequences of Political Discussion in Mass Political Behavior." Unpublished doctoral dissertation, Washington University in St. Louis.

Kenny, Christopher B., and Christopher P. Gilbert. 1988. "The Behavioral Consequences of Political Discussion: Personal Influence and Partisanship in the Local Community." Presented at the annual meeting of the Southern Political Science Association, Atlanta.

Kernell, Samuel. 1977. "Presidential Popularity and Negative Voting: An Alternative Explanation of the Midterm Congressional Decline of the President's Party." *American Political Science Review* 71: 44-66.

Knoke, David. 1974. "Religious Involvement and Political Behavior: A Log-Linear Analysis of White Americans, 1952-1968." *Sociological Quarterly* 15: 51-65.

Kuhn, Thomas. 1970. *The Structure of Scientific Revolutions*. 2d ed. Chicago: University of Chicago Press.

Lazarsfeld, Paul, Bernard Berelson, and Hazel Gaudet. 1948. *The People's Choice*. New York: Columbia University Press.

Leege, David, Lyman Kellstedt, and Kenneth Wald. 1990. "Religion and Politics: A Report on Measures of Religiosity in the 1989 NES Pilot Study." Paper presented at the annual meeting of the Midwest Political Science Association, Chicago.

Leege, David C., Joel Lieske, and Kenneth Wald. 1989. "Toward Cultural Theories of American Political Behavior: Religion, Ethnicity and Race, and Class Outlook." Revised version of paper presented at the annual meeting of the Midwest Political Science Association, Chicago.

Leege, David C., and Michael R. Welch. 1989. "Religious Roots of Political Orientation: Variations among American Catholic Parishoners." *Journal of Politics* 51: 137-162.

Leighley, Jan E. 1989. "Social Interaction as a Stimulus of Political Participation." Presented at the annual meeting of the Midwest Political Science Association, Chicago.

Lenski, Gerhard. 1961. *The Religious Factor*. Garden City, N.Y.: Doubleday-Anchor.

Lieske, Joel. 1988a. "The Cultural Nexus in U.S. Presidential Elections." Presented at the annual meeting of the American Political Science Association, Washington.

_____. 1988b. "The Cultural Origins of Political Partisanship." Presented at the annual meeting of the Western Political Science Association, San Francisco.

Lipset, Seymour Martin. 1963. *Political Man*. New York: Anchor Books.

Lopatto, Paul. 1985. *Religion and the Presidential Election*. New York: Praeger.

MacKuen, Michael, and Courtney Brown. 1987. "Political Context and Attitude Change." *American Political Science Review* 81: 471-490.

MacKuen, Michael B., Robert S. Erikson, and James A. Stimson. 1989. "Macropartisanship." *American Political Science Review* 83: 1125-1142.

_____. 1992. "Question Wording and Macropartisanship." *American Political Science Review* 86: 475-486.

Markus, Gregory, and Philip Converse. 1979. "A Dynamic Simultaneous Model of the Electoral Choice." *American Political Science Review* 73: 1055-1070.

Marty, Martin E. 1986. *Protestantism in the United States: Righteous Empire.* New York: Scribner's.

McPhee, William, with Robert B. Smith and Jack Ferguson. 1963. "A Theory of Informal Social Influence." In William McPhee, editor, *Formal Theories of Mass Behavior.* London: Collier-Macmillan, Free Press.

Mead, Sidney E. 1976. *The Lively Experiment: The Shaping of Christianity in America.* New York: Harper & Row.

Miller, Warren. 1956. "One-Party Politics and the Voter." *American Political Science Review* 50: 707-725.

Moe, Terry M. 1980. *The Organization of Interests; Incentives and the Internal Dynamics of Political Interest Groups.* Chicago: University of Chicago Press.

Newman, William M., and Peter L. Halvorson. 1980. *Patterns in Pluralism: A Portrait of American Religion, 1952-1971.* Washington, D.C.: Glenmarry Research Center.

Niebuhr, H. Richard. 1929. *The Social Sources of Denominationalism.* New York: Meridian.

Niebuhr, R. Gustav. 1991. "Mighty Fortresses: Megachurches Strive to Be All Things to All Parishoners." *Wall Street Journal,* May 13, pp. A1, A6.

Noelle-Neumann, Elisabeth. 1977. *The Spiral of Silence.* Chicago: University of Chicago Press.

Noll, Mark A., editor. 1990. *Religion and American Politics: From the Colonial Period to the 1980s.* New York: Oxford University Press.

Peterson, Steven A. 1990a. "Church Participation and Political Participation: The Spillover Effect." Presented at the annual meeting of the Midwest Political Science Association, Chicago.

_____. 1990b. *Political Behavior: Patterns in Everyday Life.* Newbury Park, Calif.: Sage Publications.

Plutzer, Eric. 1986. "Attitudes Toward Abortion: A Study of the Social and Ideological Bases of Public Opinion." Unpublished doctoral dissertation, Washington University in St. Louis.

Przeworski, Adam, and Henry Teune. 1970. *The Logic of Comparative Social Inquiry.* Malabar, Fla.: Robert E. Krieger Publishing.

Putnam, Robert D. 1966. "Political Attitudes and the Local Community." *American Political Science Review* 60: 640-654.

Robinson, W. S. 1950. "Ecological Correlations and the Behavior of Individuals." *American Sociological Review* 15: 351-357.

Salisbury, Robert, John Sprague, and Gregory Weiher. 1984. "Does Religious Pluralism Make a Difference?

Interactions among Context, Attendance and Political Behavior." Presented at the annual meeting of the American Political Science Association, Washington.

Schaeffer, Pamela. 1990. "Faith: Study Assesses Immature Christians." St. Louis Post-Dispatch, March 19: pg. B1.

Schmickle, Sharon. 1992. "Worshipers Sing Mallelujah! Thousands Flock to Service at Megamall." Minneapolis Star Tribune, August 31, pp. A1ff.

Segal, David R., and Marshall Meyer. 1974. "The Social Context of Political Partisanship." In Mattei Dogan and Stein Rokkan, editors, Social Ecology. Cambridge, Mass.: M.I.T. Press, pp. 217-232.

Sigel, Roberta S., editor. 1989. Political Learning in Adulthood: A Sourcebook of Theory and Research. Chicago: University of Chicago Press.

Sprague, John. 1982. "Is There a Micro Theory Consistent with Contextual Analysis?" In Elinor Ostrom, editor, Strategies of Political Inquiry. London: Sage Publications.

Stipak, Brian, and Carl Hensler. 1982. "Statistical Inference in Contextual Analysis." American Journal of Political Science 26: 151-175.

Tatalovich, Raymond, and Alan R. Gitelson. 1990. "Political Party Linkages to Presidential Popularity: Assessing the 'Coalition of Minorities' Thesis." Journal of Politics 52: 234-242.

Tingsten, Herbert. 1937. Political Behavior: Studies in Election Statistics. Translated by Vilgot Hammarling. Totowa, N.J.: Bedminster Press (translated version published 1963).

Wald, Kenneth. 1992. Religion and Politics in the United States. 2nd ed. Washington, D.C.: Congressional Quarterly Press.

Wald, Kenneth D., Dennis E. Owen, and Samuel S. Hill. 1988. "Churches as Political Communities." American Political Science Review 82: 531-548.

Weatherford, M. Stephen. 1982. "Interpersonal Networks and Political Behavior." American Journal of Political Science 26: 117-143.

Wilcox, Clyde. 1986. "Fundamentalists and Politics: An Analysis of the Effects of Differing Operational Definitions." Journal of Politics 48: 1041-1051.

Wolfinger, Raymond, and Steven Rosenstone. 1980. Who Votes? New Haven: Yale University Press.

Zipp, John F., and Joel Smith. 1979. "The Structure of Electoral Political Participation." American Journal of Sociology 85: 167-177.

Index

Adherence: and abortion
    attitudes, 41, 58,
    104; nature of, 10,
    18, 20, 22, 28, 60,
    171; and school prayer
    attitudes, 108
Adherents, distribution of,
    10, 45-46, 54
*American Political Science
    Review* (APSR), 14 n.1
American Political Science
    Association (APSA), 1
American Voter, The, 4, 23,
    141-42
Amplification of attitudes:
    abortion, 155-58;
    discussion partners,
    136-37, 141, 168-69,
    176; party
    identification, 145;
    school prayer, 132;
    turnout, 159-61;
    voting behavior, 82-
    83, 85, 148, 153-54,
    164-68
Anderson, John, 51, 64 n.3
Attention to public
    affairs, 35-39, 49-50,
    54, 56-57, 61-62, 172
Attitudes: abortion, 39-42,
    56-59, 62-63, 102-105,
    113 n.5, 148-53, 172;
    change over time, 158-
    59; and contextual
    effects, 3, 5, 6-7, 8,
    10, 13, 16, 18, 20-22,
    88, 91-93, 109, 112,
    129, 141, 173-74;
    discussion partners,

7, 135, 138, 176;
    government aid to
    minorities, 95-98;
    long-term versus
    short-term, 88-89;
    national defense, 93-
    95; national economic
    expectations, 97-99;
    others in church, 116,
    119, 122, 136; others
    in neighborhood, 117-
    21, 133, 175-76;
    personal economic
    expectations, 99-100;
    presidential job
    approval, 100-101;
    school prayer, 102,
    105-109, 130, 132;
    toward neighborhood,
    117-121, 133. *See
    also specific
    denominations and
    religions*

Behavior: Catholic voting,
    44, 82-84; contexts
    and, 3-4, 11, 14, 18-
    19, 22-25, 27-29, 63-
    64, 132; discussion
    partners and, 135,
    137, 176; Evangelical
    Protestant voting, 46,
    52, 85, 87;
    individual, 6-7, 8,
    172-74; mainline
    Protestant voting, 44-
    46, 85-86; personal
    influence and, 137-39;
    religion (churches)

and, 1-3, 8, 18, 21-
22, 136, 171, 176-77;
religious, 16-17;
voting, 32-35, 43-46,
51-54, 59-60, 68-70,
77-78, 88-89, 153-59,
164-68. *See also
specific denominations
and religions*
Behavioral contagion, 91-
92, 97, 102, 107, 112,
141
Berelson, Bernard, 4, 35,
73, 138
Bochel, J.M., 22
Boston, Massachusetts, 172
Bowler, Shaun, 89, 174
Boyd, Lawrence, 12
Brown, Courtney, 21, 92,
107
Bush, George, 175

Campbell, Angus, 4, 23, 35,
142
Campbell, Converse, Miller,
and Stokes, 23
Carter, Jimmy, 32, 34, 51,
53
Catholics: abortion
attitudes, 41, 42, 57-
59, 62-63, 104, 150;
church attendance, 22,
41, 57, 142, 148;
discussion partners,
140-41, 164-67; family
political views, 124;
interest in politics,
50, 60, 123;
neighborhood
satisfaction, 119,
123; political
participation and
turnout, 29; political
behavior, 31; party
identification, 47,
53-54, 60, 73-75, 83;
voting, 5, 6, 22, 23,
30, 34, 37, 43, 44,
46-47, 438, 53, 54,
64, 73, 82-83, 85,
158, 164
Catholics and John F.
Kennedy, 21, 23, 43,
44, 47-48
Center for Political
Studies, 4
Church attendance, 20-23,
32, 34, 37, 41-42, 46-

47, 54, 57, 59, 62,
68, 71-73, 88-89, 93,
102, 104, 121, 127,
136, 148, 153, 158.
*See also specific
denominations and
religions*
Churches, African-American,
10, 30
Church political
involvement, 20, 22,
67, 74, 77, 85, 88,
93, 101-102, 112, 116,
124, 173
Columbia University, 4, 75,
138
Congregation, liberal, 17
Congress, U.S., 32
Contagion model, 92. *See
also* behavioral
contagion
Contextual analysis, 3, 4,
11, 15, 22, 24, 25
n.2. *See also*
attitudes, behavior
Contextual analysis,
criticisms of, 10
Converse, Philip, 21, 43,
60, 142
Cox, Kevin, 29

Democratic party, voters,
5, 23, 32, 37, 43, 47,
51, 54, 59-61, 169
Demographic traits,
individual, 93, 117
Denver, D.F., 22
Detroit, Michigan, 22
Discussion partners: 4, 7-
8, 9, 13, 18-19, 24-
25, 135-39, 169 n.1;
coworkers, 142;
different-church, 135-
36, 140; nonspouses,
140, 158-59;
reciprocal, 140;
spouses, 140, 144,
158-59, 176; same-
church, 135-36, 140-41
Durkheim, Emile, 3

Ecological fallacy, 29
*Elections and the Political
Order* (Campbell,
Converse, Miller, and
Stokes), 23
Environment: county, 37,
42, 172-73;

church/religious, 6,
42, 68, 75, 85, 88,
92, 97, 132, 133, 135-
37, 139, 141, 145,
153-54, 158-59, 167-
69, 176-77; definition
of, 3; and
Evangelicals, 57, 85;
heterogeneous, 167;
homogeneous, 167;
local/neighborhood,
71, 85, 88, 92, 117,
172-74;
local/neighborhood,
self-evaluations, 8,
117-21, 172-73; and
mainline Protestants,
85; pluralist county,
32; Protestant church,
23, 167; and
Protestants, 45-46;
social, 4, 11, 19, 44,
62, 93, 138-39; work,
168, 174
Episcopalians, 41
Ethnicity, 5, 6, 28, 137,
142, 167
Evangelical Protestants:
abortion attitudes,
42, 57, 104, 172;
church attendance, 46;
discussion partners,
164; emerging
political activity,
32, 34, 37, 60;
political
participation and
turnout, 37, 47; party
identification, 54,
74, 75; responsiveness
to environment, 23,
60, 63; Southern, 32;
voting, 37, 46, 51-53,
85, 164-68

Family interest in
politics, 121-26
Finifter, Ada, 44, 74, 85,
158
Ford, Gerald, 32

Gallup Poll, 17
Gaudet, Hazel, 138
Glenmarry Research Center
church census, 10, 27,
28, 30
Glock, Charles, 16-17

Halvorson, Peter, 6-7, 28
Hauser, Robert, 10
Hoover, Herbert, 51
Huckfeldt, Robert, 4, 8, 9,
11, 18, 19, 20, 73,
135, 138, 159, 168

Individual political
involvement, 67, 72
Interest groups, 10, 172
Iran hostage crisis, effect
on Carter candidacy,
51, 63
Iverson, Gudmond, 12

Jews, 28, 30; abortion
attitudes, 41; party
identification, 47,
59; voting, 46
Johnson, Benton, 2, 23, 35

Kellstedt, Lyman, 5, 24,
35, 52, 60, 64 n.2, 89
n.2, 177
Kennedy, John F., 21, 23,
43
Kenny, Christopher, 7, 19,
20, 135, 138, 144, 149
Knoke, David, 20, 21
Kuhn, Thomas, 2, 4

Labeling approach, 2, 3, 5,
6, 79
Lazarsfeld, Paul, 4, 73,
138. *See also*
Berelson, Columbia
University
Leege, David, 25, 35, 137,
142, 169 n.4, 177
Leighley, Jan, 159
Lenski, Gerhard, 16, 20,
21, 22, 47, 54, 73,
75, 139
Lieske, Joel, 25, 35, 142,
169 n.4
Lipset, Seymour Martin, 22
Logit/logistic regression
model, 12, 43, 64-65
n.5, 77, 89 n.5, 106,
108, 132, 153, 164,
167; stability of
estimates, 164
Lopatto, Paul, 23-24, 70

MacKuen, Michael, 21, 61,
70, 92, 107
Mainline Protestants:
abortion attitudes,

41-42, 58-59, 62, 63-64, 172; church attendance, 57; contextual influences on, 17, 60; party identification, 34, 37, 47, 60, 73, 74-75; political participation and turnout, 37, 47, 50, 54, 61; voting, 34, 44-46, 51, 85, 164-167
Mass political behavior, church contextual influence on, 3, 4, 89, 171
McPhee, William, 19-20, 73, 77, 138-39, 168
Megachurch, 177
Meyer, Marshall, 23, 44, 64, 73
Microenvironment, 19, 138
Miller, Warren, 4, 23, 29
Moe, Terry, 10
Mondale, Walter, 5, 148
Moral issue, importance to church, 138
Mormons (Church of Jesus Christ of Latter-Day Saints), 28, 172

National Election Studies (NES), 4, 8, 10, 24, 27-28, 30, 32, 176, 177
National Council of Churches of Christ (NCCC), 10, 27, 28
Neighborhoods: Democratic, 68-71, 77; mixed, 68-71, 77; Republilcan, 68-71
Networks: opinion-leading/personal influence, 138; political discussion, 138-39, 140; social, 16-17, 67, 138
New Deal, 5
Newman, William, 6-7, 28
New York City, 172
Niebuhr, H. Richard, 15, 17
Niebuhr, R. Gustav, 177
1932 election, 51
1960 election, 21, 23, 27, 34, 43-51, 54, 59, 60-62, 64, 172
1976 election, 27-29, 32, 34, 37, 39, 43, 47, 51, 54, 56, 57-61, 172
1976 election, turnout, 37, 47
1980 election, 27, 34, 51-54, 59-61, 169, 172
1980 election, turnout, 54
1984 election, 6, 12, 23, 68, 70, 82, 93, 100, 104, 112, 121, 141, 148, 153, 159, 169
Nixon, Richard, 32, 43
Noelle-Neumann, Elisabeth, 173
Noll, Mark, 6, 24, 25 n.1, 35, 52, 60, 64 n.2
Nontraditional Protestants, 30, 89 n.2

Ordinary Least Squares regression (OLS), explanation of, 12, 89 n.5
Orthodox religions, 1, 30

Paradigm, 2, 4-5, 24
Party identification: 4, 173-74; Catholics, 74; church attendance and, 20-21; churches and, 67, 70-77, 88-89; county influences and, 29, 35-37, 47-48, 54-55, 60-61; discussion partners and, 137, 141-47, 168, 176; Evangelicals, 74; mainline Protestants, 74-75
Party loyalty, 88
Pentecostal, 35
People's Choice, The, 138
Perceptions, measures of versus objective measures, 132-33, 174-75
Personal influence, 137-39, 140-41, 168, 176
Personal Influence, 138
Peterson, Steven, 21
Pluralist neighborhood, 73
Plutzer, Eric, 12, 19, 58, 102
Political activity: church-related group, 72, 74, 85, 104, 121, 133; family, 117, 121, 126-29, 132; individual,

32, 35-36; religious,
nature of, 2, 20;
veterans group, 93,
94, 97; and voting
behavior, 77, 78
Political behavior
research, 5, 23
Political cues/signals:
direct from church
leaders or ministers,
102, 112; within
churches, 7, 13, 17,
19-21, 37, 60, 62-64,
89, 92, 93, 97, 104,
116, 125, 132, 133,
136, 168, 171, 172-75.
See also political
messages
Political discussion in
churches, 20, 62, 73,
92, 118
Political learning/
political
socialization, 3, 23,
133, 168
Political meaning, 115
Political messages, 17,
115-16
Political views, family,
121, 124
Politics in Context, 18
Prayer in public schools,
visibility during 1984
election, 113 n.4
Protestants, behavior of
versus Catholics, 23,
44, 64, 73
Protestants, definition of
subgroups, 1-2, 30, 64
n.2
Putnam, Robert, 4, 29, 85,
158

Reagan Democrats, 175
Reagan, Ronald, 51, 100-
101, 148, 175
Religion and Politics
Organized Section, 1
*Religion and Society in
Tension*, 16-17
Religion, consumer of, 17
Religious preference, lack
of, 68
Religious preference or
difference, individual
versus neighbors, 125-
28, 130-32
Religious Factor, The, 22

Religious Right, 52
Republican Party: auto
workers, 44, 74;
voters, 22, 23-24, 32,
43, 46, 51, 52, 54,
60, 70, 96, 169
Robinson, W., 29
Roe v. Wade (1973), 39

Salisbury, Robert, 28-29,
32, 64
Salt Lake City, Utah, 172
Satisfaction, individual
with neighborhood,
117-21, 132-33
Schaller, Rev. Lyle, 177
Scotland, 22
Segal, David, 23, 44, 64,
73
Self-evaluations,
individual, 8, 13,
115-17, 125, 129, 132-
33, 174-75
Smith, Joel, 127, 159
Social absorption, 138
Social interaction, 20, 92,
116, 136, 138
*Social Sources of
Denominationalism,
The*, 17
South Bend community study,
structure, 4, 5, 8-9,
14 nn.2, 3, 18, 19,
67, 135, 139-40, 176
South Bend, Indiana, 4, 5
South Bend residents,
behavior, 5
Spillover effect, 21
Spiral of Silence, The, 173
Sprague, John, 4, 8, 9, 11,
19, 20, 28-29, 32, 62,
64, 73, 77, 135, 138,
168
St. Louis, Missouri, 172
Stark, Rodney, 16-17
Subculture: Catholic, 50,
58; Evangelical, 74;
political, 7, 29;
socioreligious, 16-17,
22, 58, 74, 142
Suicide, 3

Tingsten, Herbert, 3
Tocqueville, Alexis de, 15,
27
Turnout: Catholic, 64;
voter, 35-38, 47-49,
54-56, 61, 159-63,

168, 172, 176

Two-stage Least Squares
    regression (2SLS),
    explanation of, 140,
    142, 169 n.3

Voting, 138
Voting behavior: churches
    and, 77-78, 88-89;
    county influences and,
    32-35, 43-46, 51-54,
    59-60, 68-70;
    discussion partners
    and, 153-59, 164-68

Wald, Kenneth, 5, 20, 25,

25 n.1, 35, 113 n.4,
    116, 136, 142, 159,
    168, 169 n.4, 177
Wald, Kenneth, Dennis Owen,
    and Samuel Hill, 11,
    14 n.1, 17-18, 21, 62,
    91-92, 107, 137, 176
Watergate, 32; aftermath,
    34, 63
Weiher, Gregory, 28-29, 32,
    64
White, Richard, 2, 35
Wilcox, Clyde, 89 n.2

Zipp, John, 127, 159

About the Author

CHRISTOPHER P. GILBERT, Assistant Professor of Political Science, Gustavus Adolphus College, won an E. E. Schattschneider Award of the American Political Association for the best dissertation in American government and politics. He is specializing in American politics and religious matters and is particularly interested in social science research methods.